Eric Eve is Fellow and Tutor in Theology at Harris Manchester College, Oxford. He has published a number of articles and other short pieces on various aspects of the Gospels and Jesus (usually related either to miracles or to the Synoptic Problem) and is also the author of *The Jewish Context of Jesus' Miracles* (2002) and *The Healer from Nazareth* (2009).

BEHIND THE GOSPELS

Understanding the oral tradition

ERIC EVE

Fortress Press
Minneapolis

BEHIND THE GOSPELS
Understanding the Oral Tradition

Fortress Press Edition © 2014

Cover image © Scala / Art Resource, NY
Cover design: Tory Herman

Library of Congress Cataloging-in-Publication Data available
Print ISBN: 978-1-4514-6940-0
eBook ISBN: 978-1-4514-8753-4

Manufactured in the U.S.A.

For the Principal and Fellows of
Harris Manchester College, Oxford

Contents

Contents

Note to the reader

The area bounded by the Negev to the south, Lebanon to the north, the Mediterranean Sea to the west, and the land on either side of the River Jordan to the east has gone under many names in the course of its history. In many parts of the Bible it is referred to as the land of Israel, but as a geographical term 'Israel' is ambiguous since it could refer either to the kingdom of David and Solomon or to the northern kingdom that subsequently split away from the southern kingdom of Judah. In a first-century context, which is what this book is concerned with, 'Israel' can scarcely be used as a geographical term at all, since there was no such political entity and the term 'Israel' tended to be used to refer to the covenant people as a whole. Nevertheless there were still a significant number of Jews living in what their Scriptures referred to as the Promised Land, and some term is needed, as both a noun and an adjective, to refer to this area (as opposed to other parts of the Roman Empire where mainly Greek-speaking diaspora Jews lived). In first-century terms, the area in question is roughly that covered by Judaea, Samaria, Galilee, and possibly parts of Peraea, Idumaea and the Decapolis, but this is an impossibly clumsy locution (and would become even more so as an adjective). In this book I therefore follow well-established scholarly convention and use the terms 'Palestine' and 'Palestinian' as the noun and adjective for this geographical area, without intending any implications thereby for the present-day Middle East. Although the Romans did not give the name 'Syria Palaestina' to a province covering this area until after the second Jewish revolt in 135 CE, Greek and Roman authors were already using the name 'Palestine' in the first century. Moreover, the first-century Jewish authors Philo and Josephus both use the Greek name 'Palaistinē' of the region (see, for example, Josephus, *Against Apion*, 168–71, where Josephus is commenting on Herodotus' much earlier use of the name). The scholarly convention adopted here is thus consistent with the usage of the time period to which it refers, and in no way derivative of the name 'Palestine' used of the state that existed as a British Protectorate between 1922 and 1948.

Abbreviations

‖	Synoptic or other parallel text
AJT	*Asia Journal of Theology*
Ant.	Josephus, *Jewish Antiquities*
BETL	Bibliotheca ephemeridum theologicarum lovaniensium
BNTC	Black's New Testament Commentaries
CBQ	*Catholic Biblical Quarterly*
Conf.	Augustine, *Confessions*
ETL	*Ephemerides theologicae lovanienses*
ExpTim	*Expository Times*
FRLANT	Forschungen zur Religion und Literatur des Alten und Neuen Testaments
Hist. eccl.	Eusebius, *Ecclesiastical History*
JBL	*Journal of Biblical Literature*
JSHJ	*Journal for the Study of the Historical Jesus*
JSNTSup	Journal for the Study of the New Testament: Supplement Series
J.W.	Josephus, *Jewish War*
LNTS	Library of New Testament Studies
NTS	*New Testament Studies*
OT	*Oral Tradition*
SBL	Society of Biblical Literature
SNTSMS	Society for New Testament Studies Monograph Series
WUNT	Wissenschaftliche Untersungen zum Neuen Testament

Introduction

New Testament scholars have long supposed that between the death of Jesus and the writing of the Gospels, Jesus' words and deeds were handed down by word of mouth in something called 'oral tradition'. This has never been to deny a possible role for written documents as well; hypothetical texts such as Q, miracle-story collections and sayings collections have long been proposed. The point is rather that the transmission of Jesus material by word of mouth is assumed to have played a major role in the formative stages of the Jesus tradition, and that this 'oral tradition' can be invoked as a full or partial explanation of the material available to the Evangelists (the people who wrote the Gospels).

While it is likely that the Evangelists also had written sources available to them, this book is not concerned with the question of source criticism, nor with that of the literary relationship between the Gospels, otherwise known as the Synoptic Problem. For the purposes of this book we shall assume the priority of Mark (i.e. that Mark was the first to write a Gospel and that both Matthew and Luke used his Gospel as a source) and leave open the question of 'Q' (the other source supposedly used by Matthew and Luke for the material they have in common that does not appear in Mark), except to the extent that other scholars refer to it.

For much of the last century the dominant model of oral tradition among New Testament scholars was that supplied by form criticism. As will be argued in Chapter 2 (and subsequently), it is a model that has several flaws, but it nevertheless continues to supply many New Testament scholars with their default assumptions about oral tradition, even when they have abandoned form criticism as a method. It is not as if no alternative models are available, however; the study of oral tradition has moved on a long way since form criticism represented the cutting edge of New Testament scholarship, and quite a few New Testament scholars have engaged with these developments, as we shall see. It is rather that even after all this time their collective efforts have not yet fully exorcised the form-critical ghost from the scholarly mindset. The present book represents one more attempt to do so. It also aims to inform readers who may not be all that familiar with developments in thinking about the oral tradition behind the Gospels about the various proposals currently on offer.

At a first approximation these may be classified into five approaches: the rabbinic model (associated particularly with Birger Gerhardsson; see Chapter 3), the media contrast model (Werner Kelber, Chapter 4), the model of informal controlled oral tradition (Kenneth Bailey, Chapter 5), the memory model (several contemporary scholars; see Chapters 6 and 7), and the eye-witness model (Samuel Byrskog and Richard Bauckham, Chapter 8). On closer examination, however, three of these models (the media contrast model, the informal controlled tradition model and the memory model) will be found, with some adjustment, to converge on a broadly similar approach.

As should soon become apparent, however, 'oral tradition' is a blanket term covering a wide variety of phenomena. It would be a mistake to suppose that 'oral tradition' refers to some kind of monolithic process that operates everywhere and at all times in exactly the same way. It may also be a mistake to assume that the same model of oral tradition applies equally well to all phases of the transmission of the Jesus material; this is quite unlikely to have been the case, and since we lack any direct access to what took place we certainly cannot know it to have been the case. This is a further reason for considering several models of oral tradition in this book; even if one approach turns out to be the most promising overall, it is important to be aware of other approaches and likely that each approach can contribute something towards our overall understanding.

The main task of this book is thus to present its readers with the principal lines of thinking about the oral tradition behind the Gospels (although it may turn out that 'memory' proves to be a more helpful category than 'oral tradition' and that the use of the preposition 'behind' is questionable in this context). Chapter 9 will attempt a couple of probes into the tradition as a way of testing the models on offer, and Chapter 10 will round off the discussion with a number of conclusions. But before launching into a discussion of the various models of oral tradition on offer, it will be helpful to provide the reader with some general orientation. This the first chapter will attempt to do by sketching what 'oral tradition' might mean in the context of the media situation of the first-century Roman Empire.

1

The ancient media situation

What is oral tradition?

Oral tradition is always something spoken, but not everything spoken is oral tradition. To call something oral *tradition* is to imply that it has been handed on over a period of time. It thus implies at least some degree of stability in what is handed on so that one can meaningfully talk of the same tradition at different points in time. The great majority of what is spoken is too ephemeral ever to become oral tradition. Everyday conversation is not oral tradition. Neither is casual rumour or gossip of the sort that is either quickly forgotten or rapidly distorted beyond recognition. Even if occasionally these things may become the starting point of an oral tradition, they are not themselves oral tradition.

Oral tradition is also to be distinguished from oral *history*. According to Jan Vansina, oral tradition is that which is passed down from one generation to another, or persists over a number of generations, while oral history (or reminiscence) is what you get if you ask eyewitnesses (or those whom they have informed within living memory) for their recollections.[1] This sharp dichotomy has been questioned,[2] and Vansina's requirement that something only counts as oral tradition if it has been passed down between generations is probably too restrictive, but the distinction is nevertheless not without point. To survive, an oral tradition has to be both memorable and significant to the society or group that transmits it, which means among other things that it must be shaped in such a way as to allow it to endure. Personal reminiscences do not operate under the same constraints, and may be relatively shapeless, especially if they are being produced spontaneously from episodic memory (someone's personal recollection of what took place). The distinction is not absolute, however. For one thing, oral history may be in the process of becoming oral tradition. For another, the psychological and social factors that shape oral tradition can also act

---

[1] Jan Vansina, *Oral Tradition as History* (London: James Currey, 1985), 12–13.
[2] Elizabeth Tonkin, *Narrating Our Pasts: The Social Construction of Oral History* (Cambridge Studies in Oral and Literate Culture, 22; ed. P. Burke and R. Finnegan; Cambridge: Cambridge University Press, 1995), 85–94.

on individual memories. People tend to relate their memories according to the narrative forms current in their culture. If an eyewitness habitually narrates his or her account of a salient event, it may undergo the same kind of shaping that an oral tradition would. In some cases an eyewitness may deliberately shape an account with the intention of initiating an oral tradition. A teacher might do so to help ensure the survival of his or her words (as, for example, Birger Gerhardsson argues; see Chapter 3).

Oral tradition is closely related to memory. In order to survive as oral tradition it must be memorable, and particular individuals must remember it. It also forms one part of the social or collective memory of the group to which the tradents (people who hand on the tradition) belong. But it is only one aspect of social memory, which can also include monuments, commemorative ceremonies, rituals, beliefs, ways of behaving and, not least, written texts.[3] In the context of the first-century Mediterranean, oral tradition is thus far from a purely oral phenomenon uncontaminated by any other medium of communication; it is rather but one factor (albeit often the dominant one) of a complex interplay of memory, orality and scribality (the use of texts in a pre-print culture). In the remainder of the chapter we shall examine the second and third of these factors a little further, returning to the first in Chapter 6.

Some characteristics of orality and oral tradition

Speech and writing may become intertwined in a number of ways (for example someone may write down what was originally spoken or recite what was originally written), but the two media are nevertheless distinct, and at a first approximation one may list the following ways in which speech differs from writing.

First, unlike a written or printed text, speech is an event, not a thing. The speaker speaks, and while he or she speaks, the speech event unfolds in time; when the speaker stops speaking, the sound of his or her voice falls silent, the speech event fades into the past, and there is nothing left to examine (today we could record the speech electronically, but that possibility did not exist in antiquity).

Second, speech is heard, not seen. Even while it is going on, it cannot be examined. Attending to it fully while it is being spoken allows little

---

[3] See, e.g., Paul Connerton, *How Societies Remember* (Themes in the Social Sciences; ed. J. Dunn, J. Goody, E. A. Hammel and G. Hawthorn; Cambridge: Cambridge University Press, 1989); Jan Assmann, *Cultural Memory and Early Civilization: Writing, Remembrance, and Political Imagination* (tr. David Henry Wilson; Cambridge: Cambridge University Press, 2011), 1–107.

time for critical reflection on what is being said. Once it is over, it is no longer directly available for reflection. To the extent that it lives on at all, it lives on only in memory (where, to be sure, it can be critically assessed after the event if it has been sufficiently well remembered).

Third, what is remembered of speech will vary depending on a whole host of factors, but one is most unlikely to remember every word spoken in a lengthy conversation or performance. What may stick in memory is the gist of what was said, or the impression made by the speaker, or particularly striking turns of phrase. In recalling what was said on a future occasion, one will most likely reconstruct it from remembered fragments filled in by one's own imagination and grasp of the speech conventions employed. That said, some kinds of speech are rather easier to remember with reasonable accuracy (for example short poems, witty aphorisms and the like), and oral traditions are typically shaped to be memorable.

Fourth, speech (in a situation devoid of electronic media) always involves immediate face-to-face interaction with an audience of one or more other people. What is said will be influenced to a greater or lesser extent by verbal and visual feedback from that audience (including gestures and facial expressions), and by the manner in which the speaker tailors his or her message to the audience; moreover, what is heard will be filtered through the audience's expectations.

Fifth, a speech act always takes place in a particular social situation, which may be more or less formal (for example, a casual conversation is very different from a lecture), but which will always tend to constrain what can be said and how it can be said. It is obvious, for example, that bawdy limericks or lewd jokes would be quite out of place in a board meeting or Bible study group, just as a lengthy lecture would be out of place in an informal private conversation. Some speech acts, not least those involving the deliberate handing on of oral tradition, take place as performances marked off from everyday speech by a number of factors (such as the social setting and the style of language employed).[4]

Sixth, face-to-face oral communication consists of more than just words; it includes a whole range of more or less subtle cues including gesture, facial expression, bodily deportment, and, of course, the rhythm, pacing, intonation and stress with which the words are spoken. By such means a speaker may make it very clear, for example, when irony is intended,

---

[4] Richard Bauman, *Verbal Art as Performance* (reissued 1984 edn; Long Grove, IL: Waveland Press, 1977); John Miles Foley, *The Singer of Tales in Performance* (Voices in Performance and Text; ed. J. M. Foley; Bloomington and Indianapolis: Indiana University Press, 1995), 1–59.

or which point is being emphasized. When the words are reduced to writing, such visual cues are lost, and the message may appear much more ambiguous. Indeed, the message of a speaker can be completely falsified by repeating the same words in subsequent oral performance while totally altering the intonation and facial expression. One only has to think of the different ways in which the single word 'yes' can be uttered in response to a question, and the total misrepresentation that could result from representing a cautious, sceptical, drawn-out 'yes' as a brisk, bold affirmative 'yes'.[5]

The six points just noted apply more or less to our own experience of oral communication, but we should be wary of assuming that the distinctions they imply between orality and writing apply equally well to every kind of oral utterance and every kind of writing. In this book we are particularly concerned with speech acts that form part of an oral tradition. This is an area that has been researched and written about extensively (in the context of folklore studies and cultural anthropology, for example), but we need to be a little cautious about drawing too many sweeping generalizations, first because conclusions drawn from completely non-literate cultures may not be directly applicable to the more complex media situation of the first-century Mediterranean, and second because some of the earlier conclusions (such as those suggesting a 'Great Divide' between orality and literacy) have been challenged by subsequent work. With these caveats we may nevertheless sketch a brief outline of how oral tradition has sometimes been characterized.

Much twentieth-century thinking about oral tradition grew from the seminal work of Milman Parry and Albert Lord on Homeric literature as oral poetry in connection with a study of contemporary Balkan bards. In brief and at the risk of gross oversimplification, Parry's work began from the observation that Homeric verse makes heavy use of a number of set formulas, so that, for example, in the *Iliad* and the *Odyssey* the dawn is frequently rosy-fingered, the sea wine-dark, and Achilles swift-footed, even in situations when he is not actually going anywhere. One advantage of such set formulas is that they neatly fill out one half of a Greek hexameter, and so form a useful stock of phrases for composition in performance, effectively forming the basic units of the poet's vocabulary. For according to Parry and Lord the Homeric poems were composed in performance long before they were written down. They would have been re-performed many times, but no two performances would have been exactly alike;

---

[5] For a broader discussion of the 'psychodynamics of orality' see Walter J. Ong, *Orality and Literacy: The Technologizing of the Word* (New Accents; London and New York: Routledge, 2002), 31–76.

instead the poems would have been created afresh in each new perform-ance, calling on the same stock of phrases, the same overall story outline, and the same stock of intermediate elements such as scenes following the same general outline. So, for example, more or less the same order of events is followed in the *Iliad* and *Odyssey* every time a banquet occurs or every time a hero dons his armour.[6]

It is knowing the stock of phrases and these intermediate and larger structures that is meant to have enabled the Homeric poets to recreate their epics in multiple performances without the aid of writing; no verbatim memorization was involved. In support of this thesis Parry and Lord carried out extensive fieldwork in Yugoslavia observing illiterate bards compose in performance in much the manner just described, the best of them well able to rival Homer at least in terms of the length of the epics produced.[7]

The oral formulaic theory of Parry and Lord has met with a number of criticisms. Not least, critics have challenged the sharp divide it postulates between orality and literacy. In relation to the study of the New Testament the relevance of the Parry–Lord theory has been questioned on the grounds that the synoptic tradition is plainly not epic poetry. In Chapter 6 we shall briefly describe an attempt to generalize the Parry–Lord theory to other types of oral tradition on the basis of cognitive psychology.

Stemming in part from the work of Parry and Lord, and in part from the conviction that the use of different media (speech, writing, print, electronic devices) could have profound effects both on society and on the way individuals think, the exploration of such media differences was developed by scholars such as Jack Goody, Walter J. Ong and Eric Havelock, and taken up in New Testament studies by Werner Kelber (on whom see Chapter 4).[8] It is certainly not the case either that all these scholars are in agreement with one another or that their work has gone unchallenged, but as a

---

[6] David C. Rubin, *Memory in Oral Traditions: The Cognitive Psychology of Epic, Ballads, and Counting-out Rhymes* (Oxford and New York: Oxford University Press, 1995), 210–20.

[7] Albert B. Lord, *The Singer of Tales* (Harvard Studies in Comparative Literature, 24; 2nd edn, Cambridge, MA and London: Harvard University Press, 1960); John Miles Foley, *The Theory of Oral Composition: History and Methodology* (Bloomington and Indianapolis: Indiana University Press, 1988).

[8] E.g. Jack Goody, *The Interface between the Written and the Oral* (Cambridge: Cambridge University Press, 1987); Jack Goody, *The Domestication of the Savage Mind* (Themes in the Social Sciences; Cambridge: Cambridge University Press, 1977); Ong, *Orality and Literacy*; Eric A. Havelock, *Preface to Plato* (Cambridge, MA: Harvard University Press, 1963); Eric A. Havelock, *The Muse Learns to Write: Reflections on Orality and Literacy from Antiquity to the Present* (New Haven and London: Yale University Press, 1986); Werner H. Kelber, *The Oral and the Written Gospel: The Hermeneutics of Speaking and Writing in the Synoptic Tradition, Mark, Paul and Q* (Voices in Performance and Text; Bloomington and Indianapolis: Indiana University Press, 1997).

useful first approximation it may be helpful to sketch the characterization of oral tradition that emerges from this kind of approach.

First, it is said, oral tradition (or oral transmission) is generally a series of creative performances, in which oral composition may play as much of a role as faithful recall. Such performances are rarely, if ever, attempts to repeat fixed oral 'texts'. Of course the oral performance of memorized fixed texts can and does occur, but generally only in connection with writing. The notion of a fixed text whose words are to be repeated verbatim scarcely exists except where such texts have first been written down. Indeed, it is hard to see how the notion could exist apart from a written text against which to compare successive oral performances.[9] It is probably going too far to say that oral tradition *never* allows for verbatim repetition, since there are some kinds of material (songs, short poems, liturgical and magical formulas, particularly striking pithy sayings and the like) that lend themselves to verbatim or near-verbatim repetition, especially where, for example, the efficacy of a magical formula or liturgical ceremony is assumed to depend on getting the wording exactly right, but such cases are the exception rather than the rule, and variability is possible and reasonably common even for relatively memorable metrical material.

Second, oral tradition rarely preserves the past for its own sake, that is, in the sense of retaining information about the past for purely academic, historical or antiquarian purposes. This does not mean that oral tradition never preserves anything from the past, or that it shows no interest in the past, but rather that its interest in the past is nearly always for its practical application in the present. There is a tendency in oral tradition towards what has been termed *homeostasis*, that is for orally transmitted material either to be conformed to the present interests of the social group that is using and transmitting it or to die out altogether when it ceases to be relevant. It should be stressed, however, that this is only a tendency; complete homeostasis is rarely achieved, since oral traditions often preserve archaisms whose meaning is no longer understood (certain nursery rhymes and folk songs provide modern examples of this phenomenon) as well as information about the past that is deemed interesting for its own sake (perhaps due to its very oddity).[10]

Third, oral tradition prefers the vivid and the concrete to the abstract and the general. Fourth, along with the preference for the vivid goes a

---

[9] Jocelyn Penny Small, *Wax Tablets of the Mind: Cognitive Studies of Memory and Literacy in Classical Antiquity* (Abingdon: Routledge, 1997), 5.

[10] Vansina, *Oral Tradition as History*, 114–23.

preference for the striking, the unusual, the sharply drawn, for black-and-white contrasts and situations of conflict, for the dramatic rather than the humdrum, presumably because these are more memorable than the everyday and the commonplace. Along with this is a tendency to simplify the characters oral tradition describes, making them one-dimensional heroes and villains, larger-than-life 'heavy' characters, or even caricatures. Any subtleties, complexities and ambiguities tend to get lost.

These generalizations can be helpful if used with caution. They can provide an initial orientation to the characterization of oral tradition, but it should not be assumed that all oral traditions work in the same way and display identical characteristics. Different societies value different kinds of material in different ways and may employ different techniques in handing it on. The four points listed above should be taken as indications of the way an oral tradition is quite likely to work, not as laws governing how all oral traditions must work. For example, the insistence that oral tradition is always composition-in-performance stems from the work of Parry and Lord (the 'oral-formulaic' approach), and while it may offer a good account of the performance of certain kinds of epic poetry, it does not even apply to all oral poetry, let alone all oral tradition.[11] Depending on the situation and the type of material transmitted, performances of oral tradition may be creative reworkings of remembered themes, or they may be more or less successful attempts to reproduce memorized texts, or they may be any number of things in-between, and the situation may be greatly complicated by the existence of written texts in the culture in question.[12]

Moreover, one must be wary of pressing the differences between orality and writing too hard. Other studies have tended to regard the 'Great Divide' approach as at best a useful first approximation which now needs to be nuanced and corrected. Indeed, more recent scholarship on oral tradition has tended to qualify the distinction between orality and literacy, and indeed, to question whether such broad-brush categories as 'orality' and 'literacy' have any analytical utility at all. The more recent tendency has been to stress the interpenetration of speech and writing, particularly in manuscript cultures, and also to suggest a greater gradation of cultural situations than just 'oral' and 'literate'.[13] Vernon K. Robbins, for example,

---

[11] Ruth Finnegan, *Oral Poetry: Its Nature, Significance and Social Context* (Bloomington and Indianapolis: Indiana University Press, 1992), 152; cf. John Miles Foley, *How to Read an Oral Poem* (Urbana and Chicago: University of Illinois Press, 2002), 1–21.

[12] Finnegan, *Oral Poetry*, 152.

[13] Finnegan, *Oral Poetry*, 18–19, 22–4, 160–8, 258–60, 272–3; Foley, *Singer*, 66, 79, 210–11; Foley, *Oral Poem*, 26, 36–9, 66–9.

has suggested a classification into oral, scribal, rhetorical, reading, literary, print and hypertext cultures, locating the Gospels in the third category.[14] Lest one should think that this places the greatest divide between ancient oral cultures and modern digital cultures, Bruce Lionel Mason uses the oral characteristics of internet newsgroup postings to challenge the oral–literacy divide, and points out conversely that oral rhetoric can sometimes employ literate strategies.[15]

How exactly one should characterize the oral tradition that gave rise to the Gospels will be the subject of the chapters that follow. The general characteristics of speech and oral tradition just reviewed should be regarded not as a set of firm conclusions but rather as a provisional starting point. Yet even allowing for the complex interaction of speech and writing in antiquity, an awareness of the differences between the two media is a better starting point than simply treating them as equivalent. But in order not to misunderstand the difference between them, we next need to consider how ancient writing differs from modern print.

Writing in antiquity

Earlier we emphasized the oral/aural nature of speech in contrast to the visual nature of writing. This contrast is, however, potentially misleading in relation to ancient texts. Ancient texts were designed, not primarily to be scanned by the eye, but to be read aloud and heard. Indeed, it has been suggested that silent reading was virtually unknown in antiquity and that the most famous exception proves the rule: St Augustine expressing surprise at coming across Bishop Ambrose reading to himself without uttering a sound (Augustine, *Conf.* 6.3). The interpretation of this passage as implying that Augustine was unfamiliar with silent reading has, however, been challenged on the grounds that it was not so much the silent reading as its occasion that Augustine found noteworthy.[16] Yet even if silent reading was not wholly unknown in antiquity, it seems to have been more common for people either to read aloud to themselves, or get someone else (often a slave) to read to them, or to form part of an audience listening to a work being read aloud (authors often gave public readings of their

---

[14] Vernon K. Robbins, 'Oral, Rhetorical and Literary Cultures: A Response' in Joanna Dewey (ed.), *Orality and Textuality in Early Christian Literature* (Semeia, 65; Atlanta, GA: SBL, 1995), 75–91.

[15] Bruce Lionel Mason, 'E-Texts: The Orality and Literacy Issue Revisited', *OT* 13.2 (1998), 306–29.

[16] Small, *Wax Tablets*, 52–3; Mary Carruthers, *The Book of Memory: A Study of Memory in Medieval Culture* (2nd edn; Cambridge Studies in Medieval Literature; Cambridge: Cambridge University Press, 2008), 212–15.

own works, for example). Writing was also often done aloud. The normal practice was to dictate to a scribe, and while some authors preferred to do their own writing they frequently dictated aloud to themselves, as did copyists. In sum, ancient texts often functioned in a thoroughly oral way.[17]

The difference between the ancient and modern use of texts becomes even more apparent when we consider the physical nature of ancient texts. Although a manuscript penned by a professional scribe often had a pleasingly neat appearance in which the individual letters were well formed and easily legible, ancient Greek manuscripts lacked virtually all the other visual indicators of the modern printed book. The typical manuscript had no punctuation, no paragraphing, no distinction between upper and lower case letters, and no space between words, with words generally broken at the end of a line to achieve an even right margin regardless of where in the word the break came. To read such a manuscript from beginning to end required skill enough (though the habit of reading aloud probably helped make sense of writing presented in this way); to find a particular passage in the middle of the text would have been a matter of considerable difficulty, to the extent that virtually no one would have attempted it just to check a reference to something they more or less remembered. Moreover, an ancient manuscript would have been totally devoid of any visual clues concerning the organization and structure of the text it contained. Backtracking in a text to reread a passage just read would be possible for a manuscript one was reading to oneself, or having read to oneself by one's own slave; skipping backwards and forwards, or randomly accessing particular passages elsewhere in the text would have been far more difficult. It would have been made even more difficult by the fact that books were normally in the form of scrolls.

To be sure, the early Christian Church seems to have been something of a pioneer in the adoption of the codex (the book in the page format we now take for granted), but while turning pages would have been a great deal easier than winding and unwinding a scroll, all the other visual cues were still lacking. In sum, it would not have been feasible to use an ancient manuscript text in many of the ways we use modern printed books.[18]

---

[17] Paul Achtemeier, 'Omne verbum sonat: The New Testament and the Oral Environment of Late Western Antiquity', *JBL* 109 (1990), 3–27 (12–17); Terence C. Mournet, *Oral Tradition and Literary Dependency: Variability and Stability in the Synoptic Tradition and Q* (WUNT, 195; Tübingen: Mohr Siebeck, 2005), 130–41.

[18] Achtemeier, 'Omne verbum sonat', 10–11; Small, *Wax Tablets*, 11–25.

Once pointed out, the physical limitations of ancient manuscripts are not too hard to understand. It is also not too hard to grasp how they may have prompted a greater reliance on the spoken word and on memory than we are used to in our culture. Thereafter, the ancient media situation becomes harder to grasp. The difficulty stems in part from the seeming paradox that the first-century Mediterranean world was both one in which texts proliferated and played a highly significant role, and also one in which oral habits still predominated. Writing appeared on public monuments, coins, published scrolls, private notebooks, letters and ostraca (pottery fragments used as writing surfaces). While papyrus was the preferred material and fairly readily available, one could also write on parchment (leather), notebooks made of wooden sheets, or wax tablets (the preferred medium for temporary notes, since a wax tablet was easy to erase). Both the number of various kinds of texts surviving from antiquity and the variety of surfaces used to write on suggests the great popularity of writing among those able to use it, and yet much everyday interaction continued to be oral (even more so than today).

This is partly explained by the fact that the diffusion of texts was greatly limited by the absence of printing. The only way texts could be duplicated (apart from those on coins) was to copy them by hand, a time-consuming and thus expensive procedure limiting the ownership of books in any quantity to the very wealthy. There was also a certain ambivalence towards writing; while its usefulness was clearly recognized, so were its limitations. A piece of writing could not be cross-examined in the way the oral account of an eyewitness could. Texts lacked the immediacy of face-to-face contact. Writing needed to be decoded by a reasonably competent reader able to deliver a decent oral performance despite the lack of visual aids. In addition much greater reliance was placed on memory than would be the case today, especially among the educated elites for whom high levels of memory competence could be regarded as a point of honour. In this situation, writing tended to be regarded as an aid to memory, not as a substitute for it as in our modern situation.

Estimates of ancient literacy have tended to vary, but the recent trend is to set them quite low, perhaps around 5 per cent in the population as a whole, rising to 15 per cent among urban males. It used to be thought that the Jews formed an exception, with their devotion to Scripture causing them to have a much higher literacy rate, perhaps through a system of near universal elementary education. Again more recent studies question this, suggesting that literacy rates among Jews were no higher than those among other peoples.[19] In any case, without the technology of the printing press, it is hard to see how mass literacy could have been achieved; there would not have been enough manuscript copies to go round.

In any case, 'literacy' is not an all-or-nothing term.[20] Some people could probably read short texts without being able to write. The ability to give an adequate public reading from a scroll would demand a far higher level of literacy. The ability to scratch a short list of names or items on a potsherd would have been one level of writing ability; that of being able to write at someone else's dictation another; that of being able to compose a book up to elite literary standards quite another.[21]

Be that as it may, the fact that only a minority of people could read or write would necessitate an oral approach to most of everyday living. Communication to or among the masses could only be by word of mouth. While prolific note-taking among the literary elites was far from uncommon, and the ability to write shorthand not unknown, the modern impulse to commit the noteworthy to writing could hardly exist among the population at large. Again, while the advantages of writing as an aid to memory were clearly recognized, even highly literate people were much more inclined to rely on their memories than modern people are, and those who were illiterate had no other choice. We should not, however, assume that this automatically gave everyone prodigious memories compared to people today. Memorization was a skill taught to the educated classes (those at the top of the social scale), but is a skill that modern people can equally well acquire if they choose. The difference is that memorization was much more central to ancient education than it is to modern.[22] Whether ordinary people in antiquity in fact had better memories than ordinary people today is less clear; they presumably relied on their memories far more, and that *may* have helped train their memories to be more reliable, but the fact that they were unable to check their memories against written references as we often tend to do may just as easily mean that they were less aware of their mistakes than we are.

Another seeming paradox of the ancient situation is that one did not need to be literate to become reasonably familiar with the content of

---

[19] Chris Keith, *Jesus' Literacy: Scribal Culture and the Teacher from Galilee* (LNTS, 413; ed. M. Goodacre; New York and London: T. & T. Clark, 2011), 71–85; Richard A. Horsley with Jonathan A. Draper, *Whoever Hears You Hears Me: Prophets, Performance and Tradition in Q* (Harrisburg, PA: Trinity Press International, 1999), 125–7.

[20] Tonkin, *Narrating*, 13.

[21] Keith, *Jesus' Literacy*, 85–114; L. Michael White, *Scripting Jesus: The Gospels in Rewrite* (New York: HarperOne, 2010), 94–6.

[22] See, e.g., Small, *Wax Tablets*; Carruthers, *Book of Memory*; and David M. Carr, *Writing on the Tablets of the Heart: Origins of Scripture and Literature* (Oxford: Oxford University Press, 2005).

written texts. Since nearly everyone apprehended the content of texts through hearing them read, those who could not read them for themselves were not necessarily at such a great disadvantage as might be supposed, provided they had access to a performance. To be sure, the wealthy and well-educated in centres of culture would have had much greater access to performances than peasants in a Galilean village. Nevertheless it seems likely that there would be some performances of texts open to all, particularly in cities. It also seems plausible that knowledge of the Jewish Scriptures would have extended well beyond those able to read them for themselves, since many people would gain some knowledge of the Scriptures through hearing them read. While we may doubt that every first-century Galilean village had a synagogue building housing a complete set of Torah scrolls (let alone a complete set of the Hebrew Scriptures), it is certainly possible that some towns and larger villages possessed at least some scriptural scrolls which villagers could hear read to them (this is suggested, for example, by Josephus, *J. W.* 2.229, which describes a Roman soldier burning a Torah scroll he found in a Judaean village). Scriptural knowledge was probably much more widespread among the Jewish people than the ability to read, and it may be that it was the confusion of the one with the other that in part motivated older overestimates of first-century Jewish literacy. That said, we should not be too quick to assume that popular knowledge of Israelite traditions was necessarily knowledge of the contents of any particular written texts; it may be more appropriate to regard such knowledge as more akin to folklore, or to the 'little tradition' of the peasants (on which see Chapter 7).

The interaction between speech and writing in antiquity is thus complex. Some scholars maximize the media differences between the oral and the written.[23] Others tend to minimize them by emphasizing the oral functioning of ancient written texts.[24] While the truth probably lies somewhere in-between, it is hard for us to envisage since we lack any appropriate analogue in our own experience to the ancients' use of texts.

Perhaps the closest modern analogy to an ancient text is a written (or printed) musical score.[25] Notwithstanding the fact that many musically trained people can profitably peruse a musical score by eye, the primary purpose of musical scores is performance intended for the ear, and the way in which the vast majority of people appreciate music is through

---

[23] E.g. Kelber, *The Oral and the Written Gospel*, partially in dependence on Ong, *Orality and Literacy*.
[24] E.g. Horsley and Draper, *Whoever Hears You Hears Me*, 128–44.
[25] Small, *Wax Tablets*, 23.

hearing it performed. One can be familiar with a great deal of music, be able to recognize a substantial repertoire, and able to hum or sing a wide range of melodies oneself without being able to read a note of printed music. For the vast majority of people, knowledge and appreciation of music comes through hearing it performed. It is in no way dependent on access to printed scores or the ability to read them for oneself; it is dependent only on one's access to musical performances. The ability to compose and perform one's own music is not and never has been restricted to those who can write down formal musical notation. Folk music, popular songs, ballads, religious chants, various forms of dance music and so on can all be composed, performed, learned and passed on without any recourse to writing. But there is a limitation to the sophistication of such music, especially when compared with the Western classical tradition. Music composed without the aid of writing seems unable to achieve much harmonic, contrapuntal or structural sophistication. It is perfectly possible to think up a great melody without going near pen and ink, but the ability to compose a four-movement symphony for full orchestra is hard to imagine without the ability to write out the score.

The analogy with verbal communication is only partial, since listening to a Beethoven symphony is very different from reading Plato, but the difference does tend to diminish at the other end of the scale. Reciting a folk poem and singing a folk song may be much the same thing, especially as recitals of oral tradition are often as much sung as spoken, and the public reading of texts in antiquity frequently employed a vocal technique somewhere between full-blooded singing and ordinary speech.

Consequences for the oral Jesus tradition

It should be stressed again that the present chapter is anything but the last word on oral tradition or its relation to written texts. What has been offered here is simply an initial orientation which will need to be refined and corrected in the light of the chapters to follow. Two further preliminary remarks may nevertheless be in order.

The first point concerns the possible extent of writing in the pre-Gospel tradition. As has been noted, the tendency has been to emphasize that ancient literacy was confined to the educated elites, and that few if any people from that class belonged to the primitive Church. This needs some qualification. The fact that the educated elites sometimes had their slaves read to them or take dictation implies the existence of literate slaves. There was, moreover, a measure of craft literacy. Some people earned their living as scribes, just as some earned their living as carpenters or stonemasons. Scribes might be employed by the elite (and others) but did not themselves belong to the elite. Some other people might have possessed at least rudimentary reading and writing skills that were useful in their principal trade. Physicians and engineers might typically be literate. Retainers employed to perform clerical duties for the government or for wealthy landowners would certainly have been literate. Once the Church took hold in urban settings and began to attract more than a handful of recruits, it is more probable than not that it would have some literate persons among its number, even if it had not done so before.

The significance of this is not so easy to determine, however. We should not automatically assume that people wrote Jesus traditions down simply because they could, just in order to preserve them. That would be to project the modern record-keeping habits of the present onto a much more oral past. On the other hand, given the ubiquity of note-taking in antiquity, it would not be at all surprising if literate preachers and teachers made some private notes of material they thought would be useful in their preaching and teaching. The effect of such notes is hard to gauge. While they remained little more than an aide-memoire for the oral use of the material, the fact that they were written down may not have been very significant, except insofar as papyrus may have been able to fix a little more material in a more stable form than human memory. The extent of such a practice in any case remains entirely conjectural. The possibility nevertheless reinforces the warning that models of orality drawn completely from preliterate societies need to be used with caution. If notes written in 30 CE were available to Mark in 70 CE, 40 years of oral transmission could in theory have been totally bypassed, but there is no way of knowing *a priori* whether this happened or not.

The second point is that if oral tradition is to be taken seriously as oral, it must not be treated as if it were a kind of writing. However closely writing and speech may have been intertwined in antiquity, they remained separate media with their own distinctive qualities. In particular, oral tradition is not a thing to be investigated or an artefact to be excavated. It existed in speech acts long since lapsed into silence, and in the memories of people long since turned to dust. We have no direct access to it at all, but only to its traces in the written documents that survive. How those documents can be used in the attempt to reconstruct it will form the subject of the chapters to come.

2

Form criticism

Soon after the end of the First World War, two German New Testament scholars independently launched pioneering efforts to analyse the oral tradition behind the Gospels. Their method came to be known in English as *form criticism* (from the German *Formgeschichte*, literally meaning 'form history'). It proved highly influential; so influential, in fact, that it shaped the way several generations of New Testament scholars have thought about oral tradition (and about how to do historical Jesus research), and its influence can still be felt today, even among scholars who have long since officially abandoned the method and no longer subscribe to its assumptions. Sometimes its influence is an unconscious one, a continuing unexamined acceptance of the form-critical understanding of oral tradition in default of anything better. Sometimes its effect is one of conscious rejection, since the great majority of New Testament scholars who have proposed alternative models of oral tradition have begun by exposing what they regard as form criticism's flaws. Any discussion of oral tradition in relation to the Gospels thus has to begin with form criticism, for only by understanding form criticism's strengths and weaknesses can we appreciate what subsequent proposals are reacting to and how far they succeed in advancing our understanding.

In essence, form criticism is the study of the history of individual units of (oral) tradition, based on the assumption that there is a discoverable link between their form and their social setting, or as Vincent Taylor described it:

> Form criticism is primarily concerned with the oral period ... The basal assumption is that during this period the tradition circulated mainly in separate oral units which can be classified according to their form. It is believed, further, that much may be inferred regarding the origin of these units, the causes which gave rise to them, and the changes they underwent until in course of time they were given a written form.[1]

The notion of 'separate oral units' stemmed from Karl Ludwig Schmidt's argument that the arrangement of the material in the Gospels was the

---

[1] Vincent Taylor, *The Formation of the Gospel Tradition* (London: Macmillan, 1960; 1st edn, 1933), 10.

work of the Evangelists (the authors of the Gospels), rather than the actual order of events in Jesus' ministry or in the subsequent tradition. Schmidt likened these small units of tradition to pearls, which each Evangelist threaded on a string of his own devising. The technical term for these pearls is *pericopae* (singular, *pericope*, pronounced pe*ri*kohpee) from the Greek meaning 'cut around', the idea being that each pericope is a self-contained unit, such as an individual miracle story or parable. These individual pericopae generally have no essential connection with the context in which they occur, and (it was argued) can stand alone as individual anecdotes or sayings. Moreover, Matthew, Mark and Luke frequently use the same pericopae in different settings, suggesting that there was no particular place for them dictated by the tradition.

The form critics did not set about classifying these pericopae into various forms simply for the joy of taxonomy. The idea was to identify a correlation between form and *Sitz im Leben*, a German term which may be translated as 'setting in life'. *Sitz im Leben* was intended to be a *sociological* concept; the kind of life-settings sought were not what individual people did on particular occasions, but typical uses to which the material was put by the community, such as preaching, teaching, apologetics, argumentation and polemics. Form criticism also attempted to make deductions about the origin of the material by comparing the Gospel forms with contemporary Jewish and Hellenistic parallels, and about the history of the tradition by noting how far the written form in the Gospels departed from what the pure oral form ought to look like.

While there is a general family resemblance among the form critics, they differ importantly in detail. In this chapter, therefore, we shall look at the two principal form critics in turn, and then offer some general observations.

Martin Dibelius

The pioneer in developing the form criticism of the Synoptic Gospels was the German scholar Martin Dibelius, who was inspired by Hermann Gunkel's form-critical work on the Old Testament.[2]

According to Dibelius the Jesus tradition was handed down by 'many anonymous persons' who did not always passively pass on precisely what

---

[2] Dibelius' major work on form criticism, *Die Formgeschichte des Evangeliums*, was first published in 1919. A substantially revised and enlarged edition was published in 1933. The references in this chapter will be to the English translation of the second edition published as Martin Dibelius, *From Tradition to Gospel* (tr. Bertram Lee Woolf; London: Ivor Nicholson and Watson, 1934).

they had received, but also introduced creative changes. No individual creative mind made any real impression on the tradition, however; instead the tradition developed according to its own laws, since the forms in which it was transmitted were shaped by the practical uses to which it was put. Given such impersonal laws Dibelius believed it possible to determine the *Sitz im Leben* or typical sociological setting of the various forms of traditional material. He considered even the Evangelists to be not so much authors as mere collectors and editors of the tradition. The Gospels, and any written material that preceded them, were not literature proper, but only *Kleinliteratur*, unliterary writing of a kind not intended for publication. The writing of the Gospels therefore provided no barrier to investigating the uses to which their constituent materials were put in the tradition.[3]

For Dibelius, the primary use was preaching. He arrived at this conclusion not by analysis of the Gospel material, but by his 'constructive method', which proposed typical situations in the primitive Christian Church and then attempted to correlate them with the forms of material he found in the Gospels. Dibelius started from the assumption that the words, actions and death of Jesus were rehearsed in the circle of Jesus' disciples, and asked how they would have propagated from there. Taking Luke's phrase 'eyewitnesses and ministers of the word' (Luke 1.2) to refer to a single group of people, Dibelius argued that the eyewitnesses must also have been preachers, and that the tradition grew out of what they preached. Missionary preaching would have needed to describe the Jesus in whom potential converts were being asked to believe, while preaching aimed at believers would have needed to show how Christian faith and practice were to be based on the teaching and example of Jesus. Dibelius took the missionary speeches in Acts to be representative of such early Christian sermons.[4]

Dibelius noted that at 1 Corinthians 15.3–5 Paul appeared to be handing on a formula he had received, and that there and elsewhere he used the technical terms for the receiving and handing on of traditions. The contents of this tradition no doubt varied from one church to another, but everywhere included a detailed account of the Passion as a central element of the kerygma (preaching). In addition, accounts of Jesus' deeds might have been used as sermon illustrations, while his sayings might have been used in catechetical instruction. In Dibelius' view, different laws would have applied to the handing on of narrative and sayings material.

---

[3] Dibelius, *Tradition*, 1–7.
[4] Dibelius, *Tradition*, 10–17.

Dibelius classified the forms of the tradition into Paradigms, Tales (*Novellen*), Legends, Exhortations (or Paraenesis), and Myths, with the Passion narrative as a distinct category on its own (an early connected account). The oldest and most historically reliable form in Dibelius' view was the *Paradigm*, a brief, pithy, self-contained narrative concentrating solely on essentials and ending in some saying or significant action of Jesus. Paradigms supply just enough detail to give point to the word or action with which they conclude; the British New Testament scholar Vincent Taylor accordingly dubbed this form the *Pronouncement Story*. Examples of pericopae Dibelius classified as Paradigms include the Question of Fasting (Mark 2.18–22), the Healing of the Withered Hand (Mark 3.1–6), the Tribute Money (Mark 12.13–17) and the Anointing at Bethany (Mark 14.3–9).[5]

Paradigms provide only minimal characterization of their actors, who are impersonal types, not people, and who often speak in chorus; their only importance lies in what they say. The word or deed of Jesus enshrined in the Paradigm is always something of general significance useful for preaching purposes. In Dibelius' view both the Paradigm's unworldly lack of narrative elaboration and its economy demonstrated its distinctive role as a religious form particularly suited to the needs of preaching. He believed that the Paradigms were first formulated by the eyewitnesses for the purposes of preaching, and are thus the most primitive form of Christian tradition we possess. Although they are thus relatively reliable, they are not objective police reports, since they were formulated not to convey neutral information but to convert and instruct; moreover it is a mistake to try to seek a pure form behind the Paradigms, since no such thing ever existed; the Paradigms only came into being for the purposes of preaching. On the other hand Dibelius believed that it was sometimes possible to detect secondary expansions of Paradigms, which suggested a tendency for them to grow in the course of the tradition.[6]

Several units Dibelius identified as Paradigms briefly narrate a miracle, but they were told primarily not for the sake of the miracle, but rather for the saying of Jesus or the reaction to which it led. Stories told primarily for the sake of the miracle they contain form the bulk of Dibelius' second category, the Tales. In formal terms, Tales differ from Paradigms in possessing a greater expansiveness of narrative detail and a corresponding lack of paradigmatic focus. Dibelius believed that this difference in form

---

[5] Dibelius, *Tradition*, 43.
[6] Dibelius, *Tradition*, 37–69.

betrayed a difference in origin and use. Unlike the Paradigms, the Tales were not devised for the purpose of preaching, but were rather developed by a separate group of storytellers who delighted in the narrative art for its own sake. Some of the Tales may have originated as Paradigms that were subsequently filled out with more narrative detail. Others may have been borrowed from outside the Christian tradition, it being a tendency of folk tradition to attach current stories to well-known figures.[7]

We may pass over Dibelius' other categories more rapidly. Legends are edifying narratives of a kind often told about religious figures and designed to satisfy curiosity about the virtues and trials of holy people. In the Gospels legends are found both about Jesus (for example, the birth narratives) and about the people who surrounded him (such as Peter).[8] Exhortations or Paraenetic material comprises all the sayings of Jesus that appear outside a narrative framework. Dibelius took this to resemble the kind of paraenetic material found in James, 1 Peter, *1 Clement*, the *Didache*, the *Shepherd of Hermas* and the concluding exhortations often found in the letters of Paul (although in none of these is this material explicitly attributed to Jesus as it is in the Gospels). Dibelius believed these sayings must have been handed down by a different route from that taken by the narrative material found in Mark, and must have been subject to different laws; instead they must have been handed down (and used) by Christian teachers, and gradually gathered into collections, of which Q (the hypothetical source said to have been used by Matthew and Luke in addition to Mark) would be the prime example. All this material was regarded as being inspired by the Spirit or the risen Lord, and (said Dibelius) no distinction was made between the preaching of Jesus and the preaching about Jesus.[9]

The principal exception to the rule that the Jesus tradition originally circulated in isolated units was the Passion narrative (the account of Jesus' arrest, trial and execution), which Dibelius believed existed as a connected narrative from the earliest period.[10] It was nevertheless Mark who was the first to create a connected account of Jesus' entire ministry, although there may well have been predecessors who collected groups of sayings and other related material. While Mark was basically a conservative user of the tradition he inherited, he did emphasize those parts of the tradition that showed Jesus to be the Messiah while at the same

---

[7] Dibelius, *Tradition*, 70–103.
[8] Dibelius, *Tradition*, 104–31.
[9] Dibelius, *Tradition*, 233–64.
[10] Dibelius, *Tradition*, 178–217.

time indicating why he was not recognized as such (the so-called 'messianic secret' expounded by Wrede), thereby creating a 'book of secret epiphanies' (unrecognized revelations of God at work in Jesus).[11]

Dibelius was far from wholly explicit about the model of oral tradition he was employing in all this. His references to folkloric parallels suggest that it was folklore he had in mind, although it was the *forms* rather than the *processes* of folklore that he explicitly drew attention to. That Dibelius had folklore in mind is also indicated by his references to the laws various types of tradition follow. For Dibelius, it was the community as a whole, or general groups within that community such as preachers, teachers and storytellers, who shaped and handed on the tradition, and who did so in a manner so impersonal and so collective that one could speak of the 'laws' of transmission irrespective of any individual idiosyncrasies. While Dibelius thought that different laws applied to different kinds of material, his overarching model was one of the growth of the tradition through accretion, expansion, conglomeration, the borrowing of secular motifs and narrative techniques, and the partial incursion of myth.

Although Dibelius did not go into much detail, he indicated the source of his ideas by referring to Johann Gottfried Herder's work on folk poetry and Franz Overbeck's understanding of primitive Christian literature.[12] Erhardt Güttgemanns subsequently analysed Dibelius' dependence on these predecessors, and argued that Herder's work was based more on a particular view of history than on empirical research into folklore. In particular Herder's was a 'romantic' view that equated life with orality, orality with the folk, and the folk with either the lower classes or the nation.[13] According to Güttgemanns, the brothers Grimm emphasized the collective (non-individual) origin of fairy tales with biological metaphors that Herder took over and used to metaphysically mystify his approach. Both Herder and the brothers Grimm regarded folk poetry as the product not of individuals but of living oral tradition; in Güttgemanns' view this was ultimately a circumlocution for asserting the divine origin of folk poetry, showing that the concept sprang not so much from empirical investigations into folklore but from a particular kind of metaphysics. More recent, empirically based, investigations of folklore have shown

---

[11] Dibelius, *Tradition*, 218–30.

[12] Dibelius, *Tradition*, 5.

[13] Erhardt Güttgemanns, *Candid Questions Concerning Gospel Form Criticism: A Methodological Sketch of the Fundamental Problems of Form and Redaction Criticism* (Pittsburgh Theological Monograph Series, 26; ed. Dikran Y. Hadidian; tr. William G. Doty; Pittsburgh: Pickwick Press, 1979), 127; cf. Terence C. Mournet, *Oral Tradition and Literary Dependency: Variability and Stability in the Synoptic Tradition and Q* (WUNT, 195; Tübingen: Mohr Siebeck, 2005), 3–6.

that there is no absolute distinction between folk poetry and artistic poetry, since the two co-exist in continual interaction. The 'romantic' view espoused by Herder and taken over by Dibelius overrated the creative power of the anonymous collective and ignored the fact that the originators of folk poetry might well be artistically gifted lower-class individuals.[14]

Quite apart from Dibelius' dubious model of folklore, one might also question a 'constructive' method that postulates social settings for various forms of material on the basis of such meagre evidence. Güttgemanns criticizes Dibelius' theory that preaching was central to the formation of the primitive Christian tradition on a number of grounds: first, that Dibelius set too much store on the value of Luke 1.1–4 as a historical source; second that the concept of preaching was too idealized to bear the sociological weight Dibelius put on it; and third that the speeches in Acts are Lukan constructions that cannot be used to support Dibelius' theory.[15] The 'constructive' method is not, however, the only way form criticism can be done; one could instead employ an 'analytical' method, starting not with supposed typical settings in the life of the community, but with an analysis of the material. This latter approach was the one taken by Rudolf Bultmann, whose views we shall examine next.

Rudolf Bultmann

Although Bultmann began independently of Dibelius, he shared many of the same assumptions. He too subscribed to the implied analogy with folklore with its theory of the formation of tradition by an anonymous community rather than particular individuals, the correlation between form and sociological setting, and the evaluation of primitive Christian literature as *Kleinliteratur*.[16] This led to a similar view of the development of the Christian tradition according to impersonal laws.

Where Bultmann departed most strikingly from Dibelius was in his decision to start with an 'analytic' as opposed to a 'constructive' approach, that is to start by analysing the Gospel material and deduce life-settings from the analysis rather than doing it the other way round (though Bultmann acknowledged an inevitable circularity in correlating form with social

---

[14] Güttgemanns, *Candid Questions*, 184–93. On the 'romantic' view of folk tradition see also Ruth Finnegan, *Oral Poetry: Its Nature, Significance and Social Context* (Bloomington and Indianapolis: Indiana University Press, 1992), 30–41.

[15] Güttgemanns, *Candid Questions*, 297–302.

[16] Rudolf Bultmann, *The History of the Synoptic Tradition* (tr. John Marsh; Oxford: Basil Blackwell, 1963), 1–7, together with references to folkloric parallels throughout the text.

setting).[17] This led him both to a more detailed analysis of pericopae, and to generally more sceptical conclusions about their historical authenticity, than was the case for Dibelius. Bultmann was also rather more exercised than Dibelius about assigning each piece of tradition (or form of tradition) to either a Palestinian or a Hellenistic setting.[18]

The forms into which Bultmann categorized the Gospel pericopae include Apophthegms (corresponding to Dibelius' Paradigms), Dominical Sayings, Similitudes, Miracle Stories (corresponding to Dibelius' Tales), Historical Stories and Legends. Unlike Dibelius, however, Bultmann did not think that Apophthegms originated in preaching, but rather in argumentation, in particular in the apologetics and polemics of the Palestinian Church as its members debated with outsiders or settled issues of faith and practice among themselves. He regarded the Apophthegms as Palestinian in origin due to the rabbinic style of the disputes they contain and the relative absence of any Hellenistic ideas. Bultmann also considered it possible that some Apophthegms contained genuine sayings of Jesus, or at least reflected the general tenor of his sayings. On the other hand, he regarded the narrative settings in which they placed Jesus' sayings as fictions, or 'ideal scenes' created to give concrete expression to some view that the Church wished to attribute to Jesus. Bultmann's reasons for thinking this stemmed not from the form of the Apophthegms but from an analysis of their content; for example, it seems implausible that Pharisees would be waiting around in a cornfield on the Sabbath to catch Jesus' disciples plucking ears of corn, and while the complaint is directed against the disciples, it is Jesus who is made to supply the defence of their conduct (Mark 2.23–28).[19]

Bultmann divided the other sayings of Jesus into several subcategories. The Logia (or wisdom sayings) found their parallel in the proverbial literature of all peoples, although those attributed to Jesus seem often to be based on the Old Testament and Jewish (by which Bultmann seems to have meant rabbinic) *meshalim*. Bultmann thought that many such proverbs found their way into the Jesus tradition, but that genuine sayings of Jesus could be discerned in what went beyond popular wisdom to something new.[20]

---

[17] Bultmann, *Synoptic Tradition*, 4–5.

[18] For Bultmann's understanding of the significance of this distinction, see Bultmann, 'The Study of the Synoptic Gospels' in F. C. Grant (tr. and ed.), *Form Criticism: A New Method of New Testament Research* (Chicago and New York: Willett, Clark and Co., 1934), 17–18; cf. Karl Kundsen, 'Primitive Christianity in the Light of Gospel Research', 96–139, in the same volume.

[19] Bultmann, *Synoptic Tradition*, 11–68.

[20] Bultmann, *Synoptic Tradition*, 69–105.

Bultmann proposed that many of the prophetic and apocalyptic sayings were Jewish material that had been adopted by the Christian tradition and ascribed to Jesus, but thought that those suggesting imminent eschatological expectation might go back to the historical Jesus except where they had been reformulated in the light of Church experience. In any case, Bultmann thought the Church did not distinguish between sayings of the earthly Jesus and sayings of the risen Jesus uttered through the mouths of Christian prophets.[21] The Legal Sayings and Church Rules were often rules for church discipline in the Palestinian Church. Again Bultmann saw this material as a combination of genuine sayings of Jesus, Jewish sayings adapted to a Christian context, and new coinages put into the mouth of Jesus. Towards the end of their development, largely at the written stage of tradition, these sayings were collected and edited to form a catechism, which Bultmann regarded as Mark's source for this kind of material.[22]

Bultmann next turned his attention to the various kinds of figurative speech in the Jesus tradition, such as metaphors, similitudes and story parables. In addition to discussing such formal characteristics of the parables as the conciseness of narration and the law of stage duality (only two actors or groups of actors are in view at any point in the narrative), Bultmann suggested that the applications attached to them or the contexts provided for them in the Gospels were generally secondary, and that they had sometimes undergone allegorical expansion.[23]

Turning from the sayings material to the narrative material, Bultmann next dealt with the Miracle Stories (Dibelius' Tales). After discussing the characteristic features of miracle stories in general, Bultmann noted how they underwent change and development in the tradition, for example an increase in the miraculous element. Even if historical events underlay some of the healing stories, the form in which they were narrated was the work of the tradition. The Old Testament may have made some contribution to the Jesus miracle stories, and other stories may have grown up in the Christian Church and have been projected back onto the pre-Easter Jesus, but in Bultmann's view it was more probable that the Jesus tradition has attracted folk stories of miracles and miracle motifs, as is shown by the stylistic similarity of Gospel miracle stories to Jewish and Hellenistic ones. Moreover, while Bultmann accepted that some miracles would have been attributed to Jesus in the Palestinian Church, not least because some of

---

[21] Bultmann, *Synoptic Tradition*, 108–28.

[22] Bultmann, *Synoptic Tradition*, 130–49.

[23] Bultmann, *Synoptic Tradition*, 166–205.

the Apophthegms mention miracles, some could have been fashioned in a Hellenistic milieu, from which Bultmann concluded (via the relative rarity of rabbinic miracle stories) that most probably were (in part also because Bultmann took them to exhibit a Hellenistic 'divine-man' Christology). Within the Christian tradition miracle stories underwent novelistic expansion and gained details of circumstances and place.[24]

Bultmann classified much of the other narrative material as Historical Stories and Legends, using 'Legends' in much the same sense as Dibelius. In dealing with this material Bultmann was again much exercised by the question of Palestinian versus Hellenistic origins, for example seeing the temptation story as being Palestinian in form while presupposing a Hellenistic notion of the Son of God.[25] As did Dibelius, Bultmann treated the Passion narrative as a special case of an early continuous narrative, although his primitive Passion narrative was somewhat less extensive than Dibelius'.[26] He also decided that dogmatic and apologetic motifs had thoroughly affected the Easter appearance stories and that since the virgin birth motif was unheard of in Judaism it must have been added in a Hellenistic setting.[27] Bultmann could find no unified origin or tradition history for all this diverse material. Some of it sprang from Palestinian messianic expectations, some from Hellenistic ideas and some from within the Christian tradition itself, not least from the unconscious tendency to depict the life of Jesus in the light of Christian faith and worship. Some other kinds of tendency could also be discerned in this legendary material, such as a tendency to individualize characters by naming them, the use of novelistic details, the use of the numbers two and three, and the doubling of particular figures.[28]

When it came to the editing of this material and the formation of the Gospels, Bultmann saw no definable boundary between the oral and written stages. For Bultmann, the same laws that operated in the oral tradition continued to operate when that tradition was written down, so that the composition of Mark was simply the natural culmination of an inevitable process. Along the way this process resulted in collections of sayings, controversy stories, miracle stories, parables and the like which provided the written sources Mark employed. Mark was scarcely master of the material he incorporated into his own account, but nonetheless managed to impress his own dogmatic conception on it to create a 'book of secret epiphanies'

---

[24] Bultmann, *Synoptic Tradition*, 209–43.
[25] Bultmann, *Synoptic Tradition*, 250–61.
[26] Bultmann, *Synoptic Tradition*, 262–85.
[27] Bultmann, *Synoptic Tradition*, 286–92.
[28] Bultmann, *Synoptic Tradition*, 302–20.

(a phrase Bultmann quoted approvingly from Dibelius) that managed to combine the Hellenistic Christ-myth as found in the Pauline Epistles (e.g. Philippians 2.6–11) with the Jesus traditions stemming from the Palestinian Church.[29]

In all this Bultmann did not always make it entirely clear what precise *Sitz im Leben* he intended to assign to which form, but this becomes a little clearer in his final summary of the growth of the tradition:

> *The collection of the material of the tradition began in the Primitive Palestinian Church.* Apologetic and polemic led to the collection and production of apophthegmatic sections. The demands of edification and the vitality of the prophetic spirit in the Church resulted in the handing on, the production and the collection of prophetic and apocalyptic sayings of the Lord. Further collections of dominical sayings grew out of the need of paranesis and church discipline. It is only natural that stories of Jesus should be told and handed down in the Church – biographical apophthegms, miracle stories and others. And just as surely as the miracle stories and such like were used in propaganda and apologetic as proofs of messiahship, so is it impossible to regard any one interest as the dominant factor; as it is generally not right to ask question [*sic*] about purpose and need only; for a spiritual possession objectifies itself also without any special aim.[30]

It remains unclear, however, how far the notion of sociological *Sitz im Leben* really played a central role in Bultmann's analysis of the synoptic tradition. Categories such as apologetic, polemic, paraenesis, church discipline and propaganda no more denote sociological life-settings than does Dibelius' category of preaching; rather they are vague and general labels for various kinds of ecclesiastical function, whose correlation with particular forms is asserted rather than demonstrated.

As we have noted, Bultmann was in practice rather more exercised over the distinction between Palestinian and Hellenistic settings. This distinction is problematic for a number of reasons. First, Bultmann clearly drew it purely on the basis of what he identified as either Palestinian or Hellenistic ideas; the opportunity to draw a potentially fruitful social distinction between, say, a rural Galilean setting and an urban Graeco-Roman setting was never pursued. Second, the distinction Bultmann drew between Palestinian and Hellenistic ideas is itself problematic, supposing a much sharper distinction between the two than can really be justified.[31] For Bultmann, 'Palestinian'

---

[29] Bultmann, *Synoptic Tradition*, 322–50.

[30] Bultmann, *Synoptic Tradition*, 368.

[31] See Martin Hengel, *Judaism and Hellenism: Studies in Their Encounter in Palestine during the Early Hellenistic Period*, vol. 1 (tr. John Bowden; London: SCM Press, 1974).

Form criticism

all too often meant 'rabbinic', which is problematic not so much because
the rabbinic material is later, but because we now know Palestinian Judaism
to have been far more diverse than simply proto-rabbinic Judaism.

Bultmann's classification of Josephus as 'Hellenistic' illustrates the problem,
for in origin Josephus was a Palestinian Jew of priestly descent, whose Greek
language writings generally present Josephus's Palestinian Jewish con-
victions in Hellenistic dress. The first half of Josephus's *Jewish Antiquities*
retells the story of the Old Testament in the form of Hellenistic historiography; it would be bizarre to deduce from this that the Old Testament
was of Hellenistic origin, but this is precisely the kind of fallacy Bultmann
fell into when, for example, he assigned the bulk of the Gospel miracle
stories to a Hellenistic origin on account of their apparent Hellenistic
dress.[32] Werner Kahl conducted a far more detailed analysis of the Gospel
healing stories which ended up agreeing with Bultmann that the Markan
ones resemble Hellenistic miracle stories, while their Matthean parallels
look more Jewish,[33] but this should warn us that the form of the miracle
stories as we find them in the Gospels may owe more to their use by the
Evangelists than to their origin and tradition history; Barry Blackburn,
for example, has argued that the Markan miracle stories are perfectly
understandable against a purely Jewish background.[34]

No more than Dibelius did Bultmann have a well-grounded theory of oral
tradition. Like Dibelius he occasionally noted parallels from folklore, and in
common with Dibelius he assumed a process of anonymous community
formation in which the individual played no significant role and the tradition was shaped by its own immanent laws. Apparently, then, he adopted
the same romantic notion of folklore that Dibelius employed. In any case,
in his analysis of the tendencies of the synoptic tradition, Bultmann based
nothing on the results of empirical folklore studies and everything on his
observation of the tendencies of the written tradition (such as Matthew's
and Luke's supposed redaction of Mark and Q).[35] Bultmann justified this by
asserting that there was no essential difference between the oral and written

[32] On Josephus's use of OT miracle stories, see Eric Eve, *The Jewish Context of Jesus' Miracles* (JSNTSup,
231; Sheffield: Sheffield Academic Press, 2002), 24–52.
[33] Werner Kahl, *New Testament Miracle Stories in Their Religious-Historical Setting; A Religionsgeschichtliche
Comparison from a Structural Perspective* (FRLANT, 163; Göttingen: Vandenhoeck & Ruprecht,
1994).
[34] Barry L. Blackburn, *Theios Anēr and the Markan Miracle Traditions: A Critique of the Theios Anēr
Concept as an Interpretative Background of the Miracle Traditions Used by Mark* (WUNT, 2; Tübingen:
Mohr [Siebeck], 1991); cf. Eve, *Jewish Context*.
[35] E. P. Sanders, *The Tendencies of the Synoptic Tradition* (SNTSMS, 9; Cambridge: Cambridge University
Press, 1969), 12–23.

stages of the tradition,[36] a highly questionable assertion that effectively led Bultmann into treating orality as a kind of writing.[37] This becomes apparent both when he speaks of 'editing' the tradition and in his detailed analysis. For what Bultmann did in analysing various pericopae frequently resembles a kind of microscopic redaction criticism, tracing the changes he supposed Mark or some other Evangelist had made to his pre-Gospel sources. This might make some sense on the assumption that the pre-Gospel sources reached the Evangelists in written form (and Bultmann indeed seems to have supposed that), but it makes no sense at all as a description of an oral process, which is a sequence of individual performances, not the editing of a fixed text.[38] Indeed, Bultmann's entire analysis of the synoptic tradition is in danger of reifying oral tradition into a series of archaeological layers that can be excavated, when in reality oral tradition is nothing of the sort.

Bultmann's analyses of individual pericopae often display penetrating discernment and close attention to detail, but they owe more to an assessment of the content than to form or social setting. The kinds of judgement Bultmann typically made concern internal inconsistency or historical implausibility. In particular he seemed to know in advance that the historical Jesus was an eschatological prophet who issued a radical call to repentance, so that material that reflected such a radical immanent eschatology was most likely to be authentic: his method thus delivered the historical Jesus he expected to find. But more to the present point, Bultmann's judgements about the history and authenticity of the synoptic tradition were in practice seldom based on the ostensible methods of form criticism, but on his dissection of pericopae in the light of his literary and historical judgements. It is these judgements that then drove his view of tradition history and hence his deductions about the tendencies of the tradition.

Evaluation

It has been suggested that both Bultmann and Dibelius were driven by a concern to discover both a Jesus and a primitive Church that were not

---

[36] E.g. Bultmann, *Synoptic Tradition*, 6, 87, 239, 321.

[37] So also Terence C. Mournet, 'The Jesus Tradition as Oral Tradition' in W. H. Kelber and S. Byrskog (eds), *Jesus in Memory: Traditions in Oral and Scribal Perspectives* (Waco: Baylor University Press, 2009), 39–61 (43–6); Mournet, *Oral Tradition*, 6–7, 62–3; cf. Elizabeth Tonkin, *Narrating Our Pasts: The Social Construction of Oral History* (Cambridge Studies in Oral and Literate Culture, 22; ed. P. Burke and R. Finnegan; Cambridge: Cambridge University Press, 1995), 90 on the 'talking book' fallacy in the study of other oral traditions.

[38] So also James D. G. Dunn, *Jesus Remembered* (Christianity in the Making, 1; Grand Rapids and Cambridge: Eerdmans, 2003), 194.

only distinct from but religiously superior to contemporary Judaism and Hellenistic paganism.[39] Their understanding of oral tradition was derived from a model of folklore that has been overtaken by more recent research. Their failure to appreciate the media differences between speech and writing seriously undermines the deductions they made about the former on the basis of 'the latter. Even on the basis of its own methodology form criticism cannot deliver a consistent account of the tendencies of the tradition: while Bultmann and Dibelius thought the tradition tended to expand and elaborate, Vincent Taylor argued that it tended to abbreviate and smooth out; Sanders has shown that neither is correct, and that many other supposed tendencies of the synoptic tradition cannot be demonstrated from the written record.[40] The study of other oral traditions might suggest a long-term tendency to conform to generic norms (i.e. to employ typical elements in typical structures), but we should be wary of generalizing from one oral tradition to another, and even if such a tendency existed in the synoptic tradition it might very well be masked by other factors, such as the literary creativity of the Evangelists in employing the tradition or the idiosyncrasies of particular oral performers in particular contexts of performance. In any case much of what passes as form criticism (particularly in Bultmann) is not so much an analysis of the oral tradition as a detailed literary and historical analysis of individual pericopae as they appear in the Gospels after being ripped from their context.

The form critics almost certainly underestimated the creativity of the Evangelists who, to the modern scholarly eye, appear to be much more than mere collectors of tradition. Moreover, the promise of form criticism to relate form to sociological setting is never seriously delivered, neither is adequate justification offered for the assumption that form correlates with *Sitz im Leben*, an idea that has been shown to be false in the case of oral poetry.[41] Again, the notion of an 'original' or 'pure' form that can be recovered by tracing the history of the tradition is highly problematic; material transmitted orally is likely to have been multiform from the start, so that there is no 'original form' to recover.[42] Yet another problematic assumption is that a relatively pristine primitive tradition can somehow be prised apart from the narrative setting in which it appears in the Gospels by identifying (and then reversing) the process of interpretation that has

---

[39] See Gerd Theissen and Dagmar Winter, *The Quest for the Plausible Jesus: The Question of Criteria* (tr. M. Eugene Boring; Louisville, KY: Westminster John Knox Press, 2002), 19–26, 95–121, 132–6.

[40] Taylor, *Formation*, 119–26, 202–9; Sanders, *Tendencies*, 272.

[41] Finnegan, *Oral Poetry*, 260.

[42] Mournet, *Oral Tradition*, 71–2.

taken place in-between. This ignores both the fact that the tradition will have been interpreted right from the beginning, and the likelihood that earlier interpretations will have shaped and informed those of the Evangelists. In other words one cannot arrive at primitive tradition simply by stripping away subsequent interpretation, since tradition and interpretation would have been thoroughly intertwined from the very start.[43] We shall return to some of these issues in later chapters.[44]

Yet for all its shortcomings form criticism does raise important questions about the pre-Gospel traditions, and not all of its findings can be dismissed out of hand.

The form critics would seem to have been broadly correct about the nature of the material preserved in the tradition, at least as we find it in the Gospels. There is little to suggest that the primitive Church had any purely biographical or historical interest in Jesus as a figure of the past; the material that was preserved does seem to have been such as would serve the practical interests of the Church, and to that extent Dibelius' characterization of the overall purpose of the material is probably correct: in Assmann's terminology the material found in the Gospels performs both a *formative* function in providing a foundational narrative that helps shape group identity and a *normative* function in providing instruction on how members of the Christian community ought to live.[45] That does not mean that the primitive Christians were uninterested in the earthly Jesus, but their interest in him was as a figure of authority for the present, not as an object of purely antiquarian historical curiosity. That the primitive Church would have been more concerned with knowledge of Jesus for present practical purposes than purely historical ones also seems plausible in the light of what is known of oral tradition from elsewhere, as do at least some of the form critics' observations on the nature of oral storytelling.[46]

As noted above, form criticism's claim to establish a link between form and social setting is less convincing. That there may often be a close relation

---

[43] Chris Keith, *Jesus' Literacy: Scribal Culture and the Teacher from Galilee* (LNTS, 413; ed. M. Goodacre; New York, London: T. & T. Clark, 2011), 32–41.

[44] See also the assessments of form criticism in Richard Bauckham, *Jesus and the Eyewitnesses: The Gospels as Eyewitness Testimony* (Grand Rapids and Cambridge: Eerdmans, 2006), 246–9; E. P. Sanders and Margaret Davies, *Studying the Synoptic Gospels* (London and Philadelphia: SCM Press; Trinity Press International, 1989), 127–34; and Christopher M. Tuckett, 'Form Criticism' in W. H. Kelber and S. Byrskog (eds), *Jesus in Memory: Traditions in Oral and Scribal Perspectives* (Waco: Baylor University Press, 2009), 21–38.

[45] Jan Assmann, *Cultural Memory and Early Civilization: Writing, Remembrance, and Political Imagination* (tr. David Henry Wilson; Cambridge: Cambridge University Press, 2011), 122–3.

[46] Jan Vansina, *Oral Tradition as History* (London: James Currey, 1985), 91–3.

between form, function and social setting in human communication is no doubt the case, and can easily be demonstrated from any number of modern examples such as obituary notices, advertisements and recipes.[47] Unfortunately, it is equally easy to think of modern counter-examples, particularly of short, isolated oral forms: for example jokes, amusing anecdotes and limericks. One could certainly list social settings and functions for which each of these would *not* be appropriate, but none of these forms is limited to a single function or setting, not least because any of them can be used in a larger oral or written whole (an after-dinner speech, a sermon, a novel, a newspaper article, an essay, an informal discussion between friends, a formal debate, a biography, a play, a revue, a dictionary of quotations, or even a textbook). This may also be true of many of the forms identified in the Gospel. For example, the Greek *chreia*, which resembles the Paradigm, could be employed in the popular biography of a philosopher, or in the course of a speech, or as a literary exercise, or, no doubt, in the course of preaching, teaching and argumentation as suggested by the form critics.

The notion that the units of tradition preserved in the Gospels circulated independently of one another and of the context in which they now appear does not mean that they were regularly employed without any context, or that they were always employed in the same context; the search for an original setting in the community life of the Church may thus be illusory. Moreover, the use of parallels from surviving Jewish or Graeco-Roman literature may be misleading, since this primarily illustrates the *literary* use of these forms, not the variety of ways in which they may have functioned orally.

That oral tradition often takes specific forms is not in doubt. To be handed on, oral tradition has to be memorable, and the use of set forms or genres is an aid to memory; in part they may correspond to the mnemonic scripts and schemata we shall encounter in Chapter 6.[48] As we shall again see in Chapter 6, both individual and collective memory tends to organize material using familiar narrative or poetic structures. The organization of material into set forms is thus what one might expect of an oral tradition. But we should be wary of rushing to the conclusion that the existence of such forms in the Gospels *proves* the existence of a prior oral tradition. For one thing, a writer sufficiently steeped in an oral tradition can always imitate the forms of that tradition in writing; the formal characteristics of a broadly oral-derived text can never be used to supply certain knowledge

---

[47] See, e.g., Raymond F. Collins, *Introduction to the New Testament* (2nd edn; London: SCM Press, 1992), 156–69.

[48] See also Vansina, *Oral Tradition as History*, 69–79.

about its putative oral prehistory.[49] For another, the kind of shaping into standard forms that the form critics assumed to be the result of transmission through multiple tradents could in principle also come about as the result of an eyewitness honing his or her own reminiscences through multiple performances. The most one can say, therefore, is that the formal characteristics noted by the form critics are consistent with transmission through an extended train of tradition; they do not demand it.

If one looks at the various forms form criticism has discovered in the Gospel tradition, the results in any case seem somewhat mixed; it may be no accident, for example, that E. P. Sanders largely restricts his illustrations of the form-critical method to *chreiae*, miracle stories and parables.[50] Paradigms have a fairly distinctive form that one can at least imagine being the result of frequent oral use, unless one supposes that they are literary imitations of the Hellenistic *chreia* form. Miracle Stories, Parables and Similitudes all likewise have a reasonably recognizable form, even though this may owe as much to their content as to their tradition history. Other forms of isolated sayings material present more of a puzzle, since it is quite hard to imagine a situation in which they could function as isolated units of tradition. For use in argumentation, preaching, instruction or any other such scenario proposed by the form critics, isolated sayings, or even sayings collections, would need to be embedded in some wider discourse (as we indeed find paraenetic material to be when it is deployed in the New Testament Epistles).

The form-critical view that the synoptic tradition originally consisted of isolated units of tradition with no essential chronological relation or organizing framework seems to have been widely accepted, even among scholars otherwise critical of the method.[51] It is indeed suggested by a comparison of the Synoptic Gospels, where one Evangelist may use a pericope in a context quite different from that in which it appears in the work of another. It is also suggested by the structure of the Gospels, in which one incident often follows another without any essential connection or substantial narrative link. Yet even this relatively uncontroversial finding may need to be qualified, particularly if it is taken to imply a linear development from strictly isolated individual items of traditions through aggregates of like material to fully formed Gospels.[52]

---

[49] See, e.g., John Miles Foley, *The Singer of Tales in Performance* (Voices in Performance and Text; ed. J. M. Foley; Bloomington and Indianapolis: Indiana University Press, 1995), 61–78.

[50] Sanders and Davies, *Studying the Synoptic Gospels*, 146–86.

[51] Sanders and Davies, *Studying the Synoptic Gospels*, 134, 188; Bauckham, *Eyewitnesses*, 242.

[52] Mournet, *Oral Tradition*, 72–3.

One has to ask what knowledge was presupposed in the target audience for this kind of material, and thus how isolated the fragments of tradition could actually have been in practice. What value would there be in quoting a saying of Jesus to an audience who had no idea why he should be regarded as authoritative? What significance would a miracle story about Jesus have for someone who had no other notion who Jesus was? Why would the parables of an otherwise unknown teacher be worth attending to? What apologetic function would even a connected Passion narrative have for people who have no reason to suppose that either the death or the person of Jesus held any particular significance? To be sure, people could build up a composite understanding of the significance of Jesus by hearing this material in aggregate over time, but what would attract them to listen to this material unless they had some notion of Jesus' significance in the first place? The notion of *isolated* tradition thus stands in need of revision.[53] A piece of tradition may be isolated in the sense that on any one occasion it may be uttered apart from other parts of the tradition, but that is different from supposing that it is uttered to an audience that knows no other parts of the tradition; both its actual and its intended effects may depend on other parts of the tradition latent in audience memory (as will be explored further in Chapters 6 and 7).

Finally, if form is only loosely related to function and setting, it is hardly related at all to historicity. A speaker may use the same form in narrating a historical healing or a purely fictitious one, particularly if the speaker is repeating something he or she believes to be true without having witnessed it. It is simply an assumption that proposing a present function for a piece of tradition automatically discredits its historicity, although it is an assumption Bultmann appears to have shared with Maurice Halbwachs (whom we shall meet again in Chapter 6).[54]

In sum, then, while form criticism succeeds in suggesting some useful insights and provoking some even more useful questions, it fails both as a method for investigating the traditions behind the Gospels and in supplying an adequate model for those traditions.[55] The chapters that follow will explore some of the reactions that form criticism has provoked and some of the alternative models that have been proposed in its place.

---

[53] So also Birger Gerhardsson, *The Reliability of the Gospel Tradition* (Peabody, MA: Hendrickson, 2001), 47–8.

[54] Barry Schwartz, 'Christian Origins: Historical Truth and Social Memory' in A. Kirk and T. Thatcher (eds), *Memory, Tradition, and Text: Uses of the Past in Early Christianity* (SBL Semeia Studies, 52: Atlanta: SBL, 2005), 249–61 (47–51).

[55] So also Tuckett, 'Form Criticism', 37.

3

The rabbinic model

If form criticism cannot provide an adequate account of the oral tradition behind the Gospels, then some alternative needs to be found, and one of the earliest significant alternatives came from Scandinavia, namely the view that the Jesus tradition should be thought of not as the uncontrolled (yet strangely law-like) growth of anonymous community traditions on analogy with a romantic view of folklore, but as a tightly controlled process of handing on tradition on analogy with rabbinic teaching practices. This is the view we shall examine in the present chapter.

Dibelius had noted in passing that Paul employed the technical terms for the receiving and handing on of tradition, and that he occasionally seemed to be quoting a set formula. Dibelius also briefly hinted at an analogy with rabbinic Judaism. These points did not, however, materially affect Dibelius' conception of anonymous community tradition being employed mainly in preaching.

In contrast, Harald Riesenfeld (then Professor of Exegesis at Uppsala) argued that the New Testament Epistles do not in fact show Jesus material being employed in preaching or any of the other situations Dibelius and the other form critics supposed. Although the Epistles frequently draw on the Jesus tradition, they very rarely quote it in the manner of the Gospels. Riesenfeld thus concluded that some other *Sitz im Leben* must be sought, and proposed the oral Torah of the rabbis as an analogy close to the milieu in which the Gospel tradition was formed. Like Dibelius, he noted that the New Testament uses the Greek equivalents of the rabbis' technical language of receiving and handing on tradition (*paralambanein* and *paradidonai*). Unlike Dibelius he went on to point out that this language was used not of the 'vague diffusion' of anecdotes in folk tradition, but of the highly controlled handing on of a fixed body of material, which the teacher ensured was memorized by his students. This in turn implied that the tradition was handed on not by the community at large, but by certain individuals who were particularly qualified to do so (Riesenfeld cited Paul as one example, and the 'eyewitnesses and ministers of the word' of Luke 1.2 as another).[1]

Riesenfeld went on to suggest that the *Sitz im Leben* for the transmission of the Gospel tradition would have been in community worship, where it would have been treated as a 'New Torah'. For this tradition to have been treated as a holy word it must have originated from Jesus himself. The Gospels portray Jesus as a teacher with disciples, which meant, Riesenfeld argued, that he presumably taught them in the manner of a rabbi, making them learn material by heart, given that much of the material we find in the Gospels indeed looks as if it has been formulated for memorization. This probably also applied to Jesus' deeds as well as his words, since Jesus presumably discussed his deeds (not least his miracles) with his disciples after the event. Although the tradition was subsequently moulded by the Church, in its essentials it thus went back to Jesus himself.[2]

These ideas were taken up and developed in considerably more detail by Riesenfeld's student Birger Gerhardsson, whose work will thus form the focus of this chapter.

Gerhardsson's thesis

Like Riesenfeld, Gerhardsson noted that in several places the New Testament, and particularly Paul, uses the technical language of receiving, handing on and holding fast to a tradition (e.g. 1 Corinthians 11.2, 23; 15.1, 3; Galatians 1.9; Philippians 4.9; 1 Thessalonians 2.13; 4.1; 2 Thessalonians 2.15; 3.6).[3] He pointed out that in that time and culture such language was unlikely to be used of hearing casual gossip or listening to preaching but rather implied a deliberate handing over of tradition. This in turn implied both that the person handing on the tradition would be recognized as having the authority to do so, and that the person receiving the tradition would make a conscious effort to commit it to memory.[4]

Gerhardsson took as his model the way oral Torah was handed on in rabbinic schools (where 'Torah' was taken in a broad sense as the whole

---

[1] Harald Riesenfeld, *The Gospel Tradition and Its Beginnings: A Study in the Limits of 'Formgeschichte'* (London: A. R. Mowbray, 1957), 1–22.

[2] Riesenfeld, *Gospel Tradition*, 22–30.

[3] Birger Gerhardsson, *Memory and Manuscript: Oral Tradition and Written Transmission in Rabbinic Judaism and Early Christianity* (Grand Rapids: Eerdmans/Dove: 1998; originally published Lund: Gleerup, 1961), 288–91. Birger Gerhardsson, *Tradition and Transmission in Early Christianity* (originally published Lund: Gleerup, 1964) is included in the same 1998 volume (and will also be the edition referenced below).

[4] Gerhardsson, *Memory*, 281–3.

of Israel's sacred tradition). Gerhardsson was well aware that the rabbinic schools were later than Jesus' day, so he was not suggesting that Jesus and his disciples modelled themselves on the rabbis. His point was rather that the rabbinic methods for handing on traditions were reasonably close in time and culture to the situation of Jesus and the primitive Church, and were thus worth investigating as a possible analogy for the transmission of the Jesus tradition.

According to Gerhardsson's account, the students of the rabbis had to commit large amounts of material (such as the halakah, or legal rulings, of earlier rabbis) to memory, and educational methods in rabbinic circles involved first committing the oral Torah to memory, and then learning to interpret it.[5] Although rabbinic students might keep their own private notes as an aide-memoire to learning the material, writing down the oral Torah was officially deprecated, and written versions of the oral Torah lacked any public authority.[6] Various methods might be used to aid the rote learning of this large body of material, such as cantillation (a half-singing mode of chanting) and the use of catchwords and the like, but it was mostly learned by constant repetition.[7] Moreover, the material which had to be committed to memory in this way would have been shaped for this purpose; it would not be everyday speech, but would be sharply and economically expressed (in the manner of a proverb or witty aphorism). The job of a teacher, then, would be to formulate his teaching in such pithy and memorable form, and then ensure that his pupils committed it to memory.[8]

Gerhardsson proposed that Jesus taught his disciples in an analogous fashion, and that they in turn would have been careful to hand on his teaching in the same manner. The Synoptic Gospels clearly depict Jesus as a *teacher*, and this is how a teacher in that time and culture would have operated.[9] The sayings of Jesus recorded in the Gospels (especially the Synoptics) are not casual chat; they are *meshalim*, pointed sayings designed to encapsulate Jesus' message in an economical, striking and memorable way. If Jesus actually *taught* his disciples, he would not have been content to let them overhear him preaching to the crowds; he would instead have formulated his teaching in memorable form and then repeated it to his disciples until he was sure they had committed it to memory.[10]

---

[5] Gerhardsson, *Memory*, 85–92, 122–9.
[6] Gerhardsson, *Memory*, 157–63.
[7] Gerhardsson, *Memory*, 113–36, 142–86, 163–9.
[8] Gerhardsson, *Memory*, 136–42.
[9] Gerhardsson, *Memory*, 326–9.
[10] Birger Gerhardsson, *The Reliability of the Gospel Tradition* (Peabody, MA: Hendrickson, 2001), 42–6, 77–8.

Of course the tradition of Jesus' deeds could not have come about in quite the same way, since the disciples would have first learned about them by witnessing them rather than from being taught a carefully formulated account, but Gerhardsson suggested that an 'official' way of narrating these incidents may soon have come about so that they too came to be formulated in oral texts that could be handed on in an analogous manner.[11]

To determine how the Jesus tradition continued to be handed on after Jesus' departure, Gerhardsson turned first to such post-apostolic writers as Papias and Irenaeus, who (he argued) use the language of receiving memorized traditions and (in the case of Irenaeus) committing them to memory themselves.[12] He then devoted rather more space to the evidence he found in Luke–Acts. He acknowledged that Luke was a purposeful theologian with an apologetic interest in demonstrating the reliability of the Christian tradition on the basis of eyewitnesses, but argued that this did not undermine the reliability of what Luke said. The centrality of Jerusalem in Luke–Acts mirrored the centrality of Jerusalem for the word of the Lord in Jewish writings.

In Luke's presentation, the Apostles (that is, the Twelve) were witnesses to both Jesus' resurrection and his earthly ministry. After the resurrection their primary function was witnessing and teaching the word, speaking in the name of Jesus just as the rabbis' disciples would speak in the name of their masters. Indeed, the Apostles devoted themselves to the service of the word, leaving mundane tasks to others (Acts 6.1–6), rather as the rabbinic ideal was to devote oneself to the study of (and obedience to) the Torah. This service of the word included not only teaching it, but also intense discussion to discover its full meaning. In this context 'the word', as an analogue to the rabbinic oral Torah, referred primarily to Jesus' sayings and deeds, as summarized in the speeches in Acts (Acts 2.22–36; 3.12–26; 4.8–12; 5.29–32; 10.34–43), although the Church also took over the Scriptures of Israel. In Luke's presentation Jesus laid the foundation for its Christian interpretation (Luke 24.27, 32, 44–45), and the work of continuing this interpretation was carried on by the Apostles.[13] Gerhardsson thus appears to have envisaged the Apostles as a rabbinic-like college stationed in Jerusalem meticulously studying the Jesus tradition and ensuring its accurate transmission, although he subsequently denied saying that 'the disciples formed a rabbinic academy in Jerusalem'.[14]

---

[11] Gerhardsson, *Reliability*, 46.
[12] Gerhardsson, *Memory*, 194–207.
[13] Gerhardsson, *Memory*, 208–61.
[14] Gerhardsson, *Reliability*, 73.

Whereas in *Memory and Manuscript* Gerhardsson gave the impression that he took this account of matters in Luke–Acts more or less at face value, he later qualified this. He allowed that Luke's picture is 'simplified and even tendentious', but nevertheless argued that it had historical probability on its side, in that the Twelve, as eyewitnesses of Jesus' ministry, would have been the most natural people to turn to for authoritative tradition. He also allowed that Jerusalem would not have been the only centre in which the Jesus tradition was cultivated, and that the Evangelists obtained their material from more than one source. This did not, however, materially affect his view that the Gospel traditions were reliably transmitted by people who were well informed about what Jesus had done and said.[15]

Gerhardsson also discussed the evidence from Paul. We have already seen that Paul uses the language of receiving and handing on traditions, and in passages such as 1 Corinthians 11.23–25; 15.3–7 he appears to be doing so in the form of fairly fixed formulas. Gerhardsson noted that Paul claims to have obtained his gospel directly from the Lord (Galatians 1.11–12), but argued that this primarily concerns his preaching of the law-free gospel to the Gentiles; Paul's teaching came from Jerusalem, presumably based on what Peter handed on to him during his visit there (Galatians 1.18). The very fact that Paul felt the need to check his gospel with the Jerusalem 'pillar Apostles' (Galatians 2.1–2, 9) indicates that he respected the centrality of Jerusalem as the place from which the word of God emanated. Paul's letters admittedly contain few examples of him quoting the tradition thus obtained; more often he uses the tradition by giving its substance in his own words (for example at 1 Corinthians 7.10–11; 9.14), having presumably transmitted it to his congregation in person previously. Gerhardsson thus treated the tradition Paul obtained 'from the Lord' as having come to him from Jesus via the Jerusalem Apostles and consisting of words spoken by Jesus. He noted that Paul clearly acted as someone with the authority to handle the Jesus tradition, which supports his point that the tradition was transmitted by authoritative individuals rather than the anonymous collective, and that the chain of tradition was short (Gerhardsson was quite dismissive of the notion that Paul obtained his tradition from the Hellenistic community).[16]

In sum, in Gerhardsson's view the Jesus tradition originated with Jesus making his disciples commit material to memory and was perpetuated

---

[15] Gerhardsson, *Reliability*, 38–9, 50; cf. Gerhardsson, *Memory*, 334.
[16] Gerhardsson, *Memory*, 262–323; Gerhardsson, *Reliability*, 16–25.

after Jesus' death by the circle of disciples gathered in Jerusalem continuing to nurture it in a controlled fashion. This presumably meant that they continued to rehearse the traditions about Jesus among themselves to keep them fresh in memory, and to search it for further secrets of the kingdom, but it also meant that they would have taken care to teach the tradition to others, that is to ensure that others committed it to memory. Given the Church's view of Jesus as their Lord and Israel's Messiah, they would have regarded his utterances as being of the utmost importance, and would therefore have taken the greatest care to transmit them accurately.[17]

Gerhardsson thus disputed the form-critical view that the primary modes of transmitting the Jesus tradition would have included preaching, exhortation and disputes with outsiders. These might all be situations in which the tradition was *used*, but none of them would have been the primary situation of *transmission*. The tradition was transmitted, that is deliberately handed on, when it was being deliberately taught by methods analogous to those in which the rabbis taught their students.[18]

This does not mean that Gerhardsson thought the Jesus tradition underwent no change or development. He was quite prepared to allow for some variability in the process of oral transmission. He also suggested that the disciples would have been actively engaged in what he called 'work with the word', in particular searching the Scriptures to gain a fuller understanding of the significance of Jesus and developing the Jesus tradition in the light of that study. Some changes undoubtedly occurred to the tradition in this process, partly as a result of translation from Aramaic into Greek, and partly due to the ongoing interpretation of the material. The Gospels also made some interpretive adaptations of the material and placed it in a new context. In a few cases, such as the infancy, baptism and temptation narratives (which Gerhardsson regarded as the creations of Christian scribes), much greater liberties were taken.[19] Gerhardsson's point was not that the Gospels give us a transparent window on what actually happened in Jesus' earthly career, but that both Jesus and his followers took steps to ensure the accurate transmission of his deeds and teaching. The Jesus tradition that reaches us in the Gospels is thus undoubtedly interpreted tradition, but it is basically reliable and is not, as the form critics supposed, contaminated by a great deal of extraneous material generated by the anonymous community to meet changing needs.

---

[17] Gerhardsson, *Memory*, 324–35; Gerhardsson, *Reliability*, 35–40.
[18] Gerhardsson, *Reliability*, 41–4.
[19] Gerhardsson, *Memory*, 331–2; Gerhardsson, *Reliability*, 50–7.

Evaluation

Gerhardsson's thesis has been criticized on a number of counts. First, several scholars have accused Gerhardsson of anachronism in reading later rabbinic techniques back into the first century.[20] This criticism partly misses the point, since Gerhardsson was well aware that the rabbinic material he employed came from well after the time of Jesus but suggested that the ancient world was largely conservative in its teaching methods, and that the rabbis were most unlikely to have invented completely new techniques, however much they developed existing ones to higher levels of sophistication. On that basis it would seem not unreasonable to use the rabbinic material to ascertain how first-century Jews may have gone about teaching and learning.[21] Moreover, rote learning was hardly peculiar to rabbis in antiquity but was the staple of Graeco-Roman education as well.[22] Indeed, it may well have been the staple method of most pre-print cultures where access to written texts was limited and the ability to hold a large amount of material in one's head was not only useful but virtually essential if one was to master it. Again, the rabbinic method of instruction may also have reflected a wider view of the authority of the spoken word; one learned not from a text but from a person, so that the oral transmission of memorized material would be the preferred mode of instruction.

Yet the charge of anachronism is not wholly without force, since rabbinic teaching methods developed over time, and continuity with the pre-70 Pharisees cannot simply be assumed. In particular there appears to have been a substantial change in attitudes towards writing and orality following the destruction of the Temple in 70 CE.[23] Martin Jaffee argues that it was only following the destruction that there was any conscious

---

[20] Morton Smith, 'A Comparison of Early Christian and Early Rabbinic Tradition', *JBL* 82 (1963), 169–76; Werner H. Kelber, *The Oral and the Written Gospel: The Hermeneutics of Speaking and Writing in the Synoptic Tradition, Mark, Paul and Q* (Voices in Performance and Text; Bloomington and Indianapolis: Indiana University Press, 1997), 14; Terence C. Mournet, *Oral Tradition and Literary Dependency: Variability and Stability in the Synoptic Tradition and Q* (WUNT, 195; Tübingen: Mohr Siebeck, 2005), 64.

[21] Gerhardsson, *Reliability*, 73; so also Richard Bauckham, *Jesus and the Eyewitnesses: The Gospels as Eyewitness Testimony* (Grand Rapids and Cambridge: Eerdmans, 2006), 250–1.

[22] Loveday Alexander, 'Memory and Tradition in the Hellenistic Schools' in W. H. Kelber and S. Byrskog (eds), *Jesus in Memory: Traditions in Oral and Scribal Perspectives* (Waco: Baylor University Press, 2009), 113–53 (135–9, 52).

[23] For example, Shemaryahu Talmon, 'Oral Tradition and Written Transmission, or the Heard and Seen Word in Judaism of the Second Temple Period' in Henry Wansbrough, *Jesus and the Oral Gospel Tradition*, 121–58, finds an absence of concern about the oral–written distinction in the pre-70 Qumran community. See also Peter Davids, 'The Gospels and Jewish Tradition: Twenty Years after Gerhardsson' in R. T. France and David Wenham (eds), *Gospel Perspectives*, vol. 1: *Studies of History and Tradition in the Four Gospels* (Sheffield: JSOT Press, 1980), 75–99 (79); and Martin Jaffee below.

reflection on aspects of Jewish tradition as specifically *oral* tradition. Moreover, the media preferences of the rabbis developed over time, with the insistence on the purely oral transmission of halakhic traditions being a relatively late development; even then it was partly an ideological construct (rather than a literally accurate account of pedagogical practice) designed to distinguish Israel's possession of the full Torah from the Gentiles' access to merely the written part of it. While there probably was a preference for face-to-face oral instruction, as there also was in the contemporary rhetorical schools, Jaffee argues that there never was a purely oral process of transmission; the transmission of rabbinic material involved a continuous interplay of oral performance and written text all along.[24]

The rabbinic model Gerhardsson drew on thus turns out not to be one of purely oral tradition after all. Rabbinic teaching methods were intimately bound up with written texts. This makes them unlikely to have been practised among Jesus' disciples. Indeed, the concern for rote memorization of material tends only to occur in literate circles.[25] In purely oral societies verbatim learning of large amounts of material is much less likely. The rabbis were highly literate. Children being taught to memorize large amounts of text (such as Homer) in Graeco-Roman schools were being taught to become literate. The kinds of teaching and learning methods described by Gerhardsson are the kinds of method used by educated literate elites.[26] It is unlikely that Jesus and his first disciples would have fallen into this category. E. P. Sanders noted that 'One of the real accomplishments of Gerhardsson's work is to show how difficult accurate transmission of oral tradition is and the discipline and training required to effect it'.[27] As Sanders goes on to argue, the rapidly expanding primitive Church would have been most unlikely to have contained sufficient persons with the requisite training to control the tradition in the way Gerhardsson envisaged.

Gerhardsson was aware of this objection, and countered that the New Testament presentation of Jesus and the disciples as uneducated was probably for ideological purposes, in order to stress that their teaching came

---

[24] Martin S. Jaffee, *Torah in the Mouth: Writing and Oral Tradition in Palestinian Judaism, 200 BCE – 400 CE* (Oxford: Oxford University Press, 2001), esp. 19, 32, 60–1, 67, 70, 100–2, 124, 128–30, 140, 144, 162 n. 13.

[25] Alan Kirk, 'Memory' in W. H. Kelber and S. Byrskog (eds), *Jesus in Memory: Traditions in Oral and Scribal Perspectives* (Waco: Baylor University Press, 2009), 155–72 (161–2); Jack Goody, *The Interface between the Written and the Oral* (Cambridge: Cambridge University Press, 1987), 78–122.

[26] Kirk, 'Memory', 157–63.

[27] So E. P. Sanders, *The Tendencies of the Synoptic Tradition* (SNTSMS, 9; Cambridge: Cambridge University Press, 1969), 28, 294; cf. Kelber, *Oral and Written*, 9–10, 20–1.

directly from God and not from human learning.[28] But this response is less than satisfactory. Jesus is represented as having ministered mainly in rural Galilee, where literacy rates are likely to have been very low. Three of Jesus' leading disciples, Peter, James and John, are said to have been fishermen, hardly a profession for which literacy would have been a requirement. To suggest that the Jesus tradition is misleading in all these particulars is to undermine the very reliability of the tradition that Gerhardsson is anxious to establish; such a move is surely self-defeating.[29]

R. P. C. Hanson points out that *paradosis* (tradition) occurs nine times in the New Testament in relation to Pharisaic traditions, and three times in relation to Christian traditions, which might suggest that the Christian usage is modelled on the Pharisaic, as Gerhardsson argues.[30] But the Christian usage seems to be entirely Pauline (1 Corinthians 11.2; 2 Thessalonians 2.15; 3.6). The fact that the Pharisaically educated and presumably literate Paul uses the technical language of handing on and receiving tradition may reflect the assumptions of his background rather than the teaching methods of Jesus and his first followers.[31] Loveday Alexander has argued that the kind of apostolic *collegium* Gerhardsson envisages is plausible on the analogy of Hellenistic schools, partly on the basis that Luke's picture would have to seem plausible to his audience and the existence of such a *collegium* is just what one would expect given the Hellenistic school precedent, and partly because the need to develop the tradition would have been too important to leave to chance memory.[32] Given that such a *collegium* would have operated primarily in oral mode, it is not absolutely impossible to imagine it being set up by unlettered people on the basis of a known model, but it seems more probable that Alan Kirk and Terence Mournet are both right to object that the model is too scribal – too related, that is, to the medium of writing – to be readily applicable to the formation of the Jesus tradition.[33]

One may also enquire whether the Jesus tradition exhibits the characteristics one would expect it to have if Gerhardsson's account were correct. Arguably, it does not.[34] The variability in wording of parallel passages in the Synoptic Gospels indicates a lack of concern to preserve carefully

---

[28] Gerhardsson, *Tradition and Transmission*, 24–6.

[29] So also Smith, 'Comparison', 174.

[30] R. P. C. Hanson, *Tradition in the Early Church* (London: SCM Press, 1962), 10–12.

[31] So also Smith, 'Comparison', 175–6.

[32] Alexander, 'Memory and Tradition', 152.

[33] Kirk, 'Memory', 165; Mournet, *Oral Tradition*, 65–6; Smith, 'Comparison', 172–4.

[34] So, e.g., James D. G. Dunn, *Jesus Remembered* (Christianity in the Making, 1; Grand Rapids and Cambridge: Eerdmans, 2003), 198.

memorized material in fixed form. Admittedly there tends to be less variability in the wording of Jesus' sayings than in the narrative material, which might lend support to Gerhardsson's case, but there are also notable variations in the sayings material: one only has to think of the differing Matthean and Lukan versions of the Beatitudes and the Lord's Prayer (Matthew 5.3–11 || Luke 6.20–26; Matthew 6.9–13 || Luke 11.2–4). Yet Gerhardsson might regard this kind of variation as lying within the bounds of the relative fixity he has in mind. He does, of course, recognize the existence of variations between parallel material in the Synoptic Gospels, but regards them as interpretive adaptations designed to bring out the meaning of the transmitted texts. In Gerhardsson's view such editorial changes are quite compatible with verbatim learning and are indeed paralleled in the rabbinic tradition.[35]

P. S. Alexander points out that where one can compare different versions of the same traditions in rabbinic literature, 'it is at once obvious that the material has not remained stable but has changed over time'.[36] Moreover, what the rabbinic literature tends to preserve is not the *ipsissima verba* (the very words) of the various rabbinic authorities it cites, but their reduction to a formulaic summary.[37] It is debatable whether these points are helpful or harmful to Gerhardsson's case. On the one hand it could be argued that to the extent that the variations in parallel versions of the synoptic tradition resemble the variations in parallel versions of the rabbinic traditions, the analogy between the synoptic tradition and the rabbinic tradition still holds. On the other, it could be urged that not even the rabbinic tradition really exhibits the kind of verbatim teaching and learning to which Gerhardsson appealed. If Gerhardsson were content to argue that the Jesus tradition preserved the gist rather than the wording of Jesus' sayings this might not be too problematic for him, but he makes a point of distinguishing between the way the Gospel tradition preserved Jesus' words and the way other New Testament writers such as Paul use the gist of Jesus' teaching in paraphrase.

E. P. Sanders argues that the early Jesus tradition was positively unlike the rabbinic tradition in a number of respects, including the creativity

---

[35] Gerhardsson, *Reliability*, 53–4; cf. his discussion of variations among versions of the narrative parables in Birger Gerhardsson, 'Illuminating the Kingdom: Narrative Meshalim in the Synoptic Gospels' in Henry Wansbrough (ed.), *Jesus and the Oral Gospel Tradition* (JSNTSup, 64; Sheffield: Sheffield Academic Press, 1991), 266–309 (298–9).

[36] P. S. Alexander, 'Orality in Pharisaic-Rabbinic Judaism at the Turn of the Eras' in Wansbrough (ed.), *Jesus and the Oral Gospel Tradition*, 159–84 (182).

[37] Alexander, 'Orality', 172–6.

that was probably encouraged by the belief in Jesus as living Lord, the relative brevity of the period of oral transmission prior to the writing of the Gospels, and the fact that the Gospel traditions existed in more than one language.[38] It has also been pointed out that what the rabbis memorized was a combination of written texts and commentaries on those texts, which is somewhat different from the Jesus material in its oral stage.[39]

Yet another objection to Gerhardsson's thesis is that the New Testament presents neither Jesus nor his followers handing on tradition in the manner Gerhardsson describes.[40] It is unclear how much force this objection has: if it were the case that Jesus and his followers were using teaching and learning techniques common to their culture (as Gerhardsson supposes) then there would be no particular reason for the New Testament authors to draw attention to the fact; they would be more likely simply to take it for granted.[41] Gerhardsson offers a partial argument for his model when he suggests that Jesus' explanation of his parables (e.g. at Mark 4.13–20) presupposes that the parable being explained was a fixed text previously committed to memory.[42] This argument is not particularly strong, however, both since the explanation of the parables is generally thought to be a secondary contribution rather than part of Jesus' original teaching, and because the explanation supposedly offered by Jesus would surely suffice to remind his listeners of the thrust of the parable.

Gerhardsson concedes that 'Jesus sometimes presents narrative meshalim in contexts where a single presentation would be quite enough for giving the listener the illumination intended' and that 'the composite picture of Jesus' teaching in narrative meshalim makes it quite possible that he presented his short narratives in different ways in different situations.'[43] Such concessions tend to undermine the thesis that Jesus passed on all his teaching to his disciples using formal methods akin to those attributed to the rabbis; for if some of the narrative parables in the Gospels could have found their way there from a single presentation in Jesus' ministry, it is unclear why the same could not apply to other parts of Jesus' teaching.

---

[38] Sanders, *Tendencies*, 27–8; cf. Hanson, *Tradition in the Early Church*, 16–17.

[39] Smith, 'Comparison', 173–4; Sanders, *Tendencies*, 294; Davids, 'Gospels and Jewish Tradition', 79; Erhardt Güttgemanns, *Candid Questions Concerning Gospel Form Criticism: A Methodological Sketch of the Fundamental Problematics of Form and Redaction Criticism* (Pittsburgh Theological Monograph Series, 26; ed. D. Y. Hadidian; tr. William G. Doty; Pittsburgh: Pickwick Press, 1979), 213–14; Kelber, *Oral and Written*, 9–10.

[40] Kelber, *Oral and Written*, 14; Smith, 'Comparison', 174–5.

[41] Gerhardsson, *Tradition and Transmission*, 22–3.

[42] Gerhardsson, 'Illuminating the Kingdom', 303.

[43] Gerhardsson, 'Illuminating the Kingdom', 303, 304.

Gerhardsson is justified in pointing out that the idea of Jesus *teaching* his disciples implies something rather more than casual conversation or allowing them to overhear his public proclamation, but he has not succeeded in showing that the formal teaching techniques of the rabbis provide the best model for what that something more must have been.

These considerations lead into one of Werner Kelber's main criticisms of Gerhardsson, namely that he employs a model of the purely academic memorization of material divorced from the social context of its actual use.[44] Kelber instead proposes that Jesus' teaching would have been remembered insofar as it struck a chord with its audience and continued to have some kind of resonance with the group that transmitted it. Kelber moreover implies that what Gerhardsson perceives as the deliberate formulation of pithy sayings for the purpose of memorization is simply 'the formulaic quality of oral speech'.[45] At this point, however, Kelber is not so much arguing against Gerhardsson as putting forward contrary assertions. Gerhardsson made it quite plain that he distinguished between the various occasions on which the tradition was used and the formal process of handing it on in teaching. Kelber here appears to be arguing against the latter because it ignores the social particularities of the former, but this is simply to bypass Gerhardsson's argument, not to refute it. Again, Kelber's point about the formulaic quality of oral speech is double-edged, since if such a quality is discernible in the surviving written sources it surely implies some continuity between those sources and the preceding oral tradition.

Kelber's other main criticism of Gerhardsson is that he has not sufficiently taken into account the fundamental differences between oral and written media, and that, in common with Bultmann, Gerhardsson's model remains too bound up with the world of written texts.[46] But since this criticism is not specific to Gerhardsson, and is aimed more at introducing Kelber's own approach, it can be left until we come to discuss Kelber in his own right. It should in any case be noted that Kelber has also expressed appreciation for many aspects of Gerhardsson's pioneering work.[47]

Overall, then, Gerhardsson's theory represents a serious attempt to address some of the shortcomings of form criticism but turns out to have

---

[44] Kelber, *Oral and Written*, 21–4.

[45] Kelber, *Oral and Written*, 27.

[46] Kelber, *Oral and Written*, 14–34.

[47] Werner H. Kelber, 'The Work of Birger Gerhardsson in Perspective' in W. H. Kelber and S. Byrskog (eds), *Jesus in Memory: Traditions in Oral and Scribal Perspectives* (Waco: Baylor University Press, 2009), 173–206.

a number of weaknesses of its own. On the one hand it takes seriously the language of receiving and handing on tradition found in some parts of the New Testament, just as it takes into account forms of learning and teaching likely to have been current in some quarters of the first-century Mediterranean world. Moreover the idea that the primitive Church would have been concerned to preserve traditions about Jesus and would have regarded some persons as particularly authoritative tradents is *a priori* more probable than form criticism's assumptions to the contrary, given the reverence for the person of Jesus in the primitive Church and the respect for traditional authority in the milieu in which it operated. It would be odd indeed if the Twelve ceased to have any function within a year or two of Jesus' death or if certain persons did not come to have much more control over the tradition than others; the notion that folk traditions about Jesus simply emerged from an anonymous egalitarian community probably owes more to romanticism than to the kind of social realities in which some people compete for power and influence, and others look up to those whom they regard as authoritative.

On the other hand, many aspects of Gerhardsson's model do not fit the Gospel materials. In particular, the variations we find between synoptic parallels do not seem compatible with a tightly controlled procedure for handing on a fixed tradition, and the social location of primitive Christianity was not one in which a scholastic method of strictly controlled oral transmission was likely to occur (even assuming that it was actually practised by the rabbis on whom Gerhardsson based his analogy). It is also problematic to suppose that the Jesus tradition was tightly controlled by one group of Apostles in Jerusalem. Moreover, it seems unlikely that the method of handing on Jesus tradition was uniform throughout the primitive Church from 30 CE until 70 CE (or whenever the Gospel of Mark was written). Primitive Christianity probably took different forms in rural Galilee where Jesus ministered, Jerusalem where Gerhardsson thinks the Twelve gathered, and the Gentile cities that formed the focus of Paul's ministry.[48] While the methods of handing on tradition employed by the Twelve in Jerusalem (who seem to be the main focus of Gerhardsson's theory) may have been stricter than the way tradition was used in the places where the Gospels were written a generation later, it is difficult to envisage Gerhardsson's model applying all the way from Jesus' earthly preaching to the composition of all three Synoptic Gospels.

---

[48] Mournet, *Oral Tradition*, 64, makes a similar point.

4

The media contrast model

Starting in the 1950s and continuing into the 1980s, form criticism provoked two trends that together offered a challenge to its model of oral tradition of a rather different sort from that provided by Gerhardsson. Form criticism had regarded the Evangelists, particularly Mark, merely as collectors and editors of the traditions at their disposal. With the rise of redaction criticism in the mid 1950s, increasing attention was paid to the role of the Evangelists as authors in their own right impressing their own particular theological viewpoint on the material. Willi Marxsen, who pioneered the redaction criticism of Mark, was no longer content to see Mark's Gospel 'as the "termination" of the anonymous transmission of material' but rather viewed it as a 'systematically constructed piece'.[1] In his view the scattering tendencies of the pre-Gospel traditions could not account for the unity imparted to them in the Gospels, which 'cannot be explained without taking into an account an individual, an author personality who pursues a definite goal with his work'.[2]

Once Marxsen's point is taken seriously, several cracks start to appear in the form-critical edifice. For one thing, the notion that the Gospels are simply the natural endpoints of the evolution of the oral tradition ceases to be credible. But if that is no longer credible, then the form-critical assertion that there was no significant difference between oral and written media in the synoptic tradition is also undermined. At least with the writing of Mark, something fundamentally new has occurred. Also, the more the redaction-critical approach sees Mark as master of his material, the more, that is, that redaction criticism becomes composition criticism or some form of holistic literary criticism, the less relevant the distinction between redaction and tradition starts to appear. With that step, the apparent evidence for pre-Markan collections of controversy stories and miracle stories starts to recede, as it becomes more plausible to view the arrangement of all the materials

---

[1] Willi Marxsen, *Mark the Evangelist: Studies in the Redaction History of the Gospel* (tr. James Boyce, Donal Juel, William Poehlmann, with Roy A. Harrisville; Nashville and New York: Abingdon Press, 1969), 18.

[2] Marxsen, *Mark*, 18.

in Mark as due to Mark's narrative design. With the disappearance of any need for these intermediate written collections, the evolutionary theory of Gospel origins is further undermined, and the distinction between a written Mark and the prior oral tradition looks ever more pronounced.

A separate but parallel impetus for questioning form criticism's understanding of orality stemmed from the interdisciplinary study of folklore, media and linguistics. In the 1970s and 1980s two scholars in particular stand out as pursuing this second line of enquiry, Erhardt Güttgemanns and Werner Kelber. Although writing from somewhat different perspectives (Güttgemanns was addressing what he regarded as the stagnation in German form criticism, whereas Kelber was primarily inspired by anglophone studies on orality, particularly the work of Walter Ong), there is a sufficiently common thrust to their work for it to be worth considering them together; in any case Kelber quite clearly regarded himself as continuing along the lines Güttgemanns had suggested.[3]

Erhardt Güttgemanns

We have already encountered some of Güttgemanns' critique of the form-critical understanding of orality in Chapter 2. The present chapter focuses on his critique of form criticism's minimization of the differences between oral and written media in the transmission of the synoptic tradition.

On this issue Güttgemanns began by noting the tension between form and redaction criticism inherent in the remarks of Marxsen noted above, and went on to suggest that there was more to the transition from the sociological setting of the individual units of tradition to the literary framework of the Gospels than form criticism allowed for. This was due not least to the fact that in being incorporated into a written Gospel, pericopae were removed from their original sociological setting and given an entirely new setting by being framed in a new entity. This new literary framework provided much more than the mere fixation of previously oral material; it represented the creation of a completely new genre.[4]

After discussing a number of other issues (some of which were covered in Chapter 2 above), Güttgemanns went on to discuss the question of the

---

[3] Werner H. Kelber, *The Oral and the Written Gospel: The Hermeneutics of Speaking and Writing in the Synoptic Tradition, Mark, Paul and Q* (Voices in Performance and Text; Bloomington and Indianapolis: Indiana University Press, 1997), 2.

[4] Erhardt Güttgemanns, *Candid Questions Concerning Gospel Form Criticism: A Methodological Sketch of the Fundamental Problematics of Form and Redaction Criticism* (Pittsburgh Theological Monograph Series, 26; ed. D. Y. Hadidian; tr. William G. Doty; Pittsburgh: Pickwick Press, 1979), 96–125.

oral and the written in contemporary linguistics, drawing especially on the work of Ferdinand de Saussure. He insisted that the oral and the written are two different modes of linguistic communication, since writing replaces the acoustic with the visual. This is no minor difference; the differences between the written and the oral extend to all structural levels, including phonology, morphology, syntax, vocabulary and style. Written language tends to develop greater objectification and consistency, and to free language from the immediate context of utterance.[5]

Güttgemanns turned next to the pivotal work of Albert Lord on Balkan oral epics, from which he drew a number of conclusions. First, a single performance of a work of oral poetry is not the repetition of some supposed original, but an invention in itself. Second, oral poets do not work with any concept of fixed wording or form; they have no notion of a normative 'text'. While there may be a first performance of some particular poem, this does not constitute the 'original' of which subsequent performances are 'variations', since each performance is a new creative act. Third, the advent of writing creates great difficulty for oral bards; reduction of a poem to writing results in a normative text which undermines the circumstances of oral performance. Fourth, in the oral period the bards were forced to think in formulas and formal models, and the radical effect of the transition from the oral to the written can be seen in the case of the Balkan bards. Fifth, the notion of transitional texts, something halfway between oral and written traditions, is problematic. In particular, performances taken down in dictation are not 'transitional texts'. There is no continuity in the sociology of tradition between the oral and written levels. Güttgemanns regarded these findings as placing a large question mark against the form-critical assumption of the identity of the laws of tradition history in the oral and written phases, concluding that the biblical texts as we have them are always effectively 'literary'. To get back to any preliterary stage then requires an appropriate empirical analogy.[6] (Here, unfortunately, Güttgemanns was guilty of supposing that what Lord said about Balkan bards applied to all forms of oral tradition, an assumption which is scarcely sustainable; he also drew the oral–written distinction too sharply).

Güttgemanns went on to explain Gunkel's notion of *Sitz im Leben* as 'setting in folk-life', and to explain why this notion could not simply be transferred to a written situation without modification. In particular, since

---

[5] Güttgemanns, *Candid Questions*, 196–9.
[6] Güttgemanns, *Candid Questions*, 204–10.

writing frees both the writer and the text from the immediate social situation, it is not subject to the same social-formative pressures as oral tradition and so cannot be assumed to be subject to the same laws. In any case the 'context-situation' as cultural anthropology understands it indicates that in concrete speech situations the entire culture of a people constitutes the linguistic context (this is an idea we shall see developed in later chapters); form criticism's notion of 'sociological setting' was thus too narrow.[7]

Referring once again to Marxsen's redaction-critical work on Mark, Güttgemanns asked whether the Gospel form was the result of a deliberate redactional act or of the collective tradition. For an answer, he turned not just to Marxsen's work on Mark but to the notion of a linguistic *Gestalt*. Put simply, a *Gestalt* is a composite in which the whole is more than the sum of its parts and in which the framework and the material incorporated into the framework exist in dialectic interaction (in other words, with each influencing the other). If the small units from which the Gospels were composed are 'signs', then their framing in the Gospels generates a 'super sign' which cannot be derived genetically from the tradition history of the material.[8] Neither, Güttgemanns argued, could it be derived from anything else inherent in the tradition. The notion of kerygma, the central message contained in the preaching of the gospel, turns out to be too indeterminate to bear the weight put on it, not least because the notion relied too heavily on material in Luke–Acts that was probably the work of Luke rather than a reflection of primitive Christian preaching. The notion that the written Gospels were an evolutionary development of the primitive kerygma is ill-founded, as is the notion of a 'law' of development from simpler, briefer and isolated elements into more complex, longer and aggregated ones. C. H. Dodd's notion of a primitive pre-Markan outline of Jesus' ministry was also found wanting; again partly on account of its unjustified reliance on Luke–Acts, and partly because Güttgemanns could not conceive of an appropriate social setting and circle of tradents for the transmission of Dodd's framework. Güttgemanns thus argued that there is nothing demonstrable that the Markan framework could have evolved *from*.[9]

Güttgemanns finally sought to undermine the notion of gradual evolutionary stages in the growth of the Gospel form by questioning the notion of pre-Markan redactional complexes, which he regarded as purely

---

[7] Güttgemanns, *Candid Questions*, 235–74.
[8] Güttgemanns, *Candid Questions*, 277–90.
[9] Güttgemanns, *Candid Questions*, 297–333.

hypothetical. He pointed out, for example, that differences in scholarly opinion over the extent and history of the pre-Markan Passion narrative show that too many hypothetical and subjective judgements were involved in its reconstruction. In any case, if the Passion narrative is supposed to be unique in being the only primitive connected narrative, we lack any analogies by which to gauge its pre-Markan form. A number of other proposed pre-Markan complexes were then examined (such as the group of controversy stories in Mark 2.1—3.6), but in no case was Güttgemanns convinced that their pre-Markan existence could be demonstrated. He therefore concluded that the assumption of pre-Markan redaction was an assumption whose accuracy could not be demonstrated, so that there was no observable process of gradual evolution towards the Gospel form.[10]

Many of Güttgemanns' reservations about form criticism remain pertinent, but not everything he said about the oral–written distinction would bear critical scrutiny today. One central, but perhaps questionable, thrust of his argument is that there was a substantial discontinuity between the written Gospel and the oral tradition that preceded it. This is a thesis that Werner Kelber was to develop even more strikingly, as we shall now go on to see.

Werner Kelber

The central thesis of Kelber's important book, *The Oral and the Written Gospel*, was the radical discontinuity between the Gospel of Mark as a written text and the oral tradition that preceded it. Whatever the shortcomings of his case, Kelber both injected a much needed dose of interdisciplinary expertise into the debate by drawing on the work of folklorists, anthropologists and other contemporary experts on orality and called attention to the typographic bias of much modern biblical scholarship.

After a brief review of the work of Bultmann and Gerhardsson, Kelber sketched his own view of oral transmission as 'a process of social identification and preventive censorship'.[11] He made the point that spoken and written words come into being under quite different circumstances. Speech implies an immediate audience, whose presence may affect what is said, whereas the author of a text is allowed more detachment from an immediate social context, and thus has more control. What can be said orally is limited by the requirements of memorable speech, which must

---

[10] Güttgemanns, *Candid Questions*, 333–42.
[11] Kelber, *Oral and Written*, 14.

employ devices such as oral formulas and mnemonic patterning. What is remembered of speech (in a primary oral context) is what is relevant for present living. Oral composition and transmission is thus constrained by audience response and social situation in a way that writing is not. While the first-century Jewish context was no stranger to written texts, literacy rates were low throughout the ancient world and most people communicated orally. What we know of the social profile of the primitive Church also indicates a primarily oral environment, particularly in its rural beginnings where face-to-face communication would have been the norm.[12]

Jesus himself operated orally; so far as we know he never wrote anything. He made his impact by relying on the living power of the spoken word. Against Bultmann, Kelber believed that the origin of the Christian tradition lay in Jesus' own speech. Jesus preached mainly among the people of rural Galilee, who themselves possessed oral rather than literary habits. Thereafter we should not limit the transmission of traditions to the twelve Apostles, but should suppose that anyone could have told stories about Jesus, including the 'common folk'. *Pace* Gerhardsson, nothing in the tradition suggests any stress on deliberate memorization, nor could authorities control the tradition to the extent Gerhardsson envisaged. The actual process of tradition was probably much more complex.[13]

Kelber did not rule out the existence of written notes at a fairly early stage, and he did not think that the details of the interplay between written and oral media are fully recoverable, but he clearly envisaged a process that was primarily oral. He insisted that speech always occurs in a social context. The sayings of Jesus that would have been passed on would have been those that struck a chord in their first hearers. Continuing transmission would have depended on the message's ability to find an echo in the hearts and minds of its audience, although this would not exclude the possibility that a group might also preserve what it found odd or offensive, since its very oddness might make it memorable. In general, though, the tradition would have been preserved through the law of *social identification* rather than by any techniques of verbatim memorization. As one example Kelber cited Gerd Theissen's thesis that the more radical anti-family, anti-property sayings were preserved by wandering charismatics who practised the lifestyle they proclaimed (though Kelber thought it unrealistic to confine the bearers of this tradition to such a group). As another, Kelber cited the miracle stories, which he saw as

---

[12] Kelber, *Oral and Written*, 14–17.
[13] Kelber, *Oral and Written*, 18–22.

functioning to integrate the sick into society, and so as appealing both to the sick and to the wider society.[14]

Contrary to form criticism, Kelber did not think that any one form was necessarily limited to a single social setting. For Kelber, form was more a function of the technique of oral transmission. To be memorable, speech has to fall into recognizable patterns (rhythmic and structural) and conform to mnemonic formalities. Many sayings of Jesus seem to be patterned in such a way, and it has often been noted how the miracle stories employ conventional and predictable structures. According to Kelber, this patterning is not due to the employment of a conscious oral technique, but integral to the way people steeped in oral habits primarily think. The use of oral clichés does not, however, imply verbatim repetition. Oral formulas lend themselves to habitual rather than verbatim memorization, and allow for change, flexibility and adaptability as well as stability in oral transmission.[15]

Nothing guarantees that an oral tradition will always grow and develop. Oral tradition does not only remember; it also forgets. In particular, it will tend to forget what its bearers no longer find useful or acceptable. This is what Kelber meant by *preventive censorship*, which can take many forms, including the reduction of a tradition to its most basic essentials. Conversely, a speaker may narrate a story with all sorts of additional details and digressions. The changes an oral tradition undergoes are not in any case limited to growth and loss. All sorts of other changes may occur, including the shuffling and interchange of stock features, the substitution of one theme for another, the variation of sequence, and the borrowing of features from other materials, related or otherwise. On the whole, oral transmission tends to preserve whatever is regarded as essential, while abandoning or transforming whatever no longer meets social approval. When social needs change, the tradition can be moulded to match that change, not least by attracting or creating fresh materials. In all this, contrary to what the form critics believed, there were no uniform tendencies.[16]

In Kelber's view, the notion of an original form needed to be abandoned along with that of the uniform evolution of the synoptic tradition. Each oral performance is a unique performance. If Jesus said much the same thing more than once, his first utterance should not be regarded as the 'original' of which the subsequent utterances were 'variations'. Moreover,

---

[14] Kelber, *Oral and Written*, 23–6.
[15] Kelber, *Oral and Written*, 27.
[16] Kelber, *Oral and Written*, 28–30.

oral transmission and oral composition are not separate activities but rather essentially intertwined. Oral transmission is not the handing on of something fixed, but its perpetual recreation in a series of individual performances. It is therefore futile to look for either the pure form or the original form. It is also a fundamental error to regard the development of the synoptic tradition as any kind of simple, linear process. There was no sufficiently tightly knit Christian community to control such a process, and one should instead think in terms of a multiplicity of performers generating and transmitting a tradition whose paths crossed and recrossed, diverging into a plurality of forms and directions. In sum, the oral tradition was marked by both stability and variability, both conservatism and creativity.[17]

Having sketched his general understanding of oral transmission, Kelber next turned to the ways in which Mark's Gospel both showed its debt to its oral legacy and illustrated the forms of material transmitted in the synoptic tradition. Like the form critics before him, Kelber categorized the traditional material into a number of forms, though he did not attempt to be comprehensive, since his intention was to illustrate Mark's oral legacy rather than to provide a thorough analysis. For this purpose Kelber looked at what he called Heroic Stories (healing stories), Polarization Stories (exorcisms), Didactic Stories (apophthegms or pronouncement stories) and Parabolic Stories. Unlike the form critics, Kelber was not interested in finding history of religions parallels to these forms, or in seeking an original form, or in assigning each form to a particular *Sitz im Leben*; his concern was rather to discuss what they showed about the technique of oral transmission.[18]

In the case of the Heroic (healing) Stories, Kelber noted that 'we encounter a *plurality* of brief tales that are impressive by their *uniformity* of composition and *variability* of narrative exposition'.[19] He illustrated this by briefly discussing the ten Heroic Stories he found in Mark. Each of these follows the same basic structure, but with great variation in the actual motifs employed. The three component parts of the basic structure are: *exposition of healing, performance of healing*, and *confirmation of healing*, with a number of auxiliary motifs (such as 'arrival of sick person and healer') composing each part; it is particularly in the selection and deployment of these auxiliary motifs that variability occurs, with the result that no two

---

[17] Kelber, *Oral and Written*, 30–4.
[18] Kelber, *Oral and Written*, 44–5.
[19] Kelber, *Oral and Written*, 46.

healing stories are exactly alike. Kelber suggested that this variability is similar to that which Albert Lord found in the process of oral transmission and composition, so that the combination of plurality, uniformity and variability of Heroic Stories attested to the oral nature of their composition and performance.[20]

Kelber further suggested that the Heroic (healing) Stories also exhibited an oral mode of dramatization. First (as Bultmann and others had also noted), they employ the law of scenic duality, meaning that no more than two principal actors are 'on stage' at any one point in the story (although one of the actors may be a group rather than an individual). Second, the stories do not develop the character of Jesus by, for example, assigning him any particular motives for healing; he simply heals because there is a healing to be performed and he fulfils the prescribed role of healer. It is this typecasting of Jesus into the healer role that caused Kelber to label these *Heroic* Stories. Kelber was here referring to the tendency of oral narration to eschew the mundane and ordinary and focus on the extraordinary, to reduce the human condition to a single dimension and then to exaggerate that dimension. The result is that Jesus is 'intensified and simplified'; he is made 'heroic' in the sense that he becomes larger than life (though not devoid of human frailty), thus conforming to the demands of oral rhetoric and oral presentation.[21]

In the Polarization Stories (exorcisms), Kelber found that this heroic tendency is slanted towards the agonistic (from the Greek *agōn*, meaning 'contest'). Mark's three exorcism stories (Mark 1.21–28; 5.1–20; 9.14–29) all portray a contest between Jesus and the forces of evil. This, too, Kelber regarded as characteristic of oral storytelling, which finds sharply defined struggle and competition more memorable than the everyday round and the commonplace complexities and ambiguities of ordinary life. Indeed, he went on to suggest that in agonistic oral culture the figure of Jesus practically demanded a (preferably personalized) opponent. Like the Heroic Stories, the Polarization Stories also exhibit their oral nature through their combination of structural uniformity and variation in the details of performance.[22]

Kelber classified as Didactic Stories the six controversy stories in Mark that end with a memorable saying of Jesus (Mark 2.15–17, 18–19, 23–28; 10.2–9, 17–22; 12.13–17). By combining story with statement, these stories

---

[20] Kelber, *Oral and Written*, 46–51.
[21] Kelber, *Oral and Written*, 51–2.
[22] Kelber, *Oral and Written*, 52–5.

encapsulate the values of the community in memorable form. As is usual in oral culture, they do so by providing examples of application rather than abstract generalizations.[23]

Kelber identified six Parabolic Stories in Mark (Mark 4.3–8, 26–29, 30–32; 12.1–11; 13.28, 34), although he pointed out that parabolic discourse is to be found throughout the Gospel. He could find no common pattern that fitted all six; parables were not formulaic compositions in the way that healing, exorcism and didactic stories were. At first sight the everyday agricultural setting of the parables might seem to run contrary to the rule that oral performance prefers the striking and the extraordinary, but in Kelber's view these parables are rendered memorable by the striking contrasts they contain (for example between the dismal failure and the extraordinary success of the various seeds sown in the Parable of the Sower). The initial appearance of commonplace realism in the parables is misleading; they are in fact characterized by what Paul Ricoeur calls 'extravagance', meaning elements of surprise, hyperbole and paradox, although extravagance is relatively muted in the Markan parables compared with those in Matthew and Luke. What all parables nevertheless share is a metaphorical quality; they all point beyond themselves to something they never clearly define, simultaneously suggesting and concealing understanding. This makes them a quintessentially oral form of address, strongly dependent for their interpretation on the circumstances of their utterance (including gestures, facial expression and the like as well as context; had Kelber been aware of it at the time he might well have added metonymic referentiality, a concept we shall meet in Chapter 6).[24]

Mark's oral legacy is exhibited not only in the individual units he employs, but in the way he constructs a connected narrative out of them. For one thing, Mark's Gospel remains an aggregate of individual stories (as the form critics realized). These individual units are linked by stereotypical devices that differ little from the linking devices within pericopae. Mark's large-scale compositional technique also retains a strongly oral flavour in its frequent use of folkloristic triads and its penchant for repetition (which is almost essential in a story designed to be heard). Mark's style is likewise more oral than literate, with overuse of the historic present and of parataxis (stringing sentences together with 'and'), preference for direct over indirect speech and for the third person plural active over the passive voice, and indeed in its employment of a colloquial Greek Koine. Characters

---

[23] Kelber, *Oral and Written*, 55–7.
[24] Kelber, *Oral and Written*, 57–64.

are also deployed in a manner typical of oral storytelling, which prefers to exhibit characters in action rather than attempt any kind of psychological character development. Overall then, Mark approached his composition far more as a speaker than a writer.[25]

In common with the form critics, Kelber recognized the Passion narrative as an exception to Mark's use of isolated oral units. He saw it as a tightly plotted account which shows little sign of incorporating previously oral forms. Against the form critics Kelber did not think this meant that there was a primitive pre-Markan Passion narrative composed close to the events it describes. For one thing, the various attempts to reconstruct the pre-Markan Passion narrative were so contradictory as to cast doubt on all of them; it was more plausible to see Mark's Passion narrative as woven out of whole cloth. For another, narrative coherence is by no means an index of closeness to the events narrated. Moreover, in Kelber's view, it is hard to find either a convincing setting for or a formal parallel to such an extended pre-Markan Passion narrative. Mark's Passion narrative is, for example, quite distinct from the oral formula of 1 Corinthians 15.3b–6, and it is far from clear that something like the former could grow out of something like the latter. More controversially, Kelber suggested that it required distance from the events to be able to write about the death of the Messiah at all, something he suggested would be too unheroic for orality to cope with. Instead, Kelber proposed that the Passion narrative was a Markan composition, designed to further Mark's theological agenda (in particular, the necessity of Jesus' death in the divine plan) by showing its conformity to Scripture (recycled from secondary orality to form the basis of Mark's account).[26] In response to criticism from Thomas Farrell that Mark hardly presents Jesus' death as unheroic, Kelber subsequently modified his position to suggest that Mark's Passion narrative redefines heroism in terms of the cross.[27]

Although Kelber did not stress the point, his views on the Markan Passion narrative reinforce his emphasis on the oral legacy of the remainder of the Gospel. Given that Mark could produce a relatively seamless narrative when he chose, the case for seeing the isolated accounts that make up much of Mark 1—13 as the residue of oral tradition is strengthened. This emphasis

---

[25] Kelber, *Oral and Written*, 64–70.

[26] Kelber, *Oral and Written*, 184–98.

[27] Thomas J. Farrell, 'Kelber's Breakthrough' in Lou H. Silberman (ed.), *Orality, Aurality and Biblical Narrative* (Semeia, 39; Decatur, GA: Scholars Press, 1987), 27–46 (40–1); Werner Kelber, 'Biblical Hermeneutics and the Ancient Art of Communication: A Response' in Silberman (ed.), *Orality*, 97–105 (102–3).

on the oral nature of Mark's composition (apart from the Passion narrative) raises the question whether prior to Mark there may have been a purely oral gospel of similar scope (as Herder supposed). Kelber decided not. The parallels with the possibly oral nature of epic poetry such as the *Iliad* and the *Odyssey* and the certainly oral poetry of Balkan bards was misleading, since the Gospels were not oral epic poetry but prose narratives. Moreover the Balkan bards drew on centuries of oral culture not available to Mark. But perhaps most importantly the compositional structure of Mark, which binds heterogeneous units into a single narrative, is contrary to the nature of orality which typically clusters similar material.[28]

Kelber went on to develop his thesis of the essential textual, written, nature of Mark's Gospel at some length. In part this is simply a development of Güttgemanns' insight that the Gospel is a *Gestalt*, so that removing the pericopae from their oral setting and placing them in the context of a larger, written narrative changed both their nature and their meaning, or, at the very least, allowed them to acquire new meanings from their relations to other parts of the narrative that they could never have had in their previous oral existence. So, for example, the meaning of the parables is complicated by their interaction with the surrounding text, while the healing stories take on a parabolic dimension that they could never have had in isolation (for example the placement of the stories of the healing of blind men at the start and end of Mark's travel section).[29] Moreover the fact that the Gospel is a written text meant that it could be composed away from the immediate constraints of an audience, allowing its author more control over his material.[30] In Kelber's view, Mark exercised this control by making his Gospel a kind of written parable throughout, so that the parable theory enunciated at Mark 4.10–12 becomes the hermeneutical key to the whole Gospel, with its paradoxical reversals of expectations and its unresolved ending.[31]

So far, so good, but Kelber became rather more contentious when he argued that 'To the extent that the gospel draws on oral voices, it has rendered them voiceless.'[32] In Kelber's view, this was not simply an accidental by-product of Mark's narrative form, but Mark's deliberate intention. Mark's Gospel went out of its way to portray the disciples and Jesus' family,

---

[28] Kelber, *Oral and Written*, 79–80.

[29] See Eric Eve, *The Healer from Nazareth: Jesus' Miracles in Historical Context* (London: SPCK, 2009), 92–117, for Mark's use of miracle stories, and especially 104–13 for their parabolic use.

[30] Kelber, *Oral and Written*, 105–15.

[31] Kelber, *Oral and Written*, 117–29.

[32] Kelber, *Oral and Written*, 91.

the most natural bearers of oral traditions about him, in a bad light. The ending, in which all the disciples fled and the women failed to deliver the message of the Empty Tomb, demonstrated the ultimate failure of the oral tradition. The polemic against false prophets in Mark 13.21–23 was taken to be a critique of Christian prophets in general. The absence of a resurrection appearance story showed Mark's dislike of the metaphysics of presence (of the risen Lord) and a preference for a metaphysics of absence. The relative lack of sayings material in Mark (compared with Matthew and Luke) was taken to be a principled objection to such material, an attempt to silence the living voice of the risen Lord in the oral tradition. By such means, Kelber asserted, Mark sought to undercut the authority of the oral tradents and assert his own written authority in its place.[33]

Part of the problem with this is that Kelber's assessment of what Mark chose to omit seems based on what Matthew and Luke would later add to his account. Moreover, virtually every feature of Mark's Gospel to which Kelber pointed here could plausibly be explained in other ways. But perhaps most of all, Kelber's thesis of Mark's deliberate silencing of oral voices seems to be in sharp tension with his recognition of Mark's oral legacy and oral style.

Kelber was well aware of this tension, and suggested that it could be resolved through the distinction between primary and secondary orality. He fully accepted that Mark was probably written for oral performance, but such a performance would be an instance of secondary orality, that is, orality based on a written composition, as opposed to primary orality, meaning orality not mediated by texts in the course of its transmission.[34] This distinction seems fair enough as far as it goes, but it is far from clear that it entirely meets the case. While Kelber may be correct to suggest that Mark did not write in order to preserve the oral tradition,[35] the fact that he was prepared to make such extensive use of it is a little odd if he objected to it so much in principle. At the very least, someone supposedly capable of penning the tightly plotted Passion narrative could surely have made a more thorough job of textualizing pericopae drawn from oral tradition than Mark has done, had he wished to assert the primacy of the written text over orality.

---

[33] Kelber, *Oral and Written*, 90–105.

[34] Kelber, *Oral and Written*, 217–18; note that this is very different from the sense in which Walter J. Ong, *Orality and Literacy: The Technologizing of the Word* (New Accents; London and New York: Routledge, 2002), 3, 11, 133–4, 157, uses the term 'secondary orality' to refer to orality in electronic broadcast media.

[35] Kelber, *Oral and Written*, 213.

Subsequently Kelber suggested that Mark was not simply trying to undermine ongoing oral tradition but was rather reacting to other written texts that chose a different route, namely sayings gospels as exemplified by Q and the *Gospel of Thomas*.[36] Whereas the sayings gospel 'promoted a Jesus who taught and redeemed through words of wisdom', the narrative gospel presented 'a Jesus who redeemed through the conduct of his life and death'.[37] Kelber did not, however, think that the narrative gospel evolved from the sayings gospel; rather the sayings gospel was related to the aphoristic tradition and the narrative gospel to the parable.[38]

Kelber in any case attempted to support his thesis about Mark's media preference by contrasting it with that of Paul and Q, both of whom he thought retained a principled preference for orality. He noted, for example, that Paul's letters exhibited a preference for oral–aural over visual imagery; thus the gospel was to be received by '*hearing* with faith' (Galatians 3.2, my italics). Moreover, Kelber suggested that Paul's anxieties about the law were tied up with its status as something written, and thus being fixed and external, contrary to the freedom in the Spirit imparted by his own oral gospel.[39] He likewise proposed that Q saw Jesus as a prophetic figure, speaking to his followers in the present, and making no distinction between the pre-Easter and post-Easter Jesus, or between the sayings of Jesus and those of his followers.[40] Although Q showed some signs of narrativization, its almost exclusive focus on sayings material and its lack of a Passion narrative employed an essentially oral hermeneutic of Jesus directly addressing its audience; Mark's narrativization of the life of Jesus, concluding with his death, firmly turned Jesus into a figure of the past, a kind of historical distancing that comes only with writing.[41]

More recently, Kelber's reflections on the print-centric mentality of modern scholarship have led him to question the validity of the two-source hypothesis, and hence, presumably, the existence of Q.[42] This would presumably call into question his earlier arguments about the oral hermeneutics of Q, but that need not detain us here.

---

[36] Werner Kelber, 'Narrative as Interpretation and Interpretation of Narrative: Hermeneutical Reflections on the Gospels' in Silberman (ed.), *Orality*, 107–28 (107–19); Kelber, 'Biblical Hermeneutics', 100.

[37] Kelber, 'Narrative as Interpretation', 112–13.

[38] Kelber, 'Narrative as Interpretation', 113.

[39] Kelber, *Oral and Written*, 140–83.

[40] Kelber, *Oral and Written*, 201–4.

[41] Kelber, *Oral and Written*, 209.

[42] Werner H. Kelber, 'The Case of the Gospels: Memory's Desire and the Limits of Historical Criticism', *OT* 17.1 (2002), 55–86 (70–2, 78–81).

Evaluation

Commenting on Kelber's work, J. D. G. Dunn remarks, 'Here is a thesis too quickly gone to seed.'[43] Dunn's complaint is not against Kelber's use of studies by folklorists, classicists and anthropologists to illuminate the nature of oral tradition, but that Kelber pushes the distinction between orality and writing too far, particularly in asserting that Mark deliberately set out to silence oral tradition while Paul consciously promoted an oral hermeneutic.

This complaint is not without justice. There is less justice in Dunn's complaint that Kelber ignores the fact that Mark was intended for oral performance, since, as we have seen, Kelber was well aware of that point and tried to address it. But his thesis about Mark is problematic on other grounds. That Mark did not include as high a proportion of sayings material in his Gospel as Matthew and Luke subsequently did can hardly be used as evidence of a principled objection to sayings material. For one thing, Mark seems to have been aiming at a fast-paced dramatic narrative, in which too much sayings material would have been out of place. For another, when Mark wrote, there was no obvious standard of comparison to suggest how much sayings material a narrative Gospel *ought* to contain. Moreover, it seems odd to assume that the condemnation of *false* prophets at Mark 13.21–22 is targeted at *all* prophets. It may be that Mark's target was the 'sign prophets' described by Josephus,[44] or else the propaganda put about by the supporters of Vespasian while he was making his bid for the imperial throne.[45]

The absence of a resurrection appearance in Mark may have any number of causes (perhaps Mark conceived the resurrection as an immediate translation to heaven), and need have nothing to do with Mark's media preferences. The same applies to Mark's portrayal of the disciples, which may have to do with Christological polemic, or a desire to create dramatic irony, or to use the disciples as a narrative foil, or to stress that salvation is humanly impossible and only made possible through divine omnipotence (cf. Mark 10.26–27), or as a form of pastoral encouragement; so many different explanations have been given and so little agreement reached

---

[43] James D. G. Dunn, *Jesus Remembered* (Christianity in the Making, 1; Grand Rapids and Cambridge: Eerdmans, 2003), 203.

[44] Eric Eve, *The Jewish Context of Jesus' Miracles* (JSNTSup, 231; Sheffield: Sheffield Academic Press, 2002), 296–325.

[45] Gerd Theissen, *The Gospels in Context: Social and Political History in the Synoptic Tradition* (Edinburgh: T. & T. Clark, 1992); Eric Eve, 'Spit in Your Eye: The Blind Man of Bethsaida and the Blind Man of Alexandria', *NTS* 54 (2008), 1–17.

that it would be hazardous to argue that Mark's portrayal of the disciples must be intended as polemic against oral tradition.[46] Although Terence Mournet is highly appreciative of Kelber's work overall, he criticizes him at precisely this point on the grounds that Mark wrote not to attack the disciples but to preserve the tradition.[47]

Kelber's remarks on Paul's media preferences seem similarly questionable. The prevalence of reference to speech and hearing in Paul's letters may merely reflect the media situation of the culture in which he operated rather than any deliberate policy on Paul's part. That Paul objected to the law primarily because it was written seems doubtful. Paul seems happy to cite Scripture in many contexts, and not just when reaching for the safety of the written text to curb excessive oral enthusiasm as Kelber suggests in connection with 1 Corinthians 1—3. In Galatians, Paul's protest against the law functions as part of his attempt to persuade his converts not to undergo circumcision, a procedure that would probably have killed his Gentile mission stone dead had he allowed it to become a requirement of church membership. In Romans his more nuanced complaint against the law seems to be that it commands what is right without empowering one to do it; the solution is not through receiving commands aurally but through receiving the Spirit. In both Galatians and Romans Paul also appears to object to the use of the law as a means of barring Gentile access to the God of Israel. Moreover, even if one supposes that Paul's letter to the Romans, say, was in some sense a substitute for a personal visit he was not yet able to make, and thus a substitute for oral presence, it is hard to imagine something as complex as the argument of Romans being composed, sustained and preserved in purely oral form; here, at least, Paul surely shows some active investment in textuality.

Birger Gerhardsson has also been quite critical of Kelber's position. For one thing (although this criticism is not specifically aimed at Kelber), Gerhardsson (rightly) questions whether a model of oral tradition drawn from Lord's work on Yugoslavian epic poets should be taken as normative for all oral tradition, given the very different circumstance of Jesus and the early Church.[48] To be fair, however, Kelber's views on orality were drawn from wider sources than just Lord's work and he also questioned the extent to which Lord could be used to illuminate the oral tradition

---

[46] See C. Clifton Black, *The Disciples According to Mark: Markan Redaction in Current Debate* (JSNTSup, P27; Sheffield: JSOT Press, 1989).

[47] Terence C. Mournet, *Oral Tradition and Literary Dependency: Variability and Stability in the Synoptic Tradition and Q* (WUNT, 195; Tübingen: Mohr Siebeck, 2005), 84–6.

[48] Birger Gerhardsson, *The Reliability of the Gospel Tradition* (Peabody, MA: Hendrickson, 2001), 85 n. 86.

behind Mark.[49] More specifically, Gerhardsson accuses Kelber of applying a preliterary model of orality to a society that was far from preliterary and of oversimplifying the distinction and interaction between orality and writing. In Gerhardsson's view oral texts can be just as fixed as written ones, and written ones just as flexible as oral. It is not always the case that oral presentations are adapted to the audience and so shaped by social pressures, as the rabbinic model of oral transmissions demonstrates. Moreover, Jesus was not a popular performer of folklore, but rather someone who taught in *meshalim*, carefully formulated pointed sayings.[50]

Gerhardsson seems not to be fully addressing some of the points Kelber made, but perhaps the main disagreement of substance comes down to a difference of view about the educational level of Jesus and the first disciples and the extent to which literacy had penetrated Galilean village life. Gerhardsson envisages a situation in which people were quite familiar with the text of Scripture and with the kind of formal teaching methods that go with a literate education. Kelber envisages a situation rather closer to a primarily oral culture with very low levels of literacy. Recent scholarship would tend to support Kelber's view here.[51] That said, Gerhardsson is justified in complaining that Kelber pushed the oral–written distinction too far.

Kelber also pushed his case too hard in his remarks on the media preferences of Paul, Mark and Q. In addition he probably overstated the disjunction between Markan textuality and the preceding oral tradition. In the introduction to the 1997 edition of *The Oral and the Written Gospel*, when Kelber looked back over its impact since its original publication in 1983, he acknowledged the frequent criticisms to the effect that he had overdrawn the 'Great Divide' between textuality and orality in an ancient context. He also accepted that a notion of a Great Divide between the media was not true to the realities of the interpenetration of the oral and written media in antiquity. He nevertheless argued that 'the strong thesis of *The Oral and the Written Gospel* was, and to some extent is, necessary to break theoretical ground and to challenge the chirographic-typographic hegemony that rules biblical scholarship and many of the human sciences', and further pointed out that 'once we are forewarned about the perils of the Great Divide, we need to be equally cautious not

---

[49] Kelber, *Oral and Written*, 78–9.
[50] Gerhardsson, *Reliability*, 115–23.
[51] E.g. Richard A. Horsley, *Jesus in Context: Power, People, and Performance* (Minneapolis: Fortress Press, 2008); see further Chapter 7 below.

to relapse into dominantly typographic modes of thought'.[52] These points seem to be fair enough, if they are taken to imply that Kelber's original thesis was to some extent deliberately overstated in order to carry a novel point, but that while more nuancing may now be required, maintaining awareness of the distinction between speech and writing will be a better first approximation than ignoring it.

Where Kelber is certainly correct is in insisting that however much ancient texts may have been tangled up with orality, orality should not be treated as if it were a kind of writing. His remarks on the nature of the oral tradition thus remain broadly valid (if subject to further refinement). Oral tradition is not a series of strata that can be uncovered by archaeological digging, nor does it follow inexorable laws of development that can be reverse-engineered to arrive at some putative 'original form'. Oral tradition consists in a series of individual performances. There is little reason to link particular forms with particular social settings in the manner of the form critics, but there is a sense in which form follows function: to survive, oral tradition needs to be memorable, and it achieves memorability by adopting standard patterns and motifs, by focusing on the striking and extraordinary, by making its heroes larger than life and pitting them in black-and-white contests, and by focusing on essentials. In doing so, it manifests both stability and variability; at a first approximation, stability in the core with almost infinite variability in the details of performance. But the notion both of a 'core' and of the core's stability needs some qualification; in particular there is a strong tendency for oral tradition to adapt to the current needs of the community that uses it, and little tendency for it to preserve the past as past for the sake of any notion of historical objectivity. To express the consequences of all this in Kelber's own words:

> The issue of the *historical* Jesus is of no import to the tellers and hearers of stories. The modern stance which separates 'authentic' from 'inauthentic' words or searches for the 'real' Jesus behind texts is alien to oral mentality. Stories and sayings are authenticated not by virtue of their historical reliability, but on the authority of the speaker and by the reception of hearers. This must not suggest that orality has lost all rapport with actuality. But it means that from the perspective of language that if Jesus is to continue in the hearts and minds of people, then he must be filtered through the oral medium. What is summoned for transmission is fashioned for mnemonic purposes and selected for immediate relevancy, not primarily for historical

---

[52] Kelber, *Oral and Written*, xxi–xxii.

reasons. The studied simplicity of stories is designed to meet the needs of oral expediency and social identification more than historical accuracy. In sum, orality's principal concern is not to preserve historical actuality, but to shape and break it into memorable, applicable speech.[53]

It may be that the more questionable and controversial aspects of Kelber's work have robbed its more valuable parts of the impact they deserved to have. As Dunn remarks, 'To Werner Kelber is due the credit for being the first NT [New Testament] scholar to take seriously the distinctive character of oral tradition as illuminated by a sequence of studies from classicists, folklorists, and social anthropologists.'[54] If one sets aside the overdrawn contrast between orality and writing and the dubious assertions about the conscious media preferences of Paul and Mark, the way in which Kelber characterized oral tradition (and the oral character of Mark) represents an enormous step forward, and much of what he said about it in *The Oral and the Written Gospel* remains valid. It is also broadly consonant with the picture that emerges from the social memory approach (as we shall see in Chapters 6 and 7 below), an approach Kelber has also gone on to embrace (as we shall again see in Chapter 7).

It is thus perhaps something of an irony that one scholar's influential attempt to find a middle way between form criticism and Gerhardsson's rabbinic theory seems to have totally ignored Kelber's work. As we shall see in the next chapter, it is then even more of an irony that Kenneth Bailey's attempt to construct a theory of informal controlled oral tradition ends up broadly confirming Kelber's work.

---

[53] Kelber, *Oral and Written*, 71; emphasis original.
[54] Dunn, *Jesus Remembered*, 199.

5

Informal controlled oral tradition

The models examined so far have all been theoretical, in the sense that the New Testament scholars who propounded them were drawing mainly on the writings of others or their own analysis of texts for their ideas about the workings of oral tradition. Kenneth Bailey's model of *informal controlled oral tradition*, however, is drawn primarily from his personal experience of working as a missionary and teacher in the Middle East. Despite its anecdotal basis it has proved quite influential, being espoused by, among others, J. D. G. Dunn and N. T. Wright.[1] It is worth looking at, however, not simply on account of its influence but because, for all the obvious weaknesses of an anecdotal approach, such an approach does offer both a different perspective (from a culturally relevant part of the world) and also a number of concrete examples against which more theoretical approaches can be tested and fleshed out. Once one corrects for some of the flaws in Bailey's reasoning, it turns out that his evidence tends to support Kelber's characterization of oral tradition.

Kenneth Bailey's model

Bailey locates his model between the model of informal uncontrolled oral tradition he attributes to Bultmann and that of formal controlled oral tradition he attributes to Riesenfeld and Gerhardsson (for which see Chapters 2 and 3 above). He starts by acknowledging that these two models do reflect types of oral transmission that occur in the Middle East. The informal uncontrolled type is represented by rumour transmission and atrocity stories. The formal controlled type is exemplified by the memorization of the Qur'an by Muslim sheiks and of extensive liturgies by Eastern Orthodox clergy. Bailey nonetheless suggests that there is a

---

[1] James D. G. Dunn, *Jesus Remembered* (Christianity in the Making, 1; Grand Rapids and Cambridge: Eerdmans, 2003), 205–10; N. T. Wright, *Jesus and the Victory of God* (Christian Origins and the Question of God, 2; London: SPCK, 1996), 133–6; Kenneth E. Bailey, 'Informal Controlled Oral Tradition and the Synoptic Gospels', *Themelios* 20 (1995), 4–11 (originally published in *AJT* 5 (1991), 34–54); Kenneth E. Bailey, 'Middle Eastern Oral Tradition and the Synoptic Gospels', *ExpTim* 106 (1994), 363–7.

third type, lying midway between the two, that might provide a better model for the synoptic tradition.[2]

Bailey bases his theory on 30 years of anecdotal observation in the Middle East, not least of the *haflat samar* (which he claims means 'party of preservation'), in which tales are told and handed on. At these gatherings people come and share the stories, proverbs, poems and history that constitute the lore and wisdom of the community (which, by implication from what Bailey says, might *inter alia*, be a village, an extended family, a group of friends or a church). 'At such gatherings, the community retells stories that form its identity. Many such stories are of the exploits of historical figures significant to the identity of the village or community.'[3] In practice it tends to be the elders and the more dominant that do the talking, while the others listen and absorb the community tradition. Not everything said at a *haflat samar* is of equal value. Material such as jokes, casual news, atrocity stories and accounts of tragedies in neighbouring villages is not regarded as 'wise or valuable'; it is 'irrelevant to the identity of the community' and is subject to no control. Total flexibility is allowed (including gross exaggeration), but the material does not enter the tradition. At the opposite extreme are poems and proverbs, in which no flexibility is allowed at all. Someone reciting such material in public is subject to instant correction if he or she makes a mistake, a public humiliation people in that culture would always wish to avoid. In this case control is strict, since no deviation is permitted, though it is still informal, since no one in particular is responsible for correcting mistakes.[4]

Bailey's main interest, however, lies with the kind of material that falls between these extremes, particularly '[p]arables and *recollections of historical people and events important to the identity of the community*' where 'there is flexibility *and* control. The central threads of the story cannot be changed, but flexibility in detail is allowed.'[5] Thus, where the traditions handed on in a *haflat samar* are crucial to the identity of the community, the audience provides an informal control. If someone reciting a well-known (and important) tale makes a mistake, he is corrected by a chorus of voices. A certain amount of flexibility is allowed, particularly in matters of style and dramatic detail, but the reciter is expected to preserve the basic shape and point of the story.[6]

---

[2] Bailey, 'Informal Controlled', 4–5.
[3] Bailey, 'Middle Eastern', 365.
[4] Bailey, 'Informal Controlled', 7–8; Bailey, 'Middle Eastern', 364–5.
[5] Bailey, 'Informal Controlled', 7.
[6] Bailey, 'Informal Controlled', 7–8.

It is this mode of transmission that Bailey dubs 'informal controlled oral tradition'. In his view it is a mode which 'preserves within it material of claimed great antiquity and has all the markings of an ancient methodology'.[7] He goes on to suggest that it was the methodology by which the synoptic tradition was transmitted in Palestinian villages down to the destruction wrought at the conclusion of the Jewish Revolt in 70 CE, although he qualifies this by also suggesting that the reciters of the Jesus tradition would have to have been eyewitnesses to count as ministers of the word (citing Luke 1.2). By this means, 'at least through to the end of the first century, the authenticity of that tradition was assured to the community through specially designated witnesses',[8] while the flexibility also apparent in the synoptic tradition can be accounted for. In Bailey's view, 'This understanding of how the oral tradition was passed on and preserved allows for the variations found in the Gospels. It also guarantees authenticity for the material up to the compositions of the written records and beyond.'[9]

Bailey's data

Bailey supports this theory through a number of anecdotes, including a number of stories told about John Hogg, a nineteenth-century Scottish missionary who founded Christian communities in Egypt. Bailey found that stories about Hogg were still circulating in the villages he visited, and he went on to compare these stories with versions of the same incidents reported by Rena Hogg in her biography of her father.[10] According to Bailey, there was a striking similarity between the stories reported by Rena Hogg and the stories he heard recounted in *hafalat samar* (*hafalat* being the plural of *haflat*) 60 years later, leading him to argue that this material was being faithfully preserved in informal controlled oral tradition over a considerable period of time.

Bailey has, however, come under attack from Theodore Weeden on the grounds that the evidence he relies upon does not support his case.[11] In summary Weeden finds that of the four incidents Bailey relates about John Hogg on the basis of stories he heard in Egypt, only two are found in Rena Hogg's account of her father's life. In one of these, which Bailey tells as a

---

[7] Bailey, 'Informal Controlled', 6.

[8] Bailey, 'Informal Controlled', 10.

[9] Bailey, 'Middle Eastern', 367.

[10] Rena L. Hogg, *A Master-Builder on the Nile: Being a Record of the Life and Aims of John Hogg, D.D., Christian Missionary* (New York: Fleming H. Revell, 1914).

[11] Theodore J. Weeden, Sr, 'Kenneth Bailey's Theory of Oral Tradition: A Theory Contested by Its Evidence', *JSHJ* 7 (2009), 3–43.

story about someone urinating on John Hogg's head, the Rena Hogg version is so different that one may doubt whether the same incident is being referred to (though Weeden gives it the benefit of the doubt). In the other, a story about John Hogg and his companion being accosted by robbers, the Bailey and Rena Hogg versions are indeed quite similar, but another problem arises. Although Rena Hogg indeed tells a recognizably similar version of the story to that heard by Bailey decades later, she goes on to dismiss it as 'romantic tale', and to present the accounts of the (rather more mundane) incident given by her father and his companion Shenoodeh Hanna.[12]

This example is sufficiently instructive that it is worth looking at in some detail. According to Kenneth Bailey:

> Before the first World War John Hogg's daughter dipped into this same oral tradition and in her biography of him told of how he was waylaid at night by a band of robbers who demanded valuables. He quickly surrendered a gold watch and his money but indicated that he had a treasure worth far more. They were curious. He pulled a small book from his pocket and spent the entire night telling them of the treasures it contained. By morning the band, convicted of the evil of their ways, sought to return his watch and money and pledged themselves to give up highway robbery. Hogg took the watch but insisted that they keep his money, and indeed then financed the gang personally until they could establish themselves in legal employment.[13]

This may be compared with the version of the same tale Rena Hogg says she heard 'as related by a fine old patriarch':

> At a village many miles distant from Assiut Dr. Hogg had been paying one of his periodic visits. The evening meeting was over and the missionary had sat late in conversation with his host and his friends, when to the amazement of all he rose to bid them adieu. In vain they urged him to spend the night with them, expatiating on the length of the way and the robbers that infested the district. He would neither await the daylight nor accept an escort. His work necessitated his reaching Assiut by morning, and in the Lord's keeping he was as safe as with armed men. He had not walked far in the dense darkness when he was accosted by a robber band who demanded his gold watch and purse. These he surrendered without demur, surprising his marauders with the gratuitous information that he had with him still another treasure that he would gladly add to their store. To their chagrin all that he drew from his pocket was a small book, but his audience were soon so entranced by the magic of his tongue and of that priceless Word,

---

[12] Hogg, *Master-Builder*, 215–17.
[13] Bailey, 'Informal Controlled', 4–11 (8–9).

that their greed speedily vanished, their consciences awoke, and they began to hunger for salvation. Before morning dawned the whole band had been converted and were eager to return to him his stolen goods. But the purse he refused, and as one and all, Copts and Moslems alike, had decided to abandon their life of robbery, he supported them liberally from that time forward out of his own pocket until they had learned to earn an honest living and had become respected and God-fearing members of the Church![14]

This is recognizably the same story, especially in its essentials (though it is surely noteworthy how many details appear to have been lost in the course of transmission from the earlier to the later version). Of course what we have in each case is not a verbatim transcription of anyone's oral recitation, but presumably a translation of a recollection (or a recollection of a translation) of what was said, filtered through the memories of Rena Hogg and Kenneth Bailey. Nonetheless, provided we can be confident that Bailey's account is independent of Rena Hogg's, and allowing for the kind of variations one would expect in separate oral performances of this kind of material, the oral tradition of this story does seem to have been remarkably stable between 1910 when Rena Hogg heard it, and the 1950s and 1960s when Kenneth Bailey did so. At first sight this appears to suggest that a narrative oral tradition of this kind can remain effectively stable (perhaps by a process of informal controlled oral tradition) over roughly the length of time that might have elapsed between the ministry of Jesus and the writing of Mark's Gospel.

But there is, as Weeden is quick to point out, a substantial fly in the ointment; for Rena Hogg not only records the story she heard from the patriarch, but also goes on to dismiss it as a 'romantic tale' and to narrate the actual account of the underlying events (which apparently took place in 1873) given by her father:

After a hasty breakfast on a hot Saturday in June, the two friends left the 'Ibis' [their boat] at sunrise to walk to the village of Tahta two and a half miles distance from the river. They were warmly received by the only Protestant in the place, and his house was so continuously crowded by eager listeners that for once Egyptian hospitality seemed swamped by the tide of interest, and the bodily wants of the preachers were completely overlooked. All day long they read and sang and preached and prayed, the changing audience fresh and eager, the speakers weaker and fainter with the passing hours, and all proposals to leave were overborne by the host's repeated assertion that he would feel forever disgraced if his guests should quit his house without food. At last, after fourteen hours of fasting, a sumptuous

---

[14] Hogg, *Master-Builder*, 214–15; Weeden, 'Bailey's Theory', 15–16.

meal was spread, and of this the famished men partook with more speed than wisdom before starting out with a suitable escort to ride to the river. A jolting donkey is no happy sequel to a hasty meal, and Dr. Hogg, finding his companion unable to ride and his escort restive under enforced delay, decided that they would complete their journey on foot and unaccompanied. The servants with some polite demur gladly availed themselves of the reprieve, and the two preachers started riverward alone. When they reached the water's edge, the boat was not in sight, and whether the landing lay north or south they could not tell. Some men when accosted misled them, either by mistake or of set purpose, their lack of a lantern perhaps arousing suspicions, and the night wore on in fruitless and solitary wanderings.

Suddenly they observed on the river bank a man, innocent of clothes and bearing a gun, who started towards them till arrested by the sight of their shouldered umbrellas, which in the starlight passed easily for firearms. The younger man was distracted with fear, and still more so when he heard the sound of swimmers in the river perhaps coming to join their naked friend in some bloody deed. The two wanderers walked on as if unheeding, but when a little distance was gained, turned inland, running rapidly to reach a point invisible from the beach. Avoiding Scylla, they came as it seemed upon Charybdis – a group of smokers, three men and a boy, two of them armed and with the usual vicious guard of watch-dogs. Dr. Hogg thought it best to throw himself frankly on their protection, and as the dogs sprang forward with a threatening welcome, 'Call off your dogs,' he cried, 'and I shall tell you a story that will make you laugh.'

A discussion followed, and they were soon received within the smoking circle to spend the remainder of the night in this strange company. As sleep was distant, it was proposed to pass the time in songs and tales, and Mr. Shenoodeh chose a Bible story that gave him the opportunity of dwelling on the sin of murder and the fearful punishment awaiting the guilty, a tale which brought from one of his listeners the confession that only his bro- ther's intervention had prevented him from shooting at Mr. Shenoodeh on his first approach. Towards morning the air grew cold, and the missionary, made anxious by his young friend's cough, dug a deep hole for him in the sand and buried him to the neck, after which both secured some broken sleep. At dawn one of their guard accompanied them to the boat, lying miles from the spot at which they had encamped, and received for the service a backsheesh that sent him away blessing their memory.[15]

Rena Hogg goes on to explain that while her father was of the opinion that the men they had spend the night with were merely guarding their melon crop, Hanna took them to be highway robbers.

---

[15] Hogg, *Master-Builder*, 215–16.

One can see enough of an underlying common core for this more sober account to be identified as the archetype of the other two. In both the account of the original events and the version of 1910, John Hogg sets out late in the evening after a lengthy time spent with his hosts, with some indications on the part of the hosts that unescorted travel through the dark night may be not altogether wise. In the original account Hogg and his companion undergo a series of encounters with (possibly threatening) persons before falling in with a band of people with whom they spend the night. In the subsequent account this has been simplified into a single encounter with a robber band, in the way that one might expect an oral tale to conflate several actors with broadly similar roles (various groups of threatening strangers) into one (a single robber band). In John Hogg's original account, the night is spent 'in songs and tales', to which Hanna contributes a Bible story, which brings forth a significant confession of sorts. In the later version, this is transformed into John Hogg reading to the robbers from the Bible, resulting in the general repentance and conversion of the band. Finally, the tip given to the guard who accompanies the two travellers to their boat is transmogrified into an act of extravagant financial generosity.

Rena Hogg regarded the discrepant versions of this tale as evidence of how 'fact and fancy mingled in lore'. A more accurate way of putting it might be to say that the discrepant versions show how fact is transmuted into legend. The original tale, as narrated by John Hogg, is of an interesting enough incident, but not one that succeeds in making a succinct and noteworthy point. The oral-traditional versions recorded by Rena Hogg and Kenneth Bailey are much more focused narratives, simplifying the story in a way that concentrates on essentials, and giving it a much more obviously edifying thrust. Shenoodeh Hanna drops out of the story altogether, so that the tale can focus on the exploits of John Hogg, the revered founder of Egyptian Christian communities. Since the various groups of people he encounters have coalesced into a single group of highway robbers, they are given a typically highway-robber role to perform: they rob John Hogg. This sets up a situation in which Hogg can shine as a missionary hero, and so he is portrayed. Hanna's recitation of a Bible tale eliciting a confession becomes Hogg's reading from the Bible to effect a stunning conversion. A (presumably modest) gratuity becomes an astounding act of generosity to enable the reformation of the converted robbers to be completed. The story as recast thus demonstrates both the power of the word of God to transform the sinner, and the exemplary conduct of the founding missionary, living the gospel he proclaims. All this has been achieved, not so much by introducing new elements, but by employing the elements already present to create a new story. Fact has been transmuted into legend, not so much by a process of invention, as by one of transformation.

One question this raises is at what point this transformation took place, and how long it took, given that the interval between the incident that John Hogg experienced and the account given of it by the patriarch in 1910 is again roughly comparable to that between the ministry of Jesus and the writing of Mark's Gospel. In the case of the John Hogg story this process probably got off to an early start, for Rena Hogg reports that 'Mr. Shenoodeh wove [the story of his and John Hogg's experience] into an ingenious and thrilling sermon, which greatly moved his audience.'[16]

Since it is Hanna who took the group of people they had spent the night with to be a band of robbers, it seems highly probable that it is his perception that has coloured the legendary version of the tale. The very fact that he wove it into 'an ingenious and thrilling sermon' suggests that he gave the story a strong impetus towards its later form. That it was included in a *sermon* indicates that Hanna would need to have transformed it into an edifying tale; that it was *thrilling* indicates that Hanna is likely to have dramatized it; that it was *ingenious* perhaps indicates that Hanna knew how to spin a tale with popular appeal. Moreover, the original (John Hogg) version of the tale is too long, too complicated and ultimately too inconsequential to be narrated in that form by anyone other than the participants, whereas the form heard by Rena Hogg and Kenneth Bailey is short, pointed and memorable.

It may be (though this is, of course, highly speculative) that the version of the story told by Hanna in his sermon was already closer to the 1910 version than to John Hogg's account. It seems not at all improbable that this would have been so of the versions told a few days later by the audience of Hanna's sermon. Thus, rather than envisaging a period of gradual transformation between 1873 and 1910, it may be more realistic to envisage the legendary version of the story taking shape over the period of a few days or weeks in 1873 and then remaining more or less stable thereafter, having attained a form that proved useful and sustaining to the community in which it was narrated. Given the almost universal human proclivity to prefer the good and useful story to the duller but truer one, it is doubtful whether John Hogg could have done much to check this process even if he had wanted to.

---

[16] Hogg, *Master-Builder*, 208.

Incidentally, if Hanna was indeed responsible for the form the story took, it might have interesting repercussions for the putative role of eyewitnesses in the Jesus tradition. It is often assumed that if the Gospels *were* based on eyewitness testimony, or if eyewitnesses played a significant role in controlling the Jesus tradition in the primitive Church, the historical reliability of the tradition would be thereby assured. What Hanna seems to have done with the Hogg story would appear to cast some doubt on that assumption. At the very least Hanna perceived as robbers the same people Hogg took to be innocent guarders of a melon crop. But, more than that, it could well have been Hanna's sermon that gave rise to the legendary version of the account. Hanna the eyewitness may have played a vital role in ensuring the preservation of this piece of Hogg tradition, but hardly in ensuring its historical accuracy. And even if subsequent narrations of the story took the process of legend formation further than Hanna's sermons, one wonders how vigorously Hanna would have tried to resist the process. Indeed, to the extent that the legendary version became important to the community, for Hanna to insist too much on the more mundane version might have served only to undermine his credibility as an eyewitness in the eyes of that community. It is in any case far from inconceivable that over the course of a few years Hanna's own recollection of the events could have become strongly coloured by the official community version of his story (as we shall see in the discussion on the workings of memory in Chapter 6 below).

The main feature of the model we have suggested for the story of Hogg and the robbers is that of a story that very quickly takes on a legendary or useful shape, which tends to remain reasonably stable for a relatively long time thereafter. The underlying rationale of this model is that the same forces that tend to mould the story into its socially useful form in the first place will then tend to preserve it in that form for as long as it continues to be socially useful. Some of the other anecdotes reported by Bailey also tend to support this model.

In this connection we may return to the urinating incident. According to the version Bailey says he heard in the late 1950s:

> One village proudly told of how [Hogg] was preaching in a village courtyard and the mayor, anxious to cause trouble, sent a village guard up onto the adjoining roof to urinate on him. Hogg stepped aside, took a handkerchief from his pocket, wiped his head and continued preaching without looking up. The mayor was so shamed and impressed that after enquiry and study he joined the infant church and became one of its leaders.[17]

---

[17] Bailey, 'Informal Controlled', 8.

The nearest Rena Hogg comes to narrating anything like this is where she writes:

> Not infrequently the filth of the streets was flung after [Hogg] by the way, and words as filthy were called loudly in contempt and derision as he passed, while on one occasion vile water was poured on his head through a gap in the ceiling of a room from which his audience had been forcibly ejected.[18]

Rena Hogg does not explicitly state where she obtained this information, but what she says a few pages on suggests that she most probably derived it from her father's correspondence.[19] If so, Rena Hogg's account is based on her father's recollection of what actually happened. As Weeden suggests, it may be that she found the notion of urine being poured on her father's head sufficiently offensive that in her account it became 'vile water'; if so, the same change would necessitate altering 'urinating' to 'pouring'.[20] It is also conceivable that this was how her father chose to describe it in the letter from which Rena Hogg perhaps gleaned the information. It is thus at least possible that either the father's or the daughter's sense of delicacy has made the Hogg version look less like the Bailey version than the underlying event actually was.

That said, if the 'urinating' and 'vile water' accounts do stem from one and the same incident, then it looks as if a similar process of legendization has taken place as in the robber band incident. It is harder to trace precisely what has happened since Rena Hogg's account is so compressed; indeed, it is more of an allusion to the incident than an account of it;[21] a fuller version would surely have revealed details that made the incident appear either more or less like the Bailey version. The context in which Rena Hogg places the incident, together with the notice that the water was poured down into 'a room from which [her father's] audience had been forcibly ejected' strongly suggests that the vile water incident occurred in the context of hostility to John Hogg's ministry. This is also a clear feature of the Bailey version. The notice of 'forcible ejection' suggests the hostile attention of someone able to exert force, as a mayor with village guards may well have been able to do. There is clearly a discrepancy between Hogg's head being wetted either in a room or a courtyard, but there is also some similarity between the unpleasant liquid descending from someone

---

[18] Hogg, *Master-Builder*, 214.
[19] Hogg, *Master-Builder*, 216, 251.
[20] Weeden, 'Bailey's Theory', 10.
[21] J. D. G. Dunn, 'Kenneth Bailey's Theory of Oral Tradition: Critiquing Theodore Weeden's Critique', *JSHJ* 7 (2009), 44–62 (50).

standing on a roof and someone standing in the space above the ceiling. Indeed, it is unclear from Rena Hogg's brief account whether the person pouring vile water through a gap in the ceiling was in a higher room or on the roof. What is completely missing from Rena Hogg's version is the account of her father's response and the mayor's subsequent conversion, and it is, one suspects, there that the process of legendization is most likely to have its major effect, by presenting John Hogg as the ideal self-effacing missionary with power to turn even enemies into converts. If so (and admittedly the brevity of Rena Hogg's account makes it a little speculative) then the urinating incident shows a pattern of legendization in oral transmission that is very similar to that of the robber band incident.

If these two incidents suggest how tradition might develop over time, a third narrated by Bailey suggests how the process of informal control can rapidly shape the way an incident is narrated almost from the point of inception. At a village wedding, a man coincidentally also named Hanna, a friend of Butrus, the groom, joined in with others in firing his rifle in the air, the traditional form of celebration. Or rather, he attempted to fire his rifle in the air, but it did not go off; so then 'he lowered the gun and then the defective bullet fired, passing through the groom who was killed instantly'.[22] Bailey first heard of the incident a week later, from a variety of persons, who each gave him their version as he approached their village. Although these versions varied in some details from person to person, they concurred remarkably in the way the story concluded: 'Hanna fired the gun. The gun did not go off. He lowered the gun. The gun fired [*durib al-bundugiyya* – passive]'.[23] According to Bailey this was a 'divine passive' indicating that it was God, not Hanna, who fired the gun in such a way that Butrus was killed. The purpose of this was apparently to prevent the groom's family from pursuing a blood feud against Hanna; the statement that 'The gun fired [passive]' was thus intended to encapsulate the community's judgement that Hanna was not to be blamed for the tragic accident.

A rather different account was given to the police, who were told simply, 'a camel stepped on him'. According to Bailey, each member of the community could be relied upon to give this same response to official police enquiries, but no deception was intended, since everyone involved (police included) would recognize this as a coded way of saying, 'We've dealt with this ourselves and do not need any outside interference from the police.' As Bailey explains it:

---

[22] Bailey, 'Informal Controlled', 9.
[23] Bailey, 'Informal Controlled', 9.

The police in this case knew *exactly* what had happened. *Unofficially* and privately all the details are given to them. But after the above community's theological decision and the ensuing condensation of the story, the police can *officially* examine all five thousand people in the village and receive the same answer from all.[24]

Clearly, some process of informal control seems to be operating here, though it is not, strictly speaking, informal controlled oral tradition, since one week is far too short a period to speak of an oral tradition, and it is not clear that either version of events in fact passed into an oral tradition (Bailey was of the opinion that they would not, since the persons involved were not leading figures in their village, so that the story would not survive beyond one generation). Again, on the face of it two rather different processes seem to have been at work in the version of events agreed on for internal community consumption and the official version to be told to the police. In the latter case the facts have been quite clearly falsified (even if no one is deceived as a result), whereas in the former it is not so much that the facts have been distorted (unless Hanna indeed intended to murder Butrus) as that control is being exercised on the way the facts are interpreted. It may be that 'The gun [was] fired' (meaning 'God fired the gun') intended to say something about God's role in events that can hardly be either factually correct or empirically observable, but the course of observable events in the agreed village version is otherwise no different from that described by Bailey (although how Bailey could have had independent access to what actually happened is unclear). What is striking is that what the community chose to control is not so much the facts as the significance placed on those facts; the version for internal village use thus ensured that whatever details entered into the narration, the story was always told in such a way that no human being was to blame for what happened, so there need be no ill feeling between the people of the village on account of it. One might say that this is how the village perceived the 'truth' of the matter, and it was this 'truth', rather than the empirical facts, that the internally controlled version of events was designed to promote. If so, then this accounts also for the police version, which substantially departs from the empirical facts but preserves what the community saw as the 'truth' of the matter, namely that 'We have settled this among ourselves and we don't want any police interference in the internal affairs of our community.'[25] The tentative conclusion to be drawn is that the

---

[24] Bailey, 'Informal Controlled', 9.
[25] Bailey, 'Informal Controlled', 9.

community is more concerned to preserve its version of the 'truth', insofar as that is serviceable to the community, than to preserve facts for their own sake, but this may or may not result in considerable distortion of the facts. The 'facts' offered officially to the police were considerably distorted, since this was felt necessary to prevent police interference, whereas the 'facts' narrated internally may well have remained quite close to the actual events.[26]

A further consideration, however, is that the police version was never going to be the fount of any oral tradition. One can hardly imagine generations of police officers sitting in their mess passing on the story of how a camel stepped on Butrus at his wedding; it was never intended to be that kind of story. Insofar as this incident tells us anything about the formation of tradition, it is really only the internal version of the story that can be considered directly relevant, and here Bailey could claim that the factual core was quite reasonably well preserved – except that we have no record of how the story was told 10, 20, 30 or 40 years later, if indeed it continued to be told at all. Dunn states that he first heard this story from Bailey in 1976 and retold it (and another story told him by Bailey) several times after that. Dunn goes on to say that:

> When I eventually came across the article cited (in 1998) I was fascinated to note that my own retelling had maintained the outline and the key features of the core elements, although in my retelling the supporting details had been reshaped. This oral transmission covered more than twenty years, after a single hearing of the stories, by one who normally forgets a good joke as soon as he has heard it![27]

But it is far from clear how this is meant to illustrate over 20 years of oral transmission, since it is simply Dunn's own memory that is involved here, and a memory exercised in a very different cultural and social context from that which Bailey is seeking to illuminate.

The anecdote thus illustrates how a community may very rapidly take control of how a particular incident is to be narrated when this is seen as being of sufficient importance to the community, but is unclear how, if at all, this would apply to the formation of oral tradition in general. If it does suggest that what later become oral traditions might be given their decisive shape quite early on, we may compare the speed with which

---

[26] See also Weeden, 'Bailey's Theory', 29–32 and Dunn, 'Bailey's Theory', 57–9; Dunn seems to me to get the better of the exchange on this particular point.

[27] Dunn, *Jesus Remembered*, 208 n. 185.

legends of Thomas Becket took shape, or the growth of stories about bizarre events portending the destruction of Jerusalem, or the rapid growth of the legend of the Angel(s) of Mons.[28]

Among the other examples Bailey cites, one in particular seems relevant to the process of tradition formation. Bailey tells how, when he introduced a new story in the course of preaching to the community, he would not be allowed to continue with his sermon until the congregation had had a chance to commit it to memory:

> The elder on the front row would shout across the church to a friend in a loud voice, 'Did you hear what the preacher said? He said . . .' and then would come a line or two of the story including the punch-line. People all across the church instinctively turned to their neighbours and repeated the central thrust of the story twice and thrice to each other. They wanted to retell the story that week across the village and they had to learn it on the spot.[29]

This use of repetition to aid memorization is somewhat reminiscent of Gerhardsson's model of the formal transmission of tradition, except that there are no set teacher and student roles in the process Bailey describes. Rather, 'Through such incidents it was possible to observe *informal controlled* oral tradition functioning at close range, and watch it solidify and orally record information for transmission.' The other factor that makes this tradition *informal* controlled as opposed to Gerhardsson's memorization model is its flexibility: 'As we have noted, there was a relatively inflexible central core of information and along with it a community-controlled freedom to vary the story according to individual perspectives.'[30] Bailey does not, however, supply any concrete examples of what happened to his sermon stories after they left the church.

Evaluation

As we have already seen, Bailey's theory has come in from some sharp criticism from Theodore Weeden. But we have yet to mention the issue

---

[28] David E. Aune, 'Oral Tradition and the Aphorisms of Jesus' in Henry Wansbrough (ed.), *Jesus and the Oral Gospel Tradition* (JSNTSup, 64; Sheffield: Sheffield Academic Press, 1991), 211–65 (224); S. V. McCasland, 'Portents in Josephus and in the Gospels', *JBL* 51 (1932), 323–35; Arthur Machen, *The Angels of Mons: The Bowmen and Other Legends of the War* (2nd edn; London: Simpkin, Marshall, Hamilton, Kent & Co., 1915). See also the discussion of this legend in Eric Eve, 'Meier, Miracle and Multiple Attestation', *JSJH* 3 (2005), 23–45 (29–30).

[29] Bailey, 'Informal Controlled', 10.

[30] Bailey, 'Informal Controlled', 10.

Weeden regards as most fundamental, namely the meaning of the Arabic term *haflat samar*. According to Bailey, '*Samar* in Arabic is a cognate of the Hebrew *shamar*, meaning "to preserve". The community is *preserving* its store of tradition.'[31] Weeden corresponded with a number of native Middle Eastern Arabic speakers and experts on Arabic, none of whom thought *samar* meant 'preserve', and all of whom said it meant something like 'entertainment' or, more formally, 'conversation or talking at night'. Weeden's informants appear unanimous in explaining that a *haflat samar* is a nocturnal gathering for hearing stories, not in order to preserve community traditions, but purely for amusement and entertainment.[32] In attempting to defend Bailey, Dunn accepts Weeden's research but then reproaches him for failing to take into account the possibility that Bailey was reporting the special meaning *haflat samar* had among the churches with which he was familiar, which could easily have varied from its standard Arabic meaning.[33] This looks suspiciously like special pleading. While it is possible that the churches Bailey worked with adapted the *haflat samar* to their own more serious purposes, Bailey gives no indication that the term is being used in a non-standard way, and his categorical statement that the Arabic *samar* is a cognate of the Hebrew *shamar* meaning 'to preserve' implies precisely the reverse. This does not necessarily negate Bailey's point that informal controlled oral tradition tends to conserve the core of stories regarded as important to the community, but it does place a substantial question mark over his assertion that this is what a *haflat samar* is for.

In any case, not every example Bailey gives seems immediately related to *hafalat samar*. It seems most unlikely, for example, that the *haflat samar* was the setting in which the village decided how the story of the Butrus wedding tragedy should be told. The congregation's method of memorizing Bailey's sermon story took place in a church service, not a *haflat samar*. While he does suggest that the John Hogg stories had been passed down in *hafalat samar*, that is not obviously the case with all the other examples he gives. Among these are a story about the founding of the village of Dayr Abu Hennis he says he heard from one Father Makhiel and an account of how Revd Ibrahim Dagher electrified an audience by giving a new twist to a familiar parable at a public lecture. Possibly we are meant to suppose that the former story had been passed on via a *haflat samar* and the latter

---

[31] Bailey, 'Informal Controlled', 6; cf. Bailey, 'Middle Eastern', 364.
[32] Weeden, 'Bailey's Theory', 38–42.
[33] Dunn, 'Bailey's Theory', 48–50.

one was subsequently destined to be, but Bailey does not actually say so. Perhaps, then, we are meant to understand that the *haflat samar* is the setting in which Bailey has typically observed the process of informal controlled oral tradition he describes, but that it is not the only setting in which it can operate.

One example Bailey gives of a story he heard at a *haflat samar* had the punchline 'Wafaqa Shannun Tabaqa' (Shann was pleased to accept Tabaqa). Bailey explains how he told the story to a class of boys in Beirut ten years after first hearing it. Most of the boys were already familiar with the story, and judged him to have told it correctly. They then discussed what counted as a correct recitation and came up with the following list of what must be present:

> The proverb that appeared in the story (the punch-line) had to be repeated verbatim. The three basic scenes could not be changed, but the order of the last two could be reversed without triggering the community rejection mechanism. The basic flow of the story and its conclusion had to remain the same. The names could not be changed. The summary punch-line was inviolable. However, the teller could vary the pitch of one character's emotional reaction to the other, and the dialogue within the flow of the story could at any point reflect the individual teller's style and interests. That is, the story-teller had a certain freedom to tell the story in his own way as long as the central thrust of the story was not changed.[34]

Weeden appears to take this statement as an integral part of Bailey's theory, since he lists the elements that appear in it as 'fundamental components that *must be preserved without alteration in every recitation of such stories*'.[35] He then goes on to argue that since the versions of the two John Hogg stories found both in Bailey's article and in Rena Hogg's biography of her father do not share all these elements unaltered, Bailey's theory is thereby disconfirmed. This seems unduly harsh, as Dunn argues in turn, though Dunn misses what might be the most important objection to Weeden's procedure at this point, namely that he generalizes from what Bailey says about one story (or at least, one type of story) into a claim for all informal controlled oral tradition.[36] In the case Bailey describes, he heard the punchline before he heard the story, and then asked what the story was. This thus appeared to be a story identified by its punchline. Bailey makes no

---

[34] Bailey, 'Informal Controlled', 7.
[35] Weeden, 'Bailey's Theory', 6 (emphasis original).
[36] Dunn, 'Bailey's Theory', 50–4.

claim that this applies to all stories, so Weeden's argument that, for example, the two versions of the robber band incident do not end in precisely the same way is probably beside the point. Allowing for the fact that the versions of the story recorded by Rena Hogg and Kenneth Bailey were not actually written down by them in the context of a *haflat samar*, it would be fair to say that 'the central thrust of the story was not changed', which is Bailey's main point.[37]

Dunn more than once takes Weeden to task for supposing that there is some 'original version' of an oral story against which the other recitations should be measured, or else an '"uncorrupted original account" of the event being narrated',[38] but he has perhaps missed the central point Weeden is concerned to argue, namely that the ultimate purpose of the kind of informal controlled oral tradition Bailey's anecdotes illustrate is not 'to ensure that factually accurate historical information is faithfully preserved and transmitted' but 'to ensure that the essential core of a story, considered indispensable to a community's self-identity, is preserved and faithfully transmitted', with the caveat that it may be changed to meet changing needs.[39] By applying his theory to the synoptic tradition and claiming that it guarantees the authenticity of that tradition down to the end of the first century, Bailey appears to be arguing for the transmission of factually accurate historical information. Weeden is surely justified in challenging this aspect of Bailey's theory, as Dunn effectively acknowledges in relation to his treatment of the robber band incident.[40]

In fact, it may be that where Dunn and Weeden end up in their assessment of Bailey is not quite so different as may first appear. Weeden accepts that informal controlled oral tradition may on occasion preserve 'the original and essential historical core [of] a particular story or saying' even if he does not think this is its central purpose.[41] Conversely Dunn acknowledges that Weeden's analysis of the robber band incident 'provides an appropriate warning against reading historical events too quickly from the stories to which the events gave rise'.[42] Thus neither of them sees informal controlled oral tradition as offering either a direct window or an impenetrable barrier onto historical events. Weeden (rightly) argues that Bailey's data best fits a model of informal controlled oral tradition that works in

---

[37] So also Dunn, 'Bailey's Theory', 51.

[38] Dunn, 'Bailey's Theory', 60.

[39] Weeden, 'Bailey's Theory', 33–4 n. 29.

[40] Dunn, 'Bailey's Theory', 53, 60.

[41] Weeden, 'Bailey's Theory', 36.

[42] Dunn, 'Bailey's Theory', 53.

the way Kelber and Vansina think oral tradition typically works, namely 'for the efficacious purpose of preserving and faithfully articulating stories which are congruent with and validate the social identity of an oral society in any given period of time'.[43] Dunn notes that Weeden is articulating 'a version of the well-established "social memory" thesis' which he (Dunn) regards as containing 'a good deal of sound insight'.[44] The reason Dunn and Weeden appear to be at loggerheads is that they are to a large extent arguing about different things. Dunn is primarily interested in employing Bailey's theory of informal controlled oral tradition as a useful model of the synoptic tradition; Weeden is primarily interested in refuting Bailey's apparent claims for its worth in preserving historically authentic material. Both could be right.

The conclusion to be drawn would seem to be that Bailey ends up illustrating in a concrete Middle Eastern setting the kind of picture of oral tradition we have seen described by Kelber.[45] Bailey describes a process which combines stability and flexibility, not unlike that which Kelber envisages. Taken together, the Bailey anecdotes we have discussed do not demonstrate that oral tradition in the Middle East is typically controlled in a way that reliably preserves historical fact. They do, however, suggest some kind of social control (and this would be further illustrated by the other anecdotes Bailey adduces) along the lines envisaged by Kelber.[46] This social control seems to operate to make oral material suit the needs of the community, and there is some indication that reshaping of the facts to meet this end can take place quite rapidly, and certainly while the story is being rehearsed by or in the presence of people who were eyewitnesses to what actually took place. The process of reshaping seems to involve not so much invention *de novo*, as reinterpretation, combination and idealization. Where new elements are introduced (such as the conversion of the robbers or the hostile mayor), these seem to be demanded by the logic of the new purpose the story is being made to serve (e.g. to present a founder figure in an idealized light). What the Bailey anecdotes illustrate is how

---

[43] Weeden, 'Bailey's Theory', 33.

[44] Dunn, 'Bailey's Theory', 59.

[45] So also Holly E. Hearon, 'The Implications of Orality for the Study of the Biblical Text' in Richard A. Horsley, Jonathan A. Draper and John Miles Foley (eds), *Performing the Gospel: Orality, Memory and Mark* (Minneapolis: Augsburg Fortress, 2006), 3–20 (16), citing Holly E. Hearon, *The Mary Magdalene Tradition: Witness and Counter-Witness in Early Christian Communities* (Collegeville, MN: Liturgical Press, 2004), 77–100 in support; Terence C. Mournet, *Oral Tradition and Literary Dependency: Variability and Stability in the Synoptic Tradition and Q* (WUNT, 195; Tübingen: Mohr Siebeck, 2005), 189–90.

[46] So also Weeden, 'Bailey's Theory', 32–7.

actual events can give rise to legendary accounts that are quite clearly related to the original events when both are available for comparison, but from which it would be virtually impossible to recover the original events with any degree of precision otherwise.

The final question about Bailey's theory is whether there is any reason to suppose that the anecdotes he offers about his experiences in the Middle East can be expected to shed any light on how oral tradition may have worked in Jesus' day. He offers no direct evidence that it does, and he could, of course, be criticized for building his theory on anecdotal evidence rather than sound social-anthropological methodology.[47] However, he does point out both that the Middle East of his acquaintance is likely to be rather closer to the social context of first-century Christians than is the modern West, and that in some parts of the Middle East the way of life seems to have changed little over the centuries. The latter assumption is regularly relied upon by New Testament scholars wishing to apply the fruits of Mediterranean cultural anthropology to the world of the first century, so it cannot simply be ruled out of court. Moreover, to the extent that the model sketched here on the basis of Bailey's anecdotes coheres with what more methodologically thorough students of orality and social memory have found, it can surely be used with some measure of confidence.

In places, Weeden's criticism of Bailey is a little harsh, since he is mainly concerned to demolish Bailey's theoretical constructions rather than to retrieve any alternatives. Yet in interpreting Bailey's data through the lens of Kelber and of various specialists on orality, Weeden points the way to a more constructive use of Bailey's account. We can accept Bailey's anecdotal evidence as suggestive and illustrative without necessarily accepting the theoretical construction he places upon it. We can, moreover, accept the general thesis of 'informal controlled tradition' without taking it to be as historically conservative as Bailey appears to suppose. If Bailey's anecdotes are taken primarily as illustrations of the kind of processes Kelber and others describe more abstractly, then they can help us to grasp what these abstractions might mean in practice. Even if we doubt that the kind of social situations Bailey depicts closely mirror typical situations of oral transmission in the primitive Church, Bailey is nevertheless not wrong to suggest that they do illustrate oral traditional processes that are probably a good deal closer to the conditions in which the early Church formed its traditions than anything we know

---

[47] Weeden, 'Bailey's Theory', 37.

in the modern West. Taken with due circumspection, therefore, Bailey's contribution can perhaps be used to advance our understanding of the oral tradition behind the Gospels. But Bailey's data can be viewed not only in relation to Kelber's account of oral tradition, but also in relation to theories of social memory, which will form one of the main topics of the next chapter.

6

Memory and tradition

To survive as oral tradition for any length of time, something has to be memorable. It has to be remembered by at least some individuals, and can only continue to exist for as long as some individuals remember it. But oral tradition is never just the possession of an isolated individual since the individual bearers of a tradition remember not in isolation but as part of one or more social groups, particularly the social group for whom the tradition is important. Membership of a group will affect not only the way in which individuals discuss and impart their traditions, but also the way in which they remember them. Just as there is an irreducibly social dimension to much of what we know (not least, for example, the language in which we habitually speak and think), so there is an irreducibly social dimension to our acts of remembering. Tradition, therefore, depends not only on one or more individual memories, but on something we might call 'social' or 'collective' memory, the memory of the group. Indeed one way of thinking about oral tradition is as an aspect of social memory, other aspects being such things as commemorative rituals, monuments, ceremonies, habitual practices and written texts.

To understand oral tradition, therefore, it is helpful to understand a little both about individual memory (the psychology of memory) and collective memory (the sociology of memory), both of which will be discussed shortly. But it may first be helpful to note how memory has been thought about in the past. Several scholars have described how memory was understood and employed in the pre-modern era.[1] What emerges is that memory played a far more central role in the intellectual life of the Middle Ages and antiquity than it does today and that it was conceived as encompassing aspects of imagination and mental manipulation that we tend not to think of today when we speak of 'memory'.

---

[1] Mary Carruthers, *The Book of Memory: A Study of Memory in Medieval Culture* (2nd edn, Cambridge Studies in Medieval Literature; Cambridge: Cambridge University Press, 2008); Jocelyn Penny Small, *Wax Tablets of the Mind: Cognitive Studies of Memory and Literacy in Classical Antiquity* (Abingdon: Routledge, 1997); David M. Carr, *Writing on the Tablets of the Heart: Origins of Scripture and Literature* (Oxford: Oxford University Press, 2005).

Although it may not seem immediately relevant to the question of oral tradition, something else that stands out in these historical studies is the role
played by the memorization of texts, not least sacred texts. To be compet-
ently literate in a tradition was to know its key texts by heart. The relevance
of this to the oral tradition behind the Gospels becomes more apparent when
we stop to ask what sort of people the tradents (the transmitters of the tradition) are likely to have been. Presumably the people who made the most
impact on the tradition are those who were considered to be authoritative.
Many of these are likely to have occupied positions of authority in the Church,
at least as teachers (1 Corinthians 12.28; Ephesians 4.11–13). While it is
unlikely that all authoritative tradents of the Jesus tradition were literate,
given the relative scarcity of literacy in antiquity, it seems likely that there would
be at least some tendency for literate persons to gravitate towards leader-
ship positions. While the basic ability to read and write would not necessarily
confer mastery of a written tradition, the better educated literate tradents
probably would have possessed some memory command of at least parts
of the Hebrew Scriptures and also, perhaps, of some primitive Christian texts.

Thus what some of the most potentially authoritative purveyors of the
Jesus tradition held in their individual memories and contributed to the
collective memory could well have been, not pure 'oral tradition', but a mixture
of both oral and written material, with the two rapidly becoming thoroughly
intertwined (note, however, that this is very different from Gerhardsson's
proposal that the entire Jesus tradition was tightly controlled by persons
employing formal teaching techniques akin to those of highly literate rabbis).
This is a further reason why social memory may be a better (because more
all-encompassing) category for describing the pre-Gospel Jesus tradition
than oral tradition considered as a phenomenon of pure orality.

Up until now we have used terms like 'social memory' and 'collective
memory' without explaining what they mean; the time has come to supply
that lack. But before doing so it may be helpful to give a brief sketch of the
current psychological understanding of individual memory, both because
individual memory also plays a role in the transmission of tradition and
because the more empirically based psychological approach provides a
useful check on sociological approaches that can sometimes appear rather
more speculative.

Individual memory

Even if we take the term as referring to some mental capacity of individual
human beings, memory is far from being a straightforward concept, for

there are several different types of memory relating to rather different kinds of thing. At the very least we might differentiate between the memory of events we have personally experienced in our lives (*personal* or *autobiographical* memory), memory of facts we have learned from various sources, such as the date of the Battle of Hastings or the name of the first American president (*cognitive* or *semantic* memory), and the memory of how to do things such as operate a computer or tie our shoelaces (*habit* or *procedural* memory).[2] One might well wish to subdivide some of these categories further. For example, our memory of how to perform completely routine tasks such as walking has probably become so ingrained that we do not consciously attend to it, whereas even if we are moderately competent at operating a computer we still have to attend to what we are doing; we might call the first kind of memory *habit* memory and the second *procedural* memory. Likewise, our autobiographical memories are not all of the same type. Remembering a fact about our lives (say the date on which we were born, an example of autobiographical *knowledge*) is not the same as remembering an experience by partly reliving it in our imagination (*episodic* memory).[3]

The fact that people in a primarily oral culture either cannot or at least do not regularly check information against written records has sometimes led to the supposition that their memories were much better than those of modern, literate people. Among New Testament scholars J. D. Crossan has been particularly keen to challenge such assumptions about memory by citing evidence of how unreliable it can be.[4] He points to studies that suggest that far from being a filing cabinet of stored photographic images of the past, memory is better viewed as a selective reconstruction of the past.[5] Against this Richard Bauckham has called attention to other evidence that suggests a more reliable view of (in particular, eyewitness) memory.[6]

---

[2] Paul Connerton, *How Societies Remember* (Themes in the Social Sciences; ed. J. Dunn, J. Goody, E. A. Hammel and G. Hawthorn; Cambridge: Cambridge University Press, 1989), 22–3; Barbara A. Misztal, *Theories of Social Remembering* (Theorizing Society; ed. L. Ray; Maidenhead and Philadelphia: Open University Press, 2003), 9–10; Geoffrey Cubitt, *History and Memory* (Historical Approaches; ed. G. Cubitt; Manchester and New York: Manchester University Press, 2007), 67–8.

[3] William F. Brewer, 'What Is Recollective Memory?' in David C. Rubin (ed.), *Remembering Our Past: Studies in Autobiographical Memory* (Cambridge: Cambridge University Press, 1995), 19–66; Martin A. Conway, 'Autobiographical Knowledge and Autobiographical Memories' in Rubin (ed.), *Remembering*, 67–93.

[4] John Dominic Crossan, *The Birth of Christianity: Discovering What Happened in the Years Immediately after the Execution of Jesus* (San Francisco: Harper, 1998), 59–84.

[5] Crossan, *Birth of Christianity*, 58–84; Dale C. Allison, *Constructing Jesus: Memory, Imagination and History* (London: SPCK, 2010), 1–30 similarly stresses the unreliability of certain aspects of memory.

[6] Richard Bauckham, *Jesus and the Eyewitnesses: The Gospels as Eyewitness Testimony* (Grand Rapids and Cambridge: Eerdmans, 2006), 319–57.

Both authors are able to cite psychological literature in support of their positions, and to some extent the difference between them is as much one of emphasis as one of substance. Crossan makes it abundantly clear that he is not trying to argue that human memory is radically unreliable, while Bauckham freely acknowledges that there is at least a reconstructive element to the remembering process, as indeed seems to be borne out by the psychological literature.[7]

In fact, the memory of most normal individuals is neither completely infallible nor hopelessly inefficient. For most practical purposes it works perfectly well, not least in giving us access to our own individual pasts.[8] It is, however, also capable of generating any number of errors through a combination of forgetting, distortion, unconscious invention, subsequent reinterpretation, self-interest, suggestibility and social pressure. Individual memory is thus both generally reliable and at least somewhat fallible, the degree of reliability and fallibility varying both from individual to individual and from situation to situation.

For present purposes we need note only a few further salient points about individual memory. Two of these have already been mentioned, namely that its reliability is variable and that recollection often involves an element of reconstruction, that is, recalling a memory of some event is never simply a matter of pulling a stored copy of that event out of a mental filing cabinet, and instead often involves our (unconsciously) filling in at least some details of the remembered event from our general under-standing of how things were (or are or should have been). The process of recollecting something is not primarily the reactivation of a stored image but rather an attempt to make sense of what is recalled for present purposes, which means that our current understanding of the world, our present needs and our current situation all contribute to the way we interpret and fill out our recollection of past events.[9]

In particular we both store and retrieve our memories of events in line with certain pre-existent patterns of understanding or *schemata*, which may include typical narrative patterns used for describing that kind of

---

[7] Crossan, *Birth*, 84; Bauckham, *Eyewitnesses*, 325–30; Cubitt, *History and Memory*, 77–81; Conway, 'Autobiographical'; Alan Baddeley, Michael W. Eysenck and Michael C. Anderson, *Memory* (Hove and New York: Psychology Press, 2009), 180–1.

[8] Baddeley et al., *Memory*, 1; Brewer, 'Recollective Memory', 60–1.

[9] Daniel L. Schacter, *Searching for Memory: The Brain, the Mind, and the Past* (New York: Basic Books, 1996), 69–71, 88–97; Todd Tremlin, *Minds and Gods: The Cognitive Foundations of Religion* (Oxford and New York: Oxford University Press, 2006), 152; James L. Fentress and Chris Wickham, *Social Memory* (New Perspectives on the Past; Oxford and Cambridge, MA: Basil Blackwell, 1992), 31.

event, as Crossan notes and Bauckham emphasizes at some length.[10] One kind of schema is the *script*, which defines the typical sequence of events in a given situation. For example, if I mention that I was unable to find any interesting magazines the last time I went to the dentist, due to your knowledge of our common visit-to-the-dentist script you will assume I was looking for magazines in the waiting room rather than in the dentist's chair or under the receptionist's desk. Precisely the same kind of script can be used to help us recollect or reconstruct events. Thus, for example, if you are trying to remember what happened the last time you went to a restaurant you may be helped by the fact that one typically consults the menu at the beginning of the meal and pays the bill at the end, and that there is typically a set order for the courses.

Because we need some kind of framework to make sense of our experience, we tend to remember best what best fits the frameworks we employ. If we encounter something that does not fit the schemata we customarily employ, then in our 'effort after meaning' we are liable to reshape it into something that fits better. This was famously illustrated in Frederick Bartlett's 1930s experiment with the Native American tale of the 'War of the Ghosts', which his subjects unfamiliar with Native American culture tended, when asked to reproduce it from memory, to rationalize and transform into something closer to their own world-view.[11]

Bauckham justifiably argues that such schematization, which is necessary if we are to make sense of our memories at all, does not automatically equate to falsification, but he perhaps understates the extent to which it can result in our remembering what we expected to see.[12] It might also result in our remembering what subsequent reflection (both alone and in company with others) convinces us we ought to have seen. At the very least there is likely to be a considerable interpretative element in the act of remembering (as there must in any case be in the act of narrating our memories to ourselves or others), not least because we have to cast our recollection into a conventional narrative form if we or others are to make sense of it.[13]

Another point to note is that successive acts of remembering may themselves influence the way something is remembered. The way we narrate

---

[10] F. C. Bartlett, *Remembering: A Study in Experimental and Social Psychology* (Cambridge: Cambridge University Press, 1995 [1932]), 199–214; Baddeley et al., *Memory*, 4–5, 94–6, 128–34, 320–2; Cubitt, *History and Memory*, 81–2, 96–106; Crossan, *Birth*, 82; Bauckham, *Eyewitnesses*, 326–9, 335–8; Fentress and Wickham, *Social Memory*, 32–6.

[11] Bartlett, *Remembering*, 63–4.

[12] Baddeley et al., *Memory*, 320–2.

[13] Connerton, *How Societies Remember*, 27; Craig R. Barclay, 'Autobiographical Remembering: Narrative Constraints on Objectified Selves' in Rubin (ed.), *Remembering Our Past*, 94–125.

an event to ourselves or others, including what we choose to omit, may well shape how we come to recall the event on subsequent occasions. Repeated recollections may be something of a mixed blessing: on the one hand they may serve to fix an event in memory, but on the other they may equally well serve to fix a distorted version of that event in memory or even to introduce fresh distortions.[14] For example, if soon after an event occurs we narrate it in a manner designed to make our own actions appear more praiseworthy or less culpable, and we find ourselves called upon to repeat this self-justifying account on multiple occasions, we may quickly become convinced that our now distorted version of events is an accurate memory. Conversely, while an event that is rehearsed less frequently may be more vulnerable to forgetting, it may be less prone to distortion. Distortions are not always deliberate fabrications, however; they may, for example, be due to 'source attribution' errors, that is conflating the details of one incident with another, or with something we heard about from someone else.[15]

The third point to note is that there is an irreducibly social dimension to even the most private individual remembering.[16] At the very least this is because the language, concepts, world-view and schemata we employ to encode, retrieve and interpret our memories are all drawn from our social environment, whatever our own personal idiosyncrasies may contribute to the process. Depending on our suggestibility and the particular nature of our social context, our memories may also be subject to external pressure (or simply our own desire) to conform to how the group or groups with which we most closely identify believe things should be remembered, particularly if they are matters of considerable group significance (as is likely to have been the case with the Jesus tradition).

Collective or social memory

The Jesus tradition was not handed down in a social vacuum, nor was it ever simply a matter of individuals passing on their reminiscences to other

---

[14] Schacter, *Searching for Memory*, 111–12; Cubitt, *History and Memory*, 96–7; so also Maurice Halbwachs, *On Collective Memory* (The Heritage of Sociology; ed. D. N. Levine; tr. Lewis A. Coser; Chicago and London: University of Chicago Press, 1992), 183.

[15] Schacter, *Searching for Memory*, 114–18; Cubitt, *History and Memory*, 83–4; Baddeley et al., *Memory*, 187–8, 322–3.

[16] Halbwachs, *On Collective Memory*, 53; Bartlett, *Remembering*, 237–300; Fentress and Wickham, *Social Memory*, 7; Richard A. Horsley, 'Prominent Patterns in the Social Memory of Jesus and Friends' in Alan Kirk and Tom Thatcher (eds), *Memory, Tradition and Text: Uses of the Past in Early Christianity* (SBL Semeia Studies, 52; Atlanta: SBL, 2005), 57–78 (65).

individuals in a purely private setting. While such private reminiscing may well have occurred, the recollection that was significant for the formation, maintenance and transmission of the Jesus tradition is far more likely to have occurred in wider social contexts, such as the worship and teaching of the primitive Church. In such contexts, social or collective memory will have played a substantial role.

It may not be immediately apparent what the terms 'social memory', 'collective memory' and 'cultural memory' actually mean, whether the three terms mean the same or different things, or how consistently the terms are used by different authors.[17] While the term 'collective memory' can be useful, it can also be potentially confusing if we allow ourselves to reify it into some mysterious mnemonic capacity of a social group that exists apart from the memories of the individual human beings who comprise that group.[18] In what follows, the terms 'social memory' and 'collective memory' will be used, perhaps a little loosely, in three different but related senses: first, the processes by which a group maintains, rehearses, transmits and shapes memories that are of significance to that group; second, the content of such memories; and third, what happens to the content of such memories, both in terms of stability and change and in terms of the types of shaping they might typically undergo.

While collective memories may be passed on and rehearsed in relatively informal settings (such as conversations between family members or friends),[19] social groups generally devise more formal means of rehearsing the collective memories they deem important. Such means may include not only formal verbal instruction, but also commemorative ceremonies and bodily practices (that is, a group's collective memories may be embodied not only in what its members verbalize, but in the way they behave).[20] For example, a commemorative ceremony that was central to primitive Christian communities, at least in the Pauline churches, was the Lord's Supper (1 Corinthians 11.23–26), which Paul explicitly states is a tradition he has received and handed on, and in which the words of institution he cites explicitly state remembrance as the purpose of the rite. The account of worship suggested by 1 Corinthians 14, however, indicates that the Lord's Supper was not the only thing Pauline Christians met for in their worship, and it would seem highly likely that such gatherings provided

---

[17] Cubitt, *History and Memory*, 13–14.
[18] Cubitt, *History and Memory*, 16; Fentress and Wickham, *Social Memory*, ix.
[19] But even these can have an interesting social dynamic; see William Hirst and David Manier, 'Remembering as Communication: A Family Recounts Its Past' in Rubin (ed.), *Remembering Our Past*, 271–90.
[20] Connerton, *How Societies Remember*; Cubitt, *History and Memory*, 180–1, 186–7.

occasions for the rehearsal of traditions in the form of hymns, prophecy, preaching and teaching, as well as, presumably, in the reading of Scripture or, on occasion, Paul's letters (1 Corinthians 12.28; 14.6, 19, 26; 2 Corinthians 10.10; Ephesians 4.11; 5.19; Colossians 3.16), although it may well be that Christian instruction, especially of converts, also took place outside meetings for worship.

The pioneer in the study of collective memory was Maurice Halbwachs, although his thought is not always entirely clear.[21] Like Bartlett, Halbwachs held that memory was reconstructive rather than reproductive in nature, and that social context plays a crucial role in the nature of that reconstruction, but whereas Bartlett was primarily interested in the implications for individual (and social) psychology, Halbwachs's focus was on the group.[22] In particular, although Halbwachs acknowledged that it is individuals who remember, he insisted that every act of individual remembering is necessarily social.[23] This is so in part because in order to remember anything coherently (as opposed to the confused recollection of a dream sequence) we have to place it in a stable temporal and conceptual framework, which, far from being our own individual creation, is supplied by the social group or groups to which we belong, as is the very language in which we frame our thoughts and perceptions.[24] Also, acts of remembering are frequently social acts, in which we seek to share our memories with others.

For Halbwachs the function of collective memory was to maintain the identity, values and cohesion of the group.[25] Societies thus tend to reshape their memories of the past to meet the changing needs of the present, a process that includes selectively forgetting anything that might disrupt group cohesion (a thesis that bears more than a passing resemblance to the notion of homeostasis in oral tradition).[26] Memories thus tend not to outlast the group to which they are significant, apart, perhaps, from an evanescent sentimental attachment to memories of a defunct group by some of its former members.[27]

---

[21] Cubitt, *History and Memory*, 164–5.

[22] Cubitt, *History and Memory*, 158–9.

[23] Halbwachs, *On Collective Memory*, 53; cf. Elizabeth Tonkin, *Narrating Our Pasts: The Social Construction of Oral History* (Cambridge Studies in Oral and Literate Culture, 22; ed. P. Burke and R. Finnegan; Cambridge: Cambridge University Press, 1995), 12.

[24] Halbwachs, *On Collective Memory*, 172–3; Cubitt, *History and Memory*, 159–6; Misztal, *Theories*, 54.

[25] Misztal, *Theories*, 50–2.

[26] Halbwachs, *On Collective Memory*, 182–3; cf. Jan Vansina, *Oral Tradition as History* (London: James Currey, 1985), 114–23.

[27] Cubitt, *History and Memory*, 162.

Within this model the distinctive memories of individual human beings appears to play very little role at all. Halbwachs allowed that each individual has different memories, but explained this as totally due to the fact that individuals belong to a number of different social groups and are differently situated in regard to the combination of groups to which they belong (a form of extreme sociological reductionism that seems a little implausible in the light of cognitive psychology).[28]

The idea that collective memory is a reconstruction whose primary function is to serve the interests of the group that maintains it could be taken to suggest that our notion of the past is a total fabrication designed to serve present interests. Halbwachs himself did not press his ideas quite that far, but they have subsequently been taken in that direction by a number of scholars arguing for a 'presentist' or 'invention of traditions' approach.[29] Such a position is implausible, however, since it ignores both the extent to which the actual past remains immanent in the present (the past determines the present at least as much as the present determines our view of the past) and almost certainly underestimates the resilience of individual memory.[30] Barbara Misztal outlines two further approaches that move beyond the 'presentist' approach in an attempt to address some of its more obvious shortcomings. The 'popular memory' approach also assumes that our view of the past is designed to serve present interest, but denies that this can be wholly controlled from above, instead arguing for the possibility of the construction of social memory from 'the bottom up'. This approach suffers from a number of weaknesses, however. One is the assumption that the politics of memory is always conflictual, and that the view from below is always in opposition to some dominant ideology, thus ignoring the possibility that there could be shared symbols. Another is its failure to account for why some symbols, events and heroes but not others make their way into public memory.[31]

The approach that Misztal prefers is the 'dynamics of memory' perspective, which sees social memory as a process of negotiation. It argues that 'history cannot be freely invented and reinvented and that suppression of alternative interpretations and coercion are insufficient to ensure that

---

[28] Misztal, *Theories*, 53; Cubitt, *History and Memory*, 162.

[29] Misztal, *Theories*, 56–61; cf. Alan Kirk, 'Social and Cultural Memory' in Alan Kirk and Tom Thatcher (eds), *Memory, Tradition, and Text: Uses of the Past in Early Christianity* (SBL Semeia Studies, 52; Atlanta: SBL, 2005), 1–24 (11–14); Barry Schwartz, 'Christian Origins: Historical Truth and Social Memory' in Kirk and Thatcher (eds), *Memory, Tradition, and Text*, 43–56 (44–6).

[30] So also Kirk, 'Social and Cultural Memory', 14–17.

[31] Misztal, *Theories*, 61–7.

particular interpretations will be accepted'.[32] This approach accepts that memory is fluid and unpredictable, and avoids both the social determinism of some previous approaches and the danger of reifying collective memory. While on Misztal's own estimation the 'dynamics of memory' approach lacks 'a clear focus', so that its value as a model of social memory may be limited, it nevertheless serves as a useful reminder that the social memory of a particular group is not necessarily some monolithic set of ideas about the past that all members of the group share without question, but that the contents of collective memory may be debated and contested.[33] This is potentially as true of the Jesus tradition as any other.

There have been a number of other criticisms of Halbwachs's position. Misztal argues that Halbwachs's social determinism neglected the question of how individuals' consciousness of memory might relate to the collective memory of the groups to which they belong. James Fentress and Chris Wickham similarly object that Halbwachs's theory results in 'a concept of collective consciousness curiously disconnected from the actual thought processes of any particular person'.[34] In agreement with Paul Connerton Misztal also complains that Halbwachs failed to attend to the question of how collective memories are handed on from one generation to the next, a process that Connerton sees as primarily a series of interactions between individuals, although one in which rituals also play an important role.[35] Misztal further takes Halbwachs to task for pursuing a one-dimensional approach that too readily assumes the stability of the image of the past in group memory, while Geoffrey Cubitt is concerned about Halbwachs's tendency to reify his somewhat nebulous concept of collective memory, and Tonkin complains that Halbwachs's account of social memory fails to account for change. Barry Schwartz complains that Halbwachs's ideas (like Bultmann's) took shape in the climate of disillusionment and suspicion following the First World War and that he proceeds too confidently on the basis of a dogmatic distrust by invoking extreme instances of construction as if they were the norm, while Alan Kirk accuses the constructivist approach of circular reasoning.[36]

Despite these objections, even Halbwachs's critics have adopted many of his ideas, albeit in modified form. Thus, for example, virtually all the

---

[32] Misztal, *Theories*, 71.
[33] Misztal, *Theories*, 71.
[34] Misztal, *Theories*, 54–5; Fentress and Wickham, *Social Memory*, ix.
[35] Misztal, *Theories*, 55; Connerton, *How Societies Remember*, 37–8.
[36] Misztal, *Theories*, 55; Cubitt, *History and Memory*, 13–14, 165; Tonkin, *Narrating*, 105; Schwartz, 'Christian Origins', 45–51; Kirk, 'Social and Cultural Memory', 13.

writers cited above accept that while there may be an important individual dimension to memory, it always has a social dimension as well, because it has to make use of shared language and shared ideas, and because remembering generally does take place in some kind of social context.[37] It is also accepted that social memory has a role in maintaining group identity and a world of shared meanings, and that the past may commonly be used to legitimate a present social order.[38] As might be predicted from the psychological work of Bartlett and his followers, there is indeed at least an element of construction in social memory, because social memory does have to adapt to present needs and present conceptions.[39] This may lead to social memory distorting the facts and being highly selective about what is remembered and what forgotten, but this is by no means necessarily the case.[40] Moreover, it is never simply a matter of present concerns shaping our conception of the past, since both the actual and the remembered past play a major role in shaping our understanding of the present.[41]

An important factor in social (as in individual) remembering is that of framing, or the application of schemata. The way we understand both the present and the past is conditioned by the conceptual frameworks we use to interpret our past and present experiences. What we remember, both individually and collectively, depends both on how we encoded the information to be remembered at the time we first encountered it, and how we interpret the information when we subsequently recall it and try to explain it to ourselves or others. As mentioned above, we tend to remember best what fits our habitual frameworks and to reshape the unfamiliar to better fit our customary schemata (as for example in Bartlett's experiment with the 'War of the Ghosts'). Social memory, then, tends to conform to the predominant conceptual frameworks of the group to which it belongs, although the fit can often be imperfect. Such imperfections can inspire action in the present because the mismatch may help bring about a re-evaluation of the present. Framing nonetheless plays an important role in helping us to focus on what we deem significant, rather than being overwhelmed by a flood of data and impressions.[42]

---

[37] Fentress and Wickham, *Social Memory*, 7; Cubitt, *History and Memory*, 118–20, 125–6; Misztal, *Theories*, 11–12; Kirk, 'Social and Cultural Memory', 3–5.

[38] Fentress and Wickham, *Social Memory*, 25; Connerton, *How Societies Remember*, 3; Misztal, *Theories*, 13–14; Kirk, 'Social and Cultural Memory', 10–12.

[39] Misztal, *Theories*, 13; Kirk, 'Social and Cultural Memory', 10–11.

[40] Fentress and Wickham, *Social Memory*, xii–xiii.

[41] Connerton, *How Societies Remember*, 2–4; Misztal, *Theories*, 13; Kirk, 'Social and Cultural Memory', 14–17.

[42] Connerton, *How Societies Remember*, 27; Fentress and Wickham, *Social Memory*, 32–6; Misztal, *Theories*, 15–16, 82–3, 95.

Closely related to the notion of framing is that of *keying*, which involves understanding one set of events in terms of another, or, stated more fully, employing our understanding of a significant episode in one period (the more distant past, say) to make sense of an episode in another (typically the recent past or present), so that, for example, aspects of the story of Jesus might be keyed to (i.e. understood in terms of) the sacred history of Israel.[43] As Cubitt remarks, 'Events may also take on significance from patterns of expectation that are rooted in the memory of earlier episodes. Knowledge of the earlier Hebrew prophets shaped perceptions of the life of Jesus of Nazareth, both during that life and afterwards[.]'[44]

Keying often involves telling one story in terms of another, but this is not the only role that narrativization (storing and recalling information in the form of stories) plays in social memory. There are several reasons why societies find it convenient to remember their pasts in the form of stories. The first is that stories help us make sense of the past by providing a natural way to order and connect events and explain them in a meaningful way.[45] The second is that stories are easier to remember than a collection of otherwise unrelated facts; the inner logic of the plot serves to provide some kind of stability to what is being encoded and later recalled.[46]

The requirements of storytelling may also distort what is recalled, since (not least in an oral setting) the story will probably be cast into one of a number of socially familiar forms (employing a plot structure familiar to the culture in which it is told), which may often require simplification and adaptation of the material being emplotted. 'For example, successful narratives about the past must have a beginning and an end, an interesting storyline and impressive heroes.'[47] However we might represent the past to ourselves in the privacy of our own thoughts, talking about the past to anyone else requires casting our recollections in some socially recognizable narrative form. Moreover, the very act of casting our memories into such a narrative form may affect the way in which we remember them, as may our memory of other narratives. While the internal logic of a story may aid its preservation in changing social circumstances, a change

---

[43] Misztal, *Theories*, 96–7; Barry Schwartz, 'Jesus in First Century Memory – A Response' in Kirk and Thatcher (eds), *Memory, Tradition, and Text*, 249–61 (50–1).
[44] Cubitt, *History and Memory*, 208.
[45] Fentress and Wickham, *Social Memory*, 51.
[46] Fentress and Wickham, *Social Memory*, 50, 72.
[47] Misztal, *Theories*, 10.

in circumstances, particularly one to a substantially different social setting, may result in alterations to the story to fit the new setting, especially
if the story contains elements that no longer make sense (Bartlett's
experiment with the story of 'The War of the Ghosts' again being a case
in point).[48]

Whatever the role of eyewitnesses in the primitive Church may have
been (an issue to which we shall return in Chapter 8), most of its members
would have obtained their knowledge of Jesus from other people rather
than their own autobiographical memory. It is thus appropriate to think
of the Jesus tradition as being embedded in the social memory of the
primitive Church (although as we shall see in Chapter 8, this is an assumption that Richard Bauckham challenges). We can conceive the Church as
taking not only a local form (in many cases, relatively small local house
churches) but also a wider one (the network of churches scattered across
parts of the Roman Empire, between which there would have been at least
some measure of regular communication).[49]

Since what made these groups distinctive was precisely their adherence
to Jesus Christ, we may suppose that it was their collective memory of
Jesus that was most constitutive of their group identity. But since Jesus
was held to be the Messiah of Israel and the Son of the God of Israel, it
is surely more than likely that for all or most of the groups who adhered
to him a collective memory of some version of Israelite traditions was
also significant (as noted above). This would almost certainly be the
case for Jewish followers of Jesus, but judging from the letters of Paul
and the contents of Luke–Acts (both seemingly aimed at a mainly Gentile
audience) it would probably have been true of most Gentile churches
as well. It may also be that different churches also possessed collective
memories relating to their own particular local circumstances or cultural
backgrounds, and we can be reasonably certain that not every church
community remembered Jesus in precisely the same way, for the tradition
gives every appearance of being a contested one, but, bearing in mind
these caveats, it should still be meaningful to talk about the Church's
collective memory of Jesus. How this might work out in more concrete
terms will be the subject of Chapter 7; our next immediate task is to
explore how an understanding of memory might bear on the specific issue
of oral tradition.

---

[48] Fentress and Wickham, *Social Memory*, 73–6; Cubitt, *History and Memory*, 96–7, 186.

[49] Michael B. Thompson, 'The Holy Internet: Communications between Churches in the First Christian
Generation' in Richard Bauckham (ed.), *The Gospels for All Christians* (Edinburgh: T. & T. Clark,
1998), 49–70.

Memory in oral tradition

As one might expect, stories are a particularly helpful way to transmit memories in an oral setting, especially memories that are destined to cross generations. Cubitt suggests that oral transmission preserves detailed accounts only within 'living memory' (roughly defined as meaning within the lifespan of people who could have heard of the event from eyewitnesses), and that thereafter there is a tendency to drop details and magnify mythic resonance. Oral tradition can preserve certain kinds of material quite effectively, but such material needs to be cast in special memorable form, rather than merely relayed in the language of ordinary conversation. Narratives constructed along culturally familiar lines would be one such form; proverbs would be another.[50]

Fentress and Wickham note that whereas we moderns tend to settle questions of historical authenticity by appeal to documentary evidence, in non-literate societies the acceptability of a tradition more often had to do with authority, which could be that of the speaker or that of the genre. This does not mean that genre is an indicator of historical accuracy; indeed the choice of genre is often made by people who have no means to gauge historical accuracy. It is rather an indication of the status the material is believed to have among the group that employs it. Moreover, our (modern) judgement of the inherent plausibility of various genres may be a poor guide to historical truth. 'As a rule, oral tradition combines mythology, genealogy, and narrative history rather than holding them apart.'[51]

In Fentress and Wickham's view it is a mistake to approach an ancient (or mediaeval) source with the positivist goal of arriving at a core of historical fact after correcting for the bias, obvious errors and superstition in our sources; in any case once ripped from their original context such 'facts' tend to become a mere jumble of data, deprived of the meaning given them by their original narrative contexts.[52] If this view is correct it clearly throws severe doubt on the kind of historical Jesus research that relies on 'criteria of authenticity' to establish the historical data; from the point of view of social memory theory (especially as applied to oral tradition) the notion of pure, authentic historical fact distilled from layers of later accretion is fundamentally misguided.

If social memory theory gives some indication of the likely strengths and weaknesses of oral tradition, the psychology of memory may offer

---

[50] Cubitt, *History and Memory*, 184–7.
[51] Fentress and Wickham, *Social Memory*, 82.
[52] Fentress and Wickham, *Social Memory*, 144–5.

some insights into what makes oral traditions relatively stable. David Rubin (a psychologist) has argued that oral tradition and the psychology of memory can be mutually illuminating.[53]

Rubin's starting point is to ask how it is that oral traditions can be remarkably stable over time, not in the sense of being completely unchanging but in the sense of remaining recognizable. The three types of oral tradition he specifically considers are epic poetry, folk ballads and child's counting-out rhymes. None of these may seem particularly close to the kind of oral tradition behind the Gospels, but they are presented as particular examples of a more general theory of memory in oral tradition.

In a way, Rubin is seeking to generalize the oral-formulaic theory of Milman Parry and Albert Lord developed in relation to Homeric and South Slavic epic poetry (briefly described in Chapter 1 above). Rubin agrees with Parry and Lord that oral tradition does not generally work by rote memorization of a fixed text. But while Parry and Lord stress composition in performance, Rubin prefers to talk in terms of serial cueing, the idea being that when someone sets out to perform a song or poem each line or unit prompts the memory of what comes next. Rubin's key suggestion is that oral tradition maintains stability by employing a series of multiple constraints or cues. In other words, if you are trying to remember what comes next in a poem or song, you are much more likely to get it right it you use a number of cues to remind yourself than if you rely on a single cue alone. Rubin's research suggests that multiple cues used together are orders of magnitude more effective in prompting correct memories than individual cues used in isolation.[54]

Cues that might aid recall in oral traditions include such obvious things as the overall plot and intermediate structures such as the standard scripts for various kinds of scene. They also include such factors as vivid concrete imagery; other things being equal you are much more likely to remember a story about a tiger swallowing a camel than an abstract proposition about relative size and ferocity. But Rubin also found that what he calls surface features, such as rhyme, alliteration, assonance, rhythm and melody, can be just as important in cueing recall as 'deeper' factors such as meaning, gist, imagery and structure. In other words, what a piece of oral tradition

---

[53] David C. Rubin, *Memory in Oral Traditions: The Cognitive Psychology of Epic, Ballads, and Counting-out Rhymes* (Oxford and New York: Oxford University Press, 1995).
[54] Rubin, *Memory in Oral Traditions*, 39–193.

sounds like can be just as important to its being retained in memory as what it means.

This is perhaps best illustrated by one example Rubin discusses at some length, the child's counting-out rhyme 'Eenie, Meenie, Miney, Mo', which he takes to be a piece of genuine oral tradition rather than something that children learn from books:[55]

> Eenie, meenie, miney, mo,
> Catch a *something* by the toe.
> If he hollers, let him go,
> Eenie, meenie, miney, mo.

Here, the nonsense first line cues both the last line, which repeats it, and the metre for the entire piece, four lines of seven syllables with the stress on the odd-numbered syllables in each line. The sound of 'eenie' cues the second word 'meenie' via assonance. The alliteration of 'meenie', 'miney' and 'mo' constrains the rest of the line together with the use of three vowel sounds in alphabetical order: e, i, o, an order also found, for example, in 'fee, fie, foe, fum' or 'Old MacDonald had a farm, ee-i, ee-i, oh!' The last word, 'mo', then provides the end rhyme used by every other line. The middle two lines offer the concrete image of something being caught by the toe hollering to be let go. In combination these multiple constraints make the rhyme quite hard to get wrong, but it is the sound at least as much as the sense that provides the multiple cueing that makes it so.

This short verse also illustrates the way in which a stable oral tradition can change. For there is still that placeholder 'something' that is caught by the toe. In older versions of the rhyme, the word that used to appear there is one that is no longer considered acceptable. More recent versions have therefore replaced it with something less objectionable, 'tiger' being one of the more popular variants, having the advantage of alliterating with 'toe'. The rhyme 'Eenie, Meenie, Miney, Mo' thus illustrates, not only how multiple constraints can lend stability to a piece of oral tradition, but also the kind of change that can be accommodated within such constraints when circumstances change. Of course not all oral tradition is as neatly and tightly constrained as the short rhyme 'Eenie, Meenie, Miney, Mo', but the occurrence of so many constraints in such a short piece neatly illustrates the general principle.

The application of these insights to the oral Jesus tradition may not be immediately obvious, not least because we lack access to the original

---

[55] Rubin, *Memory in Oral Traditions*, 227–52.

Aramaic tradition in which early poetic forms of Jesus sayings (for instance) can be directly discerned, even though, as Allison remarks, 'a few items in the tradition . . . look as though they were composed precisely in order to lodge themselves in memories'.[56] Rubin's insights do suggest a couple of tentative approaches, however. In more general terms they may help us to sharpen our questions about what might make some putative piece of oral tradition memorable: is it the poetic language, the concrete imagery, the familiar structure, or some combination of these? Are there enough such constraints in any given pericope for it to have survived as a relatively stable piece of tradition in the course of oral transmission? More specifically, for any given piece of supposed tradition that exists in more than one form (the Lord's Prayer, for example, which appears in slightly different forms at Matthew 6.9b–13 and Luke 11.2b–4), which is likely to be the more primitive form: the simpler, shorter, more economical version (Luke's), or the version exhibiting the greater degree of assonance, alliteration, rhythm, rhyme and parallelism that provide multiple constraints to aid oral preservation (Matthew's)?

A third approach to memory in oral tradition is provided by John Miles Foley, who starts not from modern theories of memory but from what he perceives oral practitioners as saying about memory in their poems. In Foley's view

> the oral singers tell us at least five things. First, memory in oral tradition is emphatically not a static retrieval mechanism for data. Second, it is very often a kinetic, emergent, creative activity. Third, in many cases it is linked to performance, without which it has no meaning. Fourth, memory typically entails an oral/aural communication requiring an auditor or audience. Fifth, and as a consequence of the first four qualities, memory in oral tradition is phenomenologically different from 'our memory'.[57]

In fact, as we have just seen, neither the psychology of (individual) memory nor social memory theory regards memory as 'a static retrieval mechanism for data', so memory in oral tradition may not be quite so different from 'our memory' as Foley suggests here. Of more significance is Foley's insistence that memory in oral tradition is intimately linked to performance, and it is to this aspect that we shall now turn.

---

[56] Allison, *Constructing Jesus*, 24; see also his n. 96 on the same page.

[57] John Miles Foley, 'Memory in Oral Tradition' in Richard A. Horsley, Jonathan A. Draper and John Miles Foley (eds), *Performing the Gospel: Orality, Memory and Mark* (Minneapolis: Fortress Press, 2006), 83–96 (84).

Tradition and performance

The oral-formulaic theory developed by Parry and Lord (briefly described back in Chapter 1) might create the impression that linguistic formulas in oral-traditional epic, such as Homer's oft-repeated 'rosy-fingered dawn', are simple metrical fillers, convenient pre-made clichés that can be employed by the oral poet as verbal units to fit the metre in the act of simultaneously composing and performing the poem. But John Miles Foley has argued that linguistic formulas in oral or oral-derived works may be much more than that.

Far from being mere compositional conveniences or unimaginative clichés, traditional formulas can be a special way of meaning, a way that operates through invoking resonances elsewhere in the tradition. Thus, for example, when Homeric epic repeatedly describes Achilles as swift-footed, this is not simply because the phrase 'swift-footed Achilles' neatly fits into a Greek hexameter, nor because the poet cannot be bothered to think of another adjective to describe the hero, but because to those immersed in the tradition, the phrase 'swift-footed Achilles' evokes the character of the hero in all its fullness (through familiarity with the way in which the phrase is used throughout the tradition). Foley calls this kind of allusion *metonymic*, meaning that one aspect of Achilles' character (his fleetness of foot) stands in for the whole (roughly as one might use 'hand' or 'head' to stand for the whole person in such phrases as 'all hands on deck' or 'counting heads'). Such allusion is not restricted to short phrases such as 'swift-footed Achilles' or 'grey-eyed Athena', however, but can be extended to other traditional features of oral narrative, such as scenes and story lines (the sequence of events that typically occurs in a particular type of scene such as the arming of a hero for battle, or the overall plot structure of a particular kind of story).[58]

A helpful example of how this kind of traditional referentiality might work in areas other than epic poetry is provided by Nancy Mason Bradbury's brief analysis of the Scottish ballad 'Tam Lin'.[59] Near the start, the heroine of the ballad is described as kilting up her skirt and binding up her hair, actions that are only fully meaningful if one knows that in the wider tradition that forms the background to this ballad such actions typically

---

[58] John Miles Foley, *The Singer of Tales in Performance* (Voices in Performance and Text; Bloomington and Indianapolis: Indiana University Press, 1995), 2–7.

[59] Nancy Mason Bradbury, 'Traditional Referentiality: The Aesthetic Power of Oral Traditional Structures' in John Miles Foley (ed.), *Teaching Oral Traditions* (New York: The Modern Language Association, 1998), 136–45 (139–43).

suggest an immodest woman bent on rushing headlong to an unseemly destination, or at least a determined woman in pursuit of her lover. The tradition also tends to associate picking flowers with sexual deflowering, so that when the heroine of 'Tam Lin' insists that she will pluck flowers if she wishes, the reader or audience keyed into the resonances of the tradition will be aware that she is willing for a sexual encounter. Conversely, when she is later described as 'playing ball' at home, the associations are with innocent domesticity. In each case the full meaning is far more than the literal, surface meaning of the words employed, so that only someone attuned to the tradition will pick up what is being conveyed by the poem. This kind of traditional referentiality is rather different from literary allusion, since literary allusion is a relation between a phrase in one text and another specific text. Traditional referentiality uses a formula or theme to allude, not to another specific text, but to the way that formula or theme operates in the tradition as a whole.[60]

Foley's argument in *The Singer of Tales in Performance* extends his theory of immanent art (the way in which traditional formulas and themes gain meaning by resonating with the tradition) by calling on insights from ethnopoetics and the ethnography of speaking, particularly the work of Richard Bauman on oral performance.[61] Bauman argues that the study of oral verbal art needs to attend not simply to the text that is performed but to the act of performance. A performance in Bauman's terms is something different from everyday conversation; it is a communicative act in which the performer takes 'responsibility to an audience for a display of communicative competence' and in which something occurs to tell the audience, 'interpret what I say in a special sense; do not take it to mean what the words alone, taken literally, would convey'.[62] How this is done varies from culture to culture; different communities employ different devices for keying a performance frame (i.e. signalling that a performance is taking place and what kind of performance it is) so that the audience knows what to expect and how to interpret it. Such devices may include some combination of special codes (such as archaisms), figurative language (perhaps employed in a traditional way), parallelism, special paralinguistic features (such as facial expressions and gestures), special formulas, appeals to tradition, and disclaimers of performance (e.g. 'Unaccustomed as I am

---

[60] Bradbury, 'Traditional Referentiality', 138–9.
[61] Richard Bauman, *Verbal Art as Performance* (reissued 1984 edn; Long Grove, IL: Waveland Press, 1977); see also Richard Bauman and Donald Braid, 'The Ethnography of Performance in the Study of Oral Traditions' in Foley (ed.), *Teaching Oral Traditions*, 106–22.
[62] Bauman, *Verbal Art*, 11, 9.

to public speaking . . .'), which may be regarded as forms of *metacommunication* about the nature of the performance taking place.[63]

What Bauman calls an 'interpretative frame' Foley prefers to call a 'performance arena', by which he means 'the locus where the event of performance takes place, where words are invested with their special power'.[64] This is not necessarily a place in the sense of a specific geographical location; it is more a specific social situation in which this kind of performance typically takes place (and so roughly corresponds to Bauman's conception of a particular kind of event). The point for Foley is that when an audience enters the performance arena it is in the right frame of mind to attend not purely to the literal surface meaning of whatever is said but to its 'ambient traditional meaning', the meaning to which the use of language in this kind of performance metonymically refers.[65]

Foley considers two further aspects of performance alongside the performance arena: register and communicative economy. Registers are 'major speech styles associated with recurrent types of situations'.[66] They may be marked out by, among other things, unusual kinds of language (such as archaisms), displacement of normal prose word order, formulaic phraseology, thematic structure or story pattern (so that what Foley calls 'register' corresponds to some extent to Bauman's notion of metacommunication). Modern examples might include the very different registers (typical modes of speech) employed, say, by a stand-up comic, a preacher delivering a sermon in a formal worship setting, and a lawyer making a summing-up speech in court, three very different kinds of performance calling for three very different registers. For Foley the important thing about a register is that it is a special idiom, which in turn allows 'code-switching' to alert an audience to the resonances of the performance in the appropriate tradition. To put it in Foley's terms, the special idiom enables the metonymic connotation that confers word-power on the various traditional devices employed.[67] Communicative economy arises when performer and audience are in the same performance arena and both understand the register employed. In this situation 'signals are decoded and gaps are bridged with extraordinary fluency, that is economy.' Whereas formulaic expressions such as 'swift-footed Achilles' may seem cumbersome to a modern literate

---

[63] Bauman, *Verbal Art*, 13–22; on metacommunication see also Barbara A. Babcock, 'The Story in the Story: Metanarration in Folk Narrative' in the same volume, 61–79.

[64] Foley, *Singer*, 47.

[65] Foley, *Singer*, 7–11, 47–9; Bauman, *Verbal Art*, 27–8.

[66] Foley, *Singer*, 50.

[67] Foley, *Singer*, 49–53.

audience, in their proper performance arena they act as nodes 'in a grand, untextualizable network of traditional associations. Activation of any single node brings into play an enormous wellspring of meaning that can be tapped in no other way.'[68]

This combination of performance arena, register and communicative economy enables what Foley calls 'word-power', the power of words to convey far more than their literal surface meaning through the associations they evoke (note that in this context a 'word' may be a much larger unit of utterance than what we think of as a word – i.e. an isolated lexical unit – in a print culture). In Foley's formulation, '*word-power derives from the enabling event of performance and the enabling referent of tradition*'.[69]

Where there is still a living tradition of performance (such as the Balkan singers investigated by Parry and Lord, or certain Native American traditions studied by scholars of ethnopoetics) it may be possible for an investigator to form a reasonably full understanding of the performance arena and register involved. Where all that remains of an oral tradition is its textual residue (as is the case for all mediaeval and ancient material), this may no longer be possible. Foley nevertheless believes that there can be *some* gains in studying such oral-derived text with a view to trying to reconstruct as much of the original performance arena as one can, so that one can at least part-way tune in to the appropriate register. Such a strategy is in any case likely to provide for a better interpretation of an oral-derived text than would reading it as if it were a modern literary one. Foley nevertheless warns that there is probably no generally reliable method for determining whether an ancient or mediaeval oral-derived text is a transcription of an oral performance taken down in dictation or an original written composition by someone conversant with an oral tradition.[70]

Incidentally, although Foley tends to talk in terms of oral poetry, this should not be taken as excluding the Gospel traditions because they are not in verse. In this context, 'poem' is a broader concept than our idea of verse marked out by metre, rhythm and rhyme; it should instead be understood as any instance of verbal art, speech crafted for performance as opposed to speech uttered in conversation (compare the Greek word *poiēma* which can mean 'something made' as well as 'poem'). Foley's insights are therefore potentially applicable to the Jesus tradition at at

---

[68] Foley, *Singer*, 53–4.
[69] Foley, *Singer*, 213.
[70] Foley, *Singer*, 60–98.

least three levels: the Gospels (and other early Christian documents) as oral-derived texts, the oral tradition behind the Gospels, and the historical Jesus as an oral performer. The last of these levels would involve trying to reconstruct the performance situation of the historical Jesus and making some assumptions about the existing traditions his words presupposed, which would most likely be Israelite traditions partly reflected in the Hebrew Scriptures (and quite possibly in some intertestamental literature as well). These traditions would probably have continued to be relevant at the other two levels (without necessarily excluding the possibility of other traditions coming into play from the wider Graeco-Roman cultural context), but as soon as the Jesus tradition itself began to take shape, it too would have constituted a body of tradition that its individual units could have referenced through their word-power.

Foley's concept of the 'enabling referent of the tradition' would seem to be a special case of social memory, the social memory of a performance tradition in which certain terms and themes and structures take on a special meaning that is far more than is implied by the literal surface meaning of the words actually employed. The mechanism of 'traditional referentiality' might then be seen as a special (though significant) case of keying and framing via socially shared schemata. How these insights, together with the broader insights of social memory, may be applied to the Jesus tradition will form the subject of the next chapter.

7

Memory and orality in the Jesus tradition

The last chapter examined how our understanding of oral tradition might be furthered by studies on memory, and in particular social memory, and by John Miles Foley's extension of oral formulaic theory to embrace both immanent art and the ethnography of performance. Both approaches imply that oral performance takes place in a wider context of memory and tradition that determines how a given performance is to be framed and understood. Performance tradition and social memory both constrain and enable performance. An oral performance is constrained to follow a pattern that can be recognized and appreciated by its target audience, which may oblige performers to employ types of language, formulas, themes and story patterns that are already familiar to their audience. Conversely, by taking advantage of the resources of a tradition, performers can achieve considerable communicative economy. An audience fully conversant with the relevant tradition, including any traditional style of narration involved, may understand far more from an oral performance than the literal, surface meaning of what is said, and far more than someone not familiar with the tradition would gain from reading a transcription of the performance in a written or printed text. All this has potential importance for understanding the transmission of the Jesus tradition, and a number of New Testament scholars have tried to apply one or the other set of concepts, or to combine both, as a means of doing just that. In what follows we shall pay particular attention to the work of James Dunn, Richard Horsley (with Jonathan Draper) and Rafael Rodriguez.

James Dunn – *Jesus Remembered*

The title of Dunn's 2003 book, *Jesus Remembered*, might suggest a study that paid close attention to the role of memory in the Jesus tradition.[1] The point of Dunn's title is that the only Jesus that it is accessible to us is not Jesus as he actually was, but Jesus as he was remembered through

---

[1] James D. G. Dunn, *Jesus Remembered* (Christianity in the Making, 1; Grand Rapids and Cambridge: Eerdmans, 2003).

the impact he made on his first followers.[2] In the course of this analysis there is surprisingly little discussion of the actual workings of memory, but substantial attention is paid to the workings of oral tradition.

Part of Dunn's concern is to insist that it is simply an illusion to suppose that historical enquiry can arrive at some 'objective' depiction of Jesus separated out from the faith he inspired in his first followers; since the only Jesus accessible to us is the Jesus as his followers remembered him, there is no such neutral faith-free Jesus to be had.[3] This in part follows from Dunn's conviction that most of what can be known about Jesus is contained in the synoptic tradition, and that there are no substantial neutral or hostile sources about Jesus with which to compare it. Dunn is also insistent that the impact Jesus made that inspired his followers to have faith in him was made from the very beginning, that is during his earthly ministry and on his first followers. This allows Dunn to claim that the Jesus remembered in the synoptic tradition is by and large the Jesus remembered by his first followers, the eyewitnesses to his ministry, so that although we do not have access to an objective historical Jesus, we do have access to the impact he made on those who knew him.

Dunn's conception of oral tradition plays a key role in this argument. In his view sociological logic demands that groups who identified themselves as followers of Jesus would have needed some kind of foundation story to explain to themselves and others why they formed a distinct group. From there Dunn goes on to point out that Paul several times refers to foundational traditions and that the existence of teachers in the early Church also shows that there must have been something – presumably oral traditions – to teach. He then argues that the motifs of witnessing and remembering are found throughout the New Testament, pointing out that remembering is important for identity formation. From this he concludes that 'more or less from the first those who established new churches would have taken care to provide and build a foundation of Jesus tradition'.[4] Although there is little *explicit* reference to social memory theory here, up to this point Dunn's argument is consistent with it; social groups such as early Christian communities presumably would find it important to cultivate stories in group memory that helped explain and maintain their identity.

After a brief dismissal of the oft-repeated theory that much of the sayings material attributed to Jesus came from post-Easter Christian

---

[2] Dunn, *Jesus Remembered*, 128–32, 335–6.
[3] Dunn, *Jesus Remembered*, 125–7.
[4] Dunn, *Jesus Remembered*, 175–80.

prophets,[5] Dunn turns to his main discussion of oral tradition. He begins by reviewing the contributions of Herder, Bultmann, Koester, Gerhardsson and Kelber, and finds them all wanting.[6] While Dunn is appreciative of Kelber's recognition of the character of orality and of the oral characteristics of Mark, he is highly critical of Kelber's thesis of a sharp rupture with the oral tradition caused by Mark's committing his Gospel to writing. While holding that they clearly have their axes to grind, Dunn is also appreciative of the work of Richard Horsley and Jonathan Draper (to be discussed below), and not least of their use of Foley's insights.[7] He is, however, most impressed by Kenneth Bailey's theory of informal controlled oral tradition (discussed in Chapter 5 above), partly on the basis that Bailey's anecdotal experience of the Middle East is culturally closer to the New Testament environment than the study of Balkan bards.[8] Although, as we have seen, there are a number of shortcomings with Bailey's work, the conclusions that Dunn wishes to draw from it seem largely innocuous, in part, perhaps, because Dunn is not in fact solely dependent on Bailey, and interprets him through the lens of scholars such as Jan Vansina. Thus, for example, Dunn notes (against Bultmann) that 'in oral tradition one telling of a story is in no sense an editing of a previous telling . . . each telling is a performance of the tradition itself',[9] an insight that could equally well have been gleaned from Lord, Foley, Kelber or Horsley. Nevertheless, Dunn does feel that Bailey has made a distinctive contribution, in particular:

> Bailey's thesis both informs and refines the general recognition among students of the subject that oral tradition is typically flexible . . . What he adds is significant; in particular the recognition of the likelihood that (1) a community would be concerned enough to exercise some control over its traditions; (2) the degree of control exercised would vary both in regard to form and in regard to the relative importance of the tradition for its own identity; and (3) the element in the story regarded as its core or key to its meaning would be its most firmly fixed element.[10]

By now it should be apparent that the first two numbered points are hardly contentious or original to Bailey. At this point, unlike Bailey, Dunn is making no explicit claim that what communities are likely to control

---

[5] Dunn, *Jesus Remembered*, 186–92.
[6] Dunn, *Jesus Remembered*, 199–204.
[7] Dunn, *Jesus Remembered*, 204–5.
[8] Dunn, *Jesus Remembered*, 205–10.
[9] Dunn, *Jesus Remembered*, 209.
[10] Dunn, *Jesus Remembered*, 209.

Memory and orality in the Jesus tradition

for is historical accuracy (although this is where Dunn's argument will implicitly take him). The third point looks plausible enough but is perhaps more questionable. It ignores the possibility that what is regarded as core or key in a story might change with changing circumstances, or might at least be reshaped to meet changing needs. Dunn does go on to illustrate this third point with examples from the synoptic tradition, including a number from the double tradition and Mark (with synoptic parallels). In each case Dunn argues that the degree of verbal agreement in the parallel passages he examines is so low that a theory of direct literary copying is not the best one to explain the evidence; the different accounts look not so much like literary redactions of one another as oral retellings, either of a common oral tradition, or of one Evangelist's recollection of another Evangelist's account. In support of this Dunn suggests that it is unlikely that all the material contained in Mark or Q was unfamiliar to Matthew, Luke and their communities until they came across it in a written document, so that the later Evangelists would almost certainly have been familiar with oral traditions parallel to the material they found in their written sources.[11]

This argument is questionable. For one thing, as Dunn himself acknowledges, Matthew and Luke could simply be freely reworking what they found in Mark (a possibility that becomes even stronger if they more or less knew Mark from memory and did not have to keep looking at his text). For another, as John Kloppenborg has argued in response to Dunn, the variations between the synoptic parallels Dunn appeals to are well within the bounds of those that other ancient authors made to their written sources.[12] Moreover if Rubin's multiple-constraint theory of stability in oral tradition is correct, some forms of oral tradition may actually exhibit less flexibility than that with which an author can treat a written source. The degree of agreement or disagreement between the wording of synoptic parallels is thus by no means an automatic indicator of whether the relationship between them is textual or oral.

Dunn does not believe that the relation between the Gospels can be explained on the basis of oral tradition alone; rather he insists that the oral tradition was still an active, living tradition at the time the Gospels were written, that it did not at once disappear with the writing of the Gospels, and that it played a major role in the composition of the Gospels,

---

[11] Dunn, *Jesus Remembered*, 212–38; so also James D. G. Dunn, 'Altering the Default Setting: Re-envisaging the Early Transmission of the Jesus Tradition', *NTS* 49 (2003), 139–75.

[12] John S. Kloppenborg, 'Variation and Reproduction of the Double Tradition and an Oral Q?', *ETL* 83 (2007), 53–80.

111

all of which may be true despite the shakiness of the grounds on which he argues it. He also argues that since in at least some cases the variations between parallel accounts in the Gospels is more characteristic of oral retelling than of literary editing, these variations can be taken as indicative of the extent of stability and variation within the synoptic tradition, from which he concludes that the core of the tradition was stable, even if details and emphases could be quite variable.

One possible objection to this argument is that even if one allows that the tradition was relatively stable during the period of composition of the Synoptic Gospels (say 70–100 CE), that does not prove that it was equally stable throughout the 40 years preceding the composition of Mark's Gospel, or that it was the only version of the Jesus tradition that existed in the first century. As we saw in Chapter 5, one reading of the anecdotal evidence provided by Kenneth Bailey, especially when checked against Rena Hogg's biography, is that an oral-traditional version of a story could be reshaped quite quickly into the version useful to the community and then become relatively stable thereafter, a possibility that seems to be borne out by other studies of oral tradition and social memory. The relative stability of the synoptic tradition in the last third of the first century cannot, then, be used as a direct indication of the stability of the entire Jesus tradition from its inception to the writing down of the first surviving texts in which we find it.

That Dunn wishes us to suppose that it can becomes apparent from the rhetoric of his argument. While he constantly allows that the tradition developed after Easter and that it was flexible as well as stable, it is the stability that he constantly emphasizes. For example, as opposed to form criticism's model of successive layers of tradition becoming increasingly remote from the original Jesus as time goes by, Dunn maintains that on the model of oral tradition he espouses,

> performance includes both elements of stability and elements of variability –
> stability of subject and theme, of key details or core exchanges, variability
> in the supporting details and the particular emphases to be drawn out ...
> These [conclusions from the foregoing] include the likelihood that the
> stabilities of the tradition were sufficiently maintained and the variabilities
> of the retellings subject to sufficient control for the substance of the tradi-
> tion, and often actual words of Jesus which made the first tradition-forming
> impact, to continue as integral parts of the living tradition, for at least as
> long as it took the Synoptic tradition to be written down.[13]

---

[13] Dunn, *Jesus Remembered*, 249.

Or, as Dunn can say a few pages later,

> In other words, what we today are confronted with in the Gospels is not the top layer (last edition) of a series of increasingly impenetrable layers, but the living tradition of Christian celebration which takes us with surprising immediacy to the heart of the first memories of Jesus.[14]

Dunn is reasonably explicit on how he sees the traditioning process operating. On his view, the Jesus tradition began during Jesus' ministry with his disciples discussing his deeds and teaching among themselves or with sympathizers, and it would have been initiated by the impact of Jesus (who, after all, was a *teacher* of *disciples*). This would have been a primarily *communal* process rather than the individual impressions of individual disciples, and gives us access, not to the objective words and deeds of Jesus, but to the impact Jesus made on those who knew him. Moreover the remembered impact may have taken the form, not of precise recollections of individual occasions, but of a synthesis of the impact made on a multitude of occasions (this last point is plausible enough given what is known about the workings of memory). This Jesus tradition would already have played an important role in forming community identity pre-Easter. Eyewitnesses would have had a continuing important role as respected individual authority figures. The tradition that came down to us is unlikely to be the initial preaching to potential converts but the material that was in constant use in Christian communities (as form criticism realized). Easter, the transition from Aramaic to Greek, and the shift from rural Galilee to an urban Hellenistic environment would all have made a difference as the tradition was shaped for changing circumstances. 'But the oral Jesus tradition itself provided the continuity, the living link back to the ministry of Jesus, and it was no doubt treasured for that very reason.'[15]

From there Dunn goes on to challenge what he regards as three common misconceptions about the nature of the oral tradition. The first is that it circulated purely in isolated units (the individual pericopae of classical form criticism); instead, Dunn suggests, there is evidence that stories and sayings were grouped before being written down in the Gospels, and Mark may contain sequences already familiar from the oral tradition (although Dunn concedes that this is speculative). Dunn might have strengthened his case at this point if he had considered the distinction between isolated in the sense of one unit being narrated by itself rather than in conjunction with others in any given performance, and isolated in the

---

[14] Dunn, *Jesus Remembered*, 254.
[15] Dunn, *Jesus Remembered*, 239–45.

sense of performances of individual units taking place before audiences unfamiliar with the Jesus tradition as a whole, which could provide a context of interpretation to the particular performance of a particular unit. Conjecturing catenae of units that were regularly performed together in the oral tradition is indeed speculative, while a strong case could be made against the isolation of units in the second sense.

The second assumption Dunn challenges has already been mentioned several times before, namely that the oral tradition can be conceived of as a series of layers rather than a sequence of performances (and here Dunn is surely on firm ground). The third is connected with what Dunn regards as Kelber's overstatement of the shift from orality to writing when the Gospels were composed and the more widespread failure to recognize the ongoing nature of the oral tradition.[16]

Dunn's chief interest in this is in deriving a methodology for constructing the remembered Jesus. His methodological proposals are eminently sensible, namely to suppose that whatever is characteristic (and relatively distinctive) of the synoptic tradition originates from the impact Jesus made on his first followers, without worrying about the authenticity of this or that individual saying or deed.[17] What Dunn lacks is any real treatment of the workings of memory, beyond the odd reference to its importance to social identity. Dunn thus leaves himself open to the charge that he is treating 'memory' as a direct conduit from the time of Jesus to the time of the Evangelists, appealing to it as a guarantor of continuity without stopping to consider its constructive and distorting aspects. In contrast Dale Allison tackles these issues head on, beginning his discussion by emphasizing the fallibility of memory.[18] That Allison is then able to arrive at an approach that looks broadly similar to Dunn's proposed method is due to Allison's appeal to the notion that memory is better at recalling the gist and outline of events and speeches than the precise details. In practice, then, Allison's concept of 'fuzzy memory' plays the same role as Dunn's notion of the synthesis of the impact made on a number of occasions. Allison thus shows how the gaps in Dunn's treatment of memory could be filled in without fundamentally undermining Dunn's position.

One is nevertheless left with the impression that Dunn is a little too sanguine about the continuity of the Jesus tradition. This may in part be

---

[16] Dunn, *Jesus Remembered*, 239–53.

[17] Dunn, *Jesus Remembered*, 327–36. So also Eric Eve, *The Healer from Nazareth: Jesus' Miracles in Historical Context* (London: SPCK, 2009), 118–19; Dale C. Allison, *Constructing Jesus: Memory, Imagination and History* (London: SPCK, 2010), 10–26.

[18] Allison, *Constructing Jesus*, 1–10.

due to his rhetorical strategy, designed as a corrective to more sceptical positions. It is certainly not the case that Dunn naively supposes that everything in the synoptic tradition corresponds to historical fact, as can be seen, for example, in his subsequent treatment of Jesus' trial and execution.[19] It is rather that one is left with the feeling that while Dunn has shown that it *could* be the case that the synoptic tradition preserves the original memory of Jesus as well as he supposes, he has not convincingly shown that this *must* be so.

Richard Horsley (and Jonathan Draper)

When Dunn briefly referred to the work of Richard Horsley and Jonathan Draper in the course of his survey of previous treatments of oral tradition, he had in mind their book on prophecy in Q, which argues that Q is a collection of speeches addressing social conditions in Galilean villages.[20] Since then Horsley has gone on to publish a number of pieces combining insights from Foley's theory of oral performance with social memory theory, cultural anthropology, and studies of the social, political and economic circumstances of first-century Palestine. Many of these have since been collected into a single volume which provides a convenient compendium of his views.[21] In this body of work Horsley has become one of the most prolific exponents of orality and social memory studies in the study of the New Testament (and the Gospels in particular).

A number of points recur throughout Horsley's work in this area. First of all, Horsley is anxious to challenge what he regards as the unconscious print-culture assumptions of much previous scholarship, so he frequently points out how limited literacy was in the ancient Mediterranean world, whether in classical Greece, Rome or Palestine, suggesting literacy rates of no more than 5 to 10 per cent for Greece and Rome, and as low as 3 per cent for Roman Palestine, with literacy largely confined to the upper classes and those who served them as retainers or educated slaves. He insists that communication in this environment was mainly oral, even among the literate elites, and that peasants regarded written documents with suspicion (as instruments of domination by the ruling classes, such as debt records). What we might think of as literature was performed orally, with the written text serving principally as an aide-memoire.

---

[19] Dunn, *Jesus Remembered*, 774–81.

[20] Richard A. Horsley and Jonathan A. Draper, *Whoever Hears You Hears Me: Prophets, Performance and Tradition in Q* (Harrisburg, PA: Trinity Press International, 1999).

[21] Richard A. Horsley, *Jesus in Context: Power, People, and Performance* (Minneapolis: Fortress Press, 2008).

The Jews had sacred scrolls, some of which would in time form the basis of what we call the Old Testament, but most Israelites would have been familiar with their contents only through hearing them recited orally. Writing was not much used in ordinary life, and the surviving evidence suggests that even among the educated Jewish elites, Israelite traditions were primarily cultivated orally. Since writing was relatively rare, it often had a symbolic or even magical significance; the fact that something was written down might thus be felt to be of more importance than the actual contents of the writing, so that, for example, when Mark or Q references what we think of as Scripture with the formula 'it is written', this is to be understood as an appeal to the written authority of a scroll rather than an indication that a writing is being directly cited through scribal copying; it is much more likely that the tradition is being cited from memory.[22]

This leads into Horsley's second point, which is that what we may take to be scriptural allusions and quotations in the Gospels might more appropriately be regarded as reflections of Israelite social memory. Underpinning this suggestion is the distinction between the 'great tradition' (the official tradition of the educated ruling elite) and the 'little tradition' (the tradition of the uneducated masses). The great and little traditions are not to be thought of as completely distinct, however; they may have quite a bit in common and they certainly influence each other. For example, illiterate persons might become broadly familiar with the contents of parts of Scripture through hearing it read or recited. There are nonetheless some important distinctions between the great and little traditions. First of all, whereas the great tradition may at least in part be recorded in writing, the little tradition exists solely in social memory and is rehearsed entirely through oral communication. Second, while the great tradition will tend to legitimate the interests of the ruling elite (for example, the central role of the Temple and high priesthood), the little tradition will tend to reflect the concerns of the peasantry (for example the concerns for the welfare of the poor expressed in parts of the covenant, or Elijah's stand against the oppressive rule of King Ahab). Horsley thus suggests that the distinction between the great and little traditions broadly corresponds to that between official and anti-hegemonic social memory, or between the official and the hidden transcripts.[23]

---

[22] Horsley and Draper, *Whoever Hears*, 125–44; Richard A. Horsley, *Hearing the Whole Story: The Politics of Plot in Mark's Gospel* (Louisville, KY: Westminster John Knox Press, 2001), 53–61; Horsley, *Jesus in Context*, 57–62, 89–95.

[23] Horsley and Draper, *Whoever Hears*, 98–104; Horsley, *Whole Story*, 156–61; Horsley, *Jesus in Context*, 28–30, 123–5, 146–56.

Horsley suggests that we have reasonably direct access to the Israelite great tradition (or rather, traditions, since, as he observes, the existence of dissident groups shows that the great tradition was far from unitary) through the Hebrew Bible and a number of other written texts that survive from Second Temple times. We do not have the same kind of access to the little tradition of the Israelite peasantry, however, since by its very nature it left no written remains, and the literate elites whose writings survived show very little interest in it. Horsley nevertheless proposes three ways by which we can discern something of this little tradition. First, used with caution, texts such as the Hebrew Bible can be used to illuminate the little tradition on the assumption that it would have reflected at least some parts of the great tradition. Second, we can note the kinds of tradition the Gospels, and particularly Mark and Q, appear to be appealing to. Third, the accounts of popular uprisings in the writings of Josephus can be used to indicate the cultural scripts that inspired and motivated them. From these considerations Horsley deduces the existence of popular *messianic* and *prophetic* cultural scripts among the peasantry (where the term 'cultural scripts' should be understood in terms of framing and keying in social memory). Thus, for example, Moses' deliverance of Israel from Egyptian oppression and Eljiah's resistance to the oppressive rule of Ahab and Jezebel provide scripts – patterns of expectation and interpretation – for understanding and inspiring current prophetic resistance to oppressive rule. In a similar way the young David's resistance to Philistine oppression provided a script for a popular Messiah.[24]

It is against this background that Horsley invokes Foley. While Horsley draws on Foley's concepts of performance arena and register (suggesting, for example, a prophetic register for Q), he puts the greatest weight on the notion of metonymic referencing, the thesis that in an oral-traditional performance a linguistic term or theme may carry much more than its literal, surface significance by acting *pars pro toto* (a part standing in for the whole). Horsley's main interest is in how the Jesus tradition, particularly as it appears in Q and Mark, metonymically references the Israelite little tradition. Thus, for example, where Jesus is represented as doing Moses-like or Elijah-like things such as feeding a crowd in the wilderness or healing people, we are to suppose that the entire traditional prophetic script (not least the resistance to oppressive authority) is being invoked, implying that Jesus was seen as the prophetic leader of

---

[24] Horsley and Draper, *Whoever Hears*, 95–8, 104–22; Horsley, *Whole Story*, 231–53; Horsley, *Jesus in Context*, 36–42, 67–71, 119–23, 139–45, 156–61.

a renewal movement. Similarly, where parts of the covenant are alluded to, such as sections of the Decalogue in Mark 10.19 or allusions to covenantal traditions in Luke 6.20–49, the wider context of covenant renewal is being invoked.[25]

As may be apparent from the foregoing, Horsley places the social location of Mark and Q firmly in a lower-class context. More specifically, he locates the origin of both texts in the peasant society of Galilean villages, and sees them as primarily addressing the social and economic concerns of peasants whose traditional way of life was being threatened by the pressure of several layers of taxation and the effects of the urbanization of Galilee (the rebuilding of Sepphoris and the foundation of Tiberias). Horsley takes the Galilean peasantry to be the remnants of the northern kingdom of Israel that fell to the Assyrians in 722 BCE. After spending nearly eight centuries separated from Jerusalem and Judaea, they were once again brought under Jerusalem rule and subjected to 'the laws of the Judeans' as a result of the Hasmonean expansion in the first century BCE. Prior to this the Galilean peasantry had lived in more or less autonomous villages, but the effects of first Jerusalem and then indirect Roman rule, with their increasing burdens of tithes and taxes, threatened to bring about a breakdown in traditional village social relations. It is this situation that Horsley sees the Jesus movement (as represented by Mark and Q) as addressing.

In Horsley's view the Markan Jesus is represented as the prophetic leader of a covenant renewal movement and, with considerably more (Markan) reservations, as a popular messianic figure. Horsley takes the register of Q to be that of the prophetic leader of a covenant renewal movement, with Q consisting, not of a series of independent sayings collected by a literary redactor, but of a sequence of speeches urging covenant renewal and addressing the social and economic attitudes that adherents of the movement are to take as a result. It is this renewal within Israel that constitutes what Mark and Q mean by the 'kingdom (or kingly rule) of God'; Galilean villagers are urged to live as if this kingdom had already arrived, perhaps on the basis that if Jesus' prophetic word declared it to be so, then it must be so. Horsley thus explicitly departs from more theological readings of these texts that see them concerned with the foundation of a new religion as against Judaism, insisting time and again that they are concerned with a renewal movement within

---

[25] Horsley and Draper, *Whoever Hears*, 160–74, 195–227; Horsley, *Whole Story*, 177–201; Horsley, *Jesus in Context*, 65–7, 156–61.

Israel, in opposition to the Roman Empire and its Herodian and Jerusalem representatives.[26]

It is important to note that for Horsley the foregoing description is not simply of the social context of Mark and Q, but of the oral traditions that preceded them, for according to Horsley, both Mark and Q are 'oral derived' texts (which Horsley appears to be a little too quick to equate to transcripts of oral performance, despite Foley's warnings to the contrary).[27] As noted above, Horsley and Draper argue that Q should be seen as a series of speeches, the implication being that the speeches written down in Q are more or less transcripts of speeches orally delivered to early Jesus-movement communities in rural Galilee and the surrounding areas.

This suggestion is reinforced by an analysis of portions of Q in terms of the ethnopoetics of Dell Hymes (and others) and Foley's discussion of how to approach an oral-derived text.[28] By attending to such features as 'alliteration, assonance, rhyme, tonal repetition, parallelism and rhythm' and the presence of metonymic referentiality as a marker of oral performance, Draper proceeds to illustrate the oral nature of Q 12.49–59 (i.e. the supposed Q text behind Luke 12.49–59 and its Matthean parallel) by setting it out in measured verse (exhibiting such features as couplets and triplets and stanzas grouping into threes or fives); elsewhere Horsley performs a similar analysis of Q 6.20–49.[29] The impression thus given is that Q provides a direct window into a segment of the oral tradition.

To be sure, there is far more to oral tradition than the texts of words spoken, as Horsley and Draper are well aware. One would, for example, like to know something of the context in which the Q speeches were delivered. Horsley suggests that the individual speeches would have been delivered on a variety of occasions relating to the nature of each speech, while the 'context of the performance of Q as a whole series of discourses would appear to be the periodic community or movement meetings'. The particular contexts proposed for individual speeches include covenant renewal (Q 6.20–49), mission and the sending of envoys (Q 10.2–16), the arrest and trial of community members (Q 12.2–12) and prophesying against rulers (Q 13.28–29, 34–35).[30]

---

[26] Horsley and Draper, *Whoever Hears*, 46–60; Horsley, *Whole Story*, 27–52, 99–148; Horsley, *Jesus in Context*, 1–3, 20–8, 45–7, 54–5, 190–222; Richard A. Horsley, *Jesus and the Spiral of Violence* (San Francisco: Harper & Row, 1987), 157–60, 167–208.

[27] Horsley and Draper, *Whoever Hears*, 6, 166–8; cf. John Miles Foley, *The Singer of Tales in Performance* (Voices in Performance and Text; Bloomington and Indianapolis: Indiana University Press, 1995), 63. Contrast the more careful statement at Horsley, *Whole Story*, 61–2.

[28] Foley, *Singer*, 60–98.

[29] Horsley and Draper, *Whoever Hears*, 175–94; Horsley, *Jesus in Context*, 71–85.

[30] Horsley and Draper, *Whoever Hears*, 169.

One of the contributors to a volume co-edited by Horsley, Draper and Foley argues that Mark is an oral-composed text (which would make it another example of the oral tradition in action).[31] Horsley himself does not actually claim this (so far as I know), but he comes quite close to it by insisting that Mark would have been performed from memory by people thoroughly conversant with the Jesus tradition.[32] Moreover, since Mark would have been heard in (repeated) oral performance rather than read visually in silence like a modern book, its contents would have been apprehended aurally and discussed and repeated orally in the absence of any written text. Thus on Horsley's model, Mark, like Q, should be seen as part of an ongoing oral tradition rather than its end result.

There are some problems with this reconstruction. Given that Horsley minimizes the difference between oral and written texts to the extent he does, it becomes hard to see why anyone would have bothered to write down Mark or Q in the first place, particularly if the original context of their performances was in rural Galilee where virtually no one could read or write. In discussing why John produced a written Gospel, Tom Thatcher argues that part of the reason may have been the symbolic authority accorded a written text,[33] which might accord with Horsley's views on the largely symbolic view of written documents from a peasant perspective. But this is not the only reason Thatcher gives (the other being to fix the author's vision of the tradition in a non-negotiable medium), and the fact that, from as early as we can tell, the Gospels were circulated in the form of codices rather than scrolls argues against a purely symbolic role (since a scroll, being the form in which the sacred Scriptures were kept, would have had far greater symbolic weight, while the codex, derived from the notebook, suggests convenience of use as a factor). Writing probably makes more of a difference than Horsley allows, which should make us cautious of too readily treating Mark or Q as a more or less straightforward transcript of oral performance.

A further problem, which Horsley attempts to address, is how a presumably *Aramaic* oral tradition came to be enshrined in a *Greek* text. His suggested answer is that either the Q tradition penetrated Galilean cities

---

[31] Whitney Shiner, 'Memory Technology and the Composition of Mark' in Richard A. Horsley, Jonathan A. Draper and John Miles Foley (eds), *Performing the Gospel: Orality, Memory and Mark* (Minneapolis: Fortress Press, 2006), 147–65.

[32] Horsley and Draper, *Whoever Hears*, 157–60; Horsley, *Whole Story*, 61–2; Horsley, *Jesus in Context*, 96–102.

[33] Tom Thatcher, 'Why John Wrote a Gospel: Memory and History in an Early Christian Community' in Alan Kirk and Tom Thatcher (eds), *Memory, Tradition, and Text: Uses of the Past in Early Christianity* (SBL Semeia Studies, 52; Atlanta: SBL, 2005), 79–97.

(Sepphoris and Tiberias) where more Greek was spoken, or it spread to surrounding Greek-speaking non-Israelite regions (such as the Decapolis and Syrophoenicia) which were happy to adopt Israelite traditions.[34] Neither answer is entirely convincing: it remains unclear either why speeches aimed at rural Galilean villages would come to be performed in the very different social setting of Sepphoris or Tiberias, or how their alleged metonymic referentiality would continue to communicate effectively in non-Israelite areas; Horsley's suggestion that these Greek-speaking non-Israelite areas were happy to adopt Israelite traditions is supported by no evidence whatsoever and is far from immediately plausible.

The settings proposed for the performance of Q within Galilee are not without their problems, either. One can perhaps envisage Q 6.20–49 being used at a covenant renewal ceremony, or even Q 10.2–16 being used for the commissioning of missionaries. The other suggestions offered are not so much descriptions of social contexts as of the content of the speeches, and thus somewhat vacuous as accounts of performance arenas. Even more problematic is the suggested occasion for the recital of the complete sequence of speeches; 'periodic community or movement meetings' is distressingly vague, and offers no explanation why the speeches should ever have been orally performed one after another on a single occasion in addition to the individual occasions proposed for the individual speeches.

One may also question the propriety of reconstructing an oral performance from a hypothetical reconstructed text such as Q, particularly where a putative tradition of Aramaic-language oral performance in Galilean villages is being proposed on the basis of linguistic features (such as 'alliteration, assonance, rhyme, tonal repetition, parallelism and rhythm') of a reconstructed Greek text. Dunn at least realizes that shifting from a literary to an oral paradigm radically calls into question the extent and contents of Q, but, as Rafael Rodriguez observes, Horsley and Draper blithely continue making use of a hypothetical documentary Q as if nothing has changed.[35] As Rodriguez is well aware, undermining print-culture assumptions about the ways texts were used in antiquity (as Horsley is eager to do) also undermines many of the methodological assumptions on which the last two and a half centuries of synoptic source criticism have been based, so it is unsafe simply to assume the continuing validity

---

[34] Horsley, *Jesus in Context*, 68–9.
[35] Rafael Rodriguez, *Structuring Early Christian Memory: Jesus in Tradition, Performance and Text* (LNTS, 407; ed. M. Goodacre; London: T. & T. Clark, 2010), 21–3.

of the dominant Two Document Hypothesis and the existence of Q (which, in any case, may be doubted on other grounds).[36]

Moreover, not everyone will agree with Horsley's reconstruction of the social context and function of these texts.[37] Many might feel that in his anxiety to avoid the theological reductionism of which he accuses many other scholars, Horsley has over-corrected to the extent of producing interpretations of Mark and Q from which theology has been all but totally banished. One can surely accept his point that religion, politics and economics were thoroughly bound up together in first-century Roman Palestine without being obliged to accept an interpretation in which the religious element is almost entirely reduced to the other two. Again, as Horsley himself points out, there seems to be an almost unbridgeable gap between the primitive Galilean Jesus movement as Horsley reconstructs it and subsequent Christianity.[38] Without a convincing explanation of how one gets from a rural Galilean renewal movement to Paul's letters (let alone to the fourth- or fifth-century Church), something substantial would seem to be missing from Horsley's account.

Nevertheless, despite these criticisms, Horsley, Draper and their other collaborators have contributed significantly to the study of the oral tradition. Notwithstanding the reservations just expressed, many of Horsley's insights remain valuable. These include the need to shift away from a print-culture literary mindset when considering ancient texts such as the Gospels, the desirability of employing social memory theory and the work of specialists such as Foley in constructing a model of oral tradition, and the need to take the social, economic and cultural conditions of the earliest Jesus movement fully into account in seeking to reconstruct the origins of the Jesus tradition.

Equally valuable (with some reservations) is the insistence on the importance of Israelite cultural traditions as the metonymic referent of much of the Jesus tradition, and the identification of certain cultural scripts (messianic, prophetic and covenantal) as key to their interpretation. The chief reservation, which Horsley explicitly recognizes, is that the Israelite cultural traditions he sees the Jesus tradition as metonymically referencing

---

[36] Mark Goodacre, *The Case against Q: Studies in Markan Priority and the Synoptic Problem* (Harrisburg, PA: Trinity Press International, 2002); Eric Eve, 'The Synoptic Problem without Q?' in Paul Foster, Andrew Gregory, John S. Kloppenborg and J. Verheyden (eds), *New Studies in the Synoptic Problem* (BETL, 139; Leuven: Leuven University Press, 2011), 551–70.

[37] See, e.g., Eve, *Healer from Nazareth*, 125–34, for an approach to some of these matters that draws much from Horsley's work while departing from it in a number of ways.

[38] Horsley, *Jesus in Context*, 53–4.

are rather different in nature from the performance traditions that Foley appears to have had in mind.[39] Horsley's insistence on the importance of Israelite cultural traditions in no way excludes the possibility that parts of the Jesus tradition may also metonymically reference the Jesus tradition as a whole (so that, for example, anyone hearing an individual miracle story would be well aware that the same Jesus performing the healing also told parables, clashed with the authorities, called disciples and was crucified by order of the Roman governor, and would 'hear' the story in the light of all those other aspects of Jesus as well as the prophetic script of which the healing story might form a part).

That said, it is not entirely clear how much the apparatus of metonymic referencing really adds to what could be said from the perspective of social memory. A tentative suggestion is that it may alert us to the possibility that aspects of the tradition of performance of Israelite and Jesus traditions are being referenced in this way, so that, for example, phrases such as 'scribes and Pharisees' or the way in which miracle stories are narrated may be metonymically referencing such phrases or narrative patterns elsewhere in a tradition of performance now largely lost to us. In a similar vein, it may be that we should regard the description of John the Baptist's mode of dress at Mark 1.6 not so much as a direct allusion to 2 Kings 1.8 as a metonymic reference to the way in which prophetic attire is typically described in a performance tradition. Such ideas are at least worth exploring, and are explored further by Rafael Rodriguez, whose contribution we shall examine next.

Rafael Rodriguez – *Structuring Early Christian Memory*

Rafael Rodriguez's recent book, *Structuring Early Christian Memory*, constitutes another substantial attempt to incorporate the insights of social memory theory and oral tradition studies into New Testament interpretation, applying them in particular to Jesus' healings and exorcisms in the sayings tradition.[40] While Rodriguez resembles Horsley in drawing both on theories of memory and the work of John Miles Foley, he explicitly aligns himself more with Dunn. In contrast to Horsley and Draper, Rodriguez is not looking for signs of oral composition within the written texts, nor (probably rightly) does he think that linguistic features such as formulas, repetitions and rhythmic patterns can be used to raise questions

---

[39] Horsley and Draper, *Whoever Hears*, 173–4.
[40] See note 35 above.

about the oral traditions enveloping the texts. It is not that he doubts that they were so enveloped, but he prefers to proceed on the basis of such factors as historical hypotheses about low literacy rates and the robustness of the Jesus tradition.[41]

Rodriguez begins by noting the paradox that Gospel scholarship focuses on texts and employs methods (such as redaction criticism) appropriate to texts while increasingly recognizing the importance of the oral environment and oral tradition. The texts happen to be all that survive of the tradition, but they were far from being the whole of the tradition. The Gospels were embedded in and surrounded by the tradition rather than being new sources of tradition, although many of the features of the oral performance of the tradition are now lost to us. Scholarship is exercised by the question of the fluidity and stability of the oral tradition, but according to Rodriguez, the same applies to texts in the first century; scribal operations on texts were not limited to copying, and texts could be influenced by performance. Conversely, a tradent did not need a written text in order to perform the tradition. In Rodriguez's view Kelber's oral–written contrast is far too sharp; texts did not silence speech since the tradition continued in memory, bridging the divide. Moreover, memory is not necessarily memorization; it is generally something more variable and dynamic.[42]

Rodriguez's discussion of social memory begins with the by now familiar insistence that all remembering takes place in a social context, but swiftly moves on to challenge taking this fact in a radically constructivist sense. It may be that memory distorts the past, but there are two rather different senses of 'distortion'. In the dominant form-critical model 'distortion' tends to suggest a deliberate falsification of the past to serve present interests. But there is a less radical sense of 'distortion' in which it merely refers to the act of interpretation in the light of the present that necessarily attends any act of recall, although it may then be impossible to separate historical 'fact' from subsequent interpretation. While it is true that memories can become embroiled in the ideological struggles of the present, that is only one side of the story. The other is that the past continues to influence the present in a number of ways, such as providing templates and frames for apprehending the present, and that many features of the past constitute given features of our present lives, even when they are inconvenient, not least through a commitment to an identity shaped by the past. Moreover,

---

[41] Rodriguez, *Structuring*, 23–6.
[42] Rodriguez, *Structuring*, 3–6.

the presence of conflicting interest groups limits the extent to which the past can simply be rewritten.

Rodriguez appeals in particular to the work of Barry Schwartz, both to the model of keying and framing as a way of understanding recent events in the light of older ones and to the notion that the social memory of the past contains a stable core, around which peripheral elements are added or subtracted to meet current interests, although this stability persists at the level of meaning rather than text. This stable core does not necessarily correspond to historical reality, but in Rodriguez's opinion historical Jesus research has tended to underestimate the stability of memory in the face of social change.[43]

One form a stable core may take is that of a persistent historical reputation. Rodriguez notes that Jesus scholars often refer to Jesus' reputation without stopping to analyse the notion of 'reputation', a lack Rodriguez goes on to supply by outlining a social theory of reputation. He defines reputation as a socially constructed and shared *persona*. As against a strict constructionist approach, however, Rodriguez espouses a contextual constructionist one in which objective factors also play a role; a reputation cannot be pure invention, and among other things it has to resonate with existing shared values, even while it makes selective use of the past.

Establishing a reputation requires *social entrepreneurship*. This in turn requires an element of self-interest (however complex) to motivate the effort required to establish a reputation, the ability to construct a narrative that resonates with a wider group, and the occupation of a position of authority. This, says Rodriguez, makes the entrepreneurial success of the Gospels surprising. The reputations of heroes and villains, remembered in black-and-white terms, are relatively unproblematic, but there are also difficult reputations, the reputations of ambiguous people and failures, where the reasons of failure may turn out to be more memorable than the individuals concerned. Occasionally, however, people who seemed likely to be forgotten as failures manage to shake off anonymity and become remembered in their own right. Social changes and shifts in cultural logic can result in the widespread acceptance of a previously difficult past; Rodriguez cites Abraham Lincoln and Masada as examples.

---

[43] Rodriguez, *Structuring*, 50–64; cf. James L. Fentress and Chris Wickham, *Social Memory* (New Perspectives on the Past; Oxford and Cambridge, MA: Basil Blackwell, 1992), 59; Barry Schwartz, 'Christian Origins: Historical Truth and Social Memory' in Alan Kirk and Tom Thatcher (eds), *Memory, Tradition, and Text: Uses of the Past in Early Christianity* (SBL Semeia Studies, 52; Atlanta: SBL, 2005), 43–56.

Finally, reputations are symbolic; they mediate between past and present, but may mean different things to different people, although, like rituals, they have to maintain some link to shared ultimate values.[44] Rodriguez does not make the application of all this to Jesus' reputation entirely clear; presumably the implication is that Jesus, who ended his life executed as a criminal, would have had a potentially difficult reputation which nevertheless managed to be salvaged.

Rodriguez observes that orality studies have received far more attention than social memory in New Testament scholarship, but regards this as something of a mixed blessing since, in his view, it has given rise to some confusion, which he consequently sets out to dispel. While Kelber is right to emphasize the element of composition-in-performance in oral tradition, he is wrong if he means thereby to stress the variability of the tradition. Performance does not recreate tradition anew, but retells it from memory. The tradition lacks a fixed textual form and is embodied in the act of performance. Written versions of the Jesus tradition would have been received as other performances, not definitive accounts. Rodriguez proposes that the variability and stability of the tradition are rooted in the memory both of Jesus' words and deeds and of previous performances of the tradition. On this understanding each performance transmits the same thing since the tradition is the story/memory, not the precise words used to convey it. Over time, multiple performances tend to stabilize the tradition as performers feel the weight, not only of the stories they are narrating, but also of the tradition of past performances. Such previous performances serve to create a tradition in the context of which new performances are understood; so, for example, an individual healing story would resonate not only with Israelite traditions but with other stories about Jesus in the tradition, and the image of Jesus created by the tradition of performances. This stability is not, however, stability of verbal form (at least, not in the first century), nor is the tradition limited by any textual embodiment of it. Verbal multiformity remains, even though certain words, phrases and expressions may become salient in the tradition.[45]

Rodriguez, like Horsley and Draper, goes on to appeal to Foley's theory of performance, word-power and metonymic referencing. While noting that the twin phenomena of variability and stability lie at the root of the Synoptic Problem, he suggests that instead of seeing these as the result of the Evangelists' editorial practices we should regard the Gospels as different

---

[44] Rodriguez, *Structuring*, 64–79.
[45] Rodriguez, *Structuring*, 81–8.

instantiations of the same tradition. The Gospels reference that wider tradition *pars pro toto* (in the manner Foley ascribes to oral performance). The Evangelists did not merely *use* oral tradition; they were part of it, having been performers and tradents of that tradition before they wrote their Gospels.

Making further use of Foley's work, Rodriguez insists that it is important to take into account the audience's role in performance, and their need to be conversant in the traditional idiom to recognize the metonymic reference of the 'words' performed as opposed to their apparent denotative meaning. He observes that Foley uses the receptionist theory of Hans Robert Jauss and Wolfgang Iser; but in this case the tradition imparts stability to what would otherwise be a multitude of readings of a pluriform text. In a living oral tradition interpreters can observe these processes at work, but we only have texts to work with. Foley proposes a spectrum of relations between text and tradition in the case of oral-derived texts from transcripts of performance to 'literary' texts still rooted in oral tradition. For Foley, appreciation of traditional verbal art involves attending not only to its metonymic references but also to the lacunae within the text that an audience must fill in through its knowledge of the tradition, a process of consistency building (which, albeit in a different way, must also be carried out by a modern reader of a modern text). According to Rodriguez, we need thus to consider not only the Gospels' *composition* but their *reception*. Referring to Foley's notions of performance arena and register, Rodriguez goes on to propose as a working hypothesis that the Gospels preserve language in the special register of oral-traditional performance; he accordingly suggests that we thus need to enquire how that register incorporates traditional metonymic signification and how the texts relate to traditional oral performances.[46]

Of all the authors considered so far, Rodriguez takes the most self-consciously nuanced approach to the relation between the Gospels as written text and the oral tradition in which they are enveloped. Negatively, he insists that the Gospels are neither transcripts of nor scripts for oral performances (presumably Rodriguez does not thereby mean to deny that the Gospels would have been read aloud to an audience, so he must mean that they were not intended to perpetuate a particular oral performance of the Jesus tradition). Nevertheless, while the written Gospels were not transcribed oral performances, there was a continuity of reception across oral performances and the written text. The Gospels presented images of

---

[46] Rodriguez, *Structuring*, 88–102.

Jesus within the context of images already established by multiple oral performances; it would be hard to explain the widespread acceptance of the Gospels if they had made a substantial break with this tradition.

Given this continuity, Rodriguez suggests that we need to look out for the ways in which the Gospels' register invokes the performance arena so that the written phraseology continues to invoke its metonymic character. He also invokes Foley's fourfold typology of oral-derived texts to represent the spectrum of possibilities: Oral Performance, Voiced Texts, Voices from the Past, and Written Oral Poems.[47] In Rodriguez's view, the Gospels fall into the third of these categories. He states that they are not 'voiced texts' because they were not *required* for the oral performance of the Jesus tradition, and points out that Foley also classifies the Gospels as Voices from the Past, meaning texts that 'were composed according to the rules of actualizing the Jesus tradition in oral performance'[48] without there being any certainty concerning the processes of the texts' composition, performance and reception.

There is thus continuity between the oral tradition and the written Gospel texts – and certainly rather more continuity than Kelber allowed for – but the continuity is less than perfect (writing has made *some* difference). For one thing, Rodriguez maintains, the written Gospels would have been constrained by the need to be acceptable to audiences already familiar with the oral Jesus tradition. The oral-performative tradition exerts a certain inertia; while it allows disparate and even conflicting portrayals of Jesus, it does impose limits. For another, while Rodriguez does not wish to deny that there may be some sort of literary relationship between the Gospels, he suggests that they should be seen as instances of the ambient tradition rather than as redactions of one another (how far this does justice to the considerations that convince the majority of scholars that there must be a literary relationship between the Synoptic Gospels is not an issue that can be pursued here).[49]

In what follows Rodriguez is not so much interested in trying to reconstruct the workings or social contexts of the pre-Gospel oral tradition (his general approach suggests that he is in any case quite sceptical of such attempts) as in exploring the relation between the Gospel texts and the Jesus tradition of which they form a part. The orality of the tradition matters to Rodriguez primarily in two respects: first in the carry-over

---

[47] John Miles Foley, *How to Read an Oral Poem* (Urbana and Chicago: University of Illinois Press, 2002), 38–53.

[48] Rodriguez, *Structuring*, 106.

[49] Rodriguez, *Structuring*, 102–12.

of the oral dynamics of metonymic referentiality into the Gospels as oral-derived texts, and second in viewing parallel accounts of similar material in two or more Gospels not in terms of literary editing ('redaction') but in terms of variant instantiations of the ambient tradition in oral-dynamic mode (here one might wish to bear in mind the criticisms of Dunn's proposals earlier in this chapter).

It is in this light that Rodriguez goes on to examine three passages in some detail: the Response of Jesus to John the Baptist's Enquiry (Matthew 11.2–6 || Luke 7.18–23), Jesus' Inaugural Sermon at Nazareth (Luke 4.16–30) and the Beelzebul Controversy (Mark 3.20–26 || Matthew 12.22–28 || Luke 11.14–20). In doing so Rodriguez argues not so much for the faithful reporting of objective historical fact in these passages as for continuity in the presentation of Jesus' reputation. Thus, for example, while Rodriguez allows that Luke 4.16–20, which depicts Jesus reading from a scroll of Isaiah, can hardly be an accurate account of an actual historical occurrence, he insists that in presenting Jesus as he does here, Luke calls on pre-Lukan traditional material employed in Luke 7.18–32, and in doing so does not significantly alter Jesus' reputation, although he does refocus it and dramatize it.[50] More broadly, Rodriguez is interested in exploring how these three passages resonate with Israelite tradition, not least in respect of the exodus, Isaianic, and Elijah–Elisha traditions, and in insisting that there must have been something about Jesus' reputation that made it appear *appropriate* to interpret him in terms of these traditions.[51] To a considerable extent, then, for Rodriguez Jesus' reputation serves a role that is analogous to the role of Jesus' impact for Dunn, part of the difference being that Rodriguez has attempted to theorize more explicitly about the concept of reputation than Dunn does about the notion of impact.

Rodriguez concurs with Horsley that the Israelite traditions metony-mically referenced in the Jesus tradition indicate a Jesus who was concerned with the restoration of Israel. He also fully concurs with Dunn that it is most unlikely that Matthew and Luke were unaware of much of the material in Mark until they encountered his Gospel; rather, Rodriguez suggests, it is much more likely that the Gospels were embedded in an oral tradition, and that the performance of this oral tradition was the primary means by which the Evangelists knew stories about Jesus.[52] Thus,

---

[50] Rodriguez, *Structuring*, 140–6; cf. the treatment of Luke 4.16–20 by another scholar who takes a social memory approach to the Jesus tradition, Chris Keith, *Jesus' Literacy: Scribal Culture and the Teacher from Galilee* (LNTS, 413; ed. M. Goodacre; New York and London: T. & T. Clark, 2011), 142–5.

[51] Rodriguez, *Structuring*, 138–210.

[52] Rodriguez, *Structuring*, 27–31.

like Dunn, Rodriguez does not think that the synoptic tradition should be treated purely in terms of a literary relationship between texts; oral storytelling dynamics and an ongoing oral tradition also need to be taken into account. In fact Rodriguez is prepared to go further than Dunn here in hinting that such considerations might call the dominant Two Document Hypothesis into question, although this is not a question he chooses to pursue. Also like Dunn, Rodriguez emphasizes the stability and continuity of the Jesus tradition, although he also appears more willing to give equal weight to its malleability. Overall Rodriguez appears much less sanguine than Dunn that the synoptic tradition can be used as a kind of window into the direct impact Jesus made on his original disciples, and rather more willing to recognize that history – even history interpreted from the perspective of faith – cannot necessarily be read off from a stable tradition in any straightforward sense.

Instead, Rodriguez ends with three important conclusions. First, he notes that his discussion has proceeded on the basis of social memory theory rather than through any appeal to the criteria of authenticity. He accordingly (and in my view, rightly) suggests that future historical Jesus scholarship should abandon the simplistic attempt to divide the Gospel material into 'authentic' and 'inauthentic' bins, not least because one has to consider the meaning of the Gospel material in its context. Second, in addition to application to historical Jesus research, Rodriguez believes that the combination of social memory and oral-traditional theory has implications for other areas of New Testament study. Source criticism needs to take into account more recent work on the dynamics of orality rather than reifying oral tradition as one source among many, as well as re-examining its assumptions about the functioning of ancient texts; for example, Rodriguez suggests, Matthew could have incorporated Mark without ever laying hands on a written copy of it. Tradition criticism may not be possible at all. Third, the process of atomizing and decontextualizing bits of the Jesus tradition in the attempt to identify authentic material that can then be used in the reconstruction of the historical Jesus has been shown to be culturally inappropriate.[53]

These are all important conclusions, though it seems to me that the first and third of them are also supportable on other grounds.[54] In relation to the second, while I would agree that synoptic source criticism needs

---

[53] Rodriguez, *Structuring*, 213–25.

[54] See, e.g., Eric Eve, 'Meier, Miracle and Multiple Attestation', *JSHJ* 3.1 (2005), 23–45; Allison, *Constructing Jesus*, 10–30; Rafael Rodriguez, 'Authenticating Criteria: The Use and Misuse of a Critical Method', *JSHJ* 7 (2009), 152–67.

revisiting in the light of the issues raised in this chapter and the previous one, some of Rodriguez's specific proposals in this area are less convincing, not least the suggestion that Matthew need never have had access to a written copy of Mark. If that were the case, one wonders how one could then account for the degree of verbatim agreement that does occur between these two Gospels, as well as the agreement in order; it may well be that Matthew had memory command of Mark, but for that he would surely have required access to the written text at some point. So perhaps what needs questioning is not so much the fact of literary dependence between the Gospels as what literary dependence might actually mean in this context.[55]

Other contributions

This chapter has focused almost entirely on the work of three scholars who in one way or another have tried to address the questions of memory and orality in the Jesus tradition. This selection of scholars is by no means exhaustive; others could have been chosen instead or in addition. For example, in their survey of the use of social memory theory in Gospel research, the more recent scholars whom Alan Kirk and Tom Thatcher interact with include John Dominic Crossan, Burton Mack and Jens Schröter, although of these three it is perhaps only Schröter who engages with social memory theory in the manner covered in this chapter (Kirk and Thatcher mention the other two only to disagree with them; Crossan for being too individualistic in his concept of memory and Mack for being too constructivist).[56] Otherwise, Kirk and Thatcher's emphases to some extent resemble those of Rodriguez, namely to reject a purely presentist or constructivist notion of social memory in favour of a model in which the past exerts a continuing influence on the present even while the present provides frameworks for viewing the past. Also in common with Rodriguez, Kirk and Thatcher insist that 'oral tradition' and 'social memory' are related terms.

Interestingly, Schröter's contribution to another volume comes to conclusions that look rather more sceptical than those of the three authors discussed in this chapter, in that he argues that from its inception the Jesus

---

[55] On which see Andrew Gregory, 'What Is Literary Dependence?' in Paul Foster, Andrew Gregory, John S. Kloppenborg and J. Verheyden (eds), *New Studies in the Synoptic Problem* (BETL, 139; Leuven: Leuven University Press, 2011), 87–114.

[56] Alan Kirk and Tom Thatcher, 'Jesus Tradition as Social Memory' in Alan Kirk and Tom Thatcher (eds), *Memory, Tradition, and Text: Uses of the Past in Early Christianity* (SBL Semeia Studies, 52; Atlanta: SBL, 2005), 25–42.

tradition was 'a free and living' one in which there was no interest in distinguishing the authentic words of Jesus from material drawn from elsewhere; on this understanding, what imparted relative stability to the Jesus tradition as it developed into the second century was not so much the impact or reputation of the original Jesus as the Church's rule of faith.[57] While Schröter's insistence on the variability of the *wording* of the sayings of Jesus does not contradict anything that Rodriguez, for example, argues, one senses that in Schröter the balance between the stability and the variability of the tradition has tilted rather further towards the latter.

Werner Kelber's contributions in this area did not stop with *The Oral and the Written Gospel*. In a now oft-quoted metaphor he has since likened tradition to a biosphere, by which he means 'an invisible nexus of references and identities from which people draw sustenance, in which they live, and in relation to which they make sense of their lives'.[58] This notion of a 'biosphere' makes much the same point about the resonance of traditional oral performances as the treatments of social memory theory and Foley's theory of word-power, and has been warmly welcomed by Foley.[59] In the same article Kelber also draws attention to the interplay of stability and flexibility in oral poetics, as well as making a number of other points about the nature of oral performance and the functions of texts in a chirograph (pre-print) culture that by now should have become familiar. In another essay Kelber returns Foley's compliment by welcoming his theory of metonymic referentiality as a particularly valuable extension to the Parry–Lord theory.[60]

While some of the other scholars reviewed in this chapter, not least Horsley, have tended to minimize the distinction between oral and written texts in antiquity, Kelber has continued to emphasize the distinction. While allowing that he may have overstated it in *The Oral and the Written Gospel*, and while explicitly disavowing the Great Divide thesis, he offers a number of arguments to suggest that the ancients were just as aware of the media difference between orality and writing as we are. He points out, for example, that dictation would affect thought processes by slowing down speech, and that the act of written composition was in any case often

---

[57] Jens Schröter, 'Jesus and the Canon: The Early Jesus Traditions in the Context of the Origins of the New Testament Canon' in Richard A. Horsley, Jonathan A. Draper and John Miles Foley (eds), *Performing the Gospel: Orality, Memory and Mark* (Minneapolis: Augsburg Fortress, 2006), 104–46.

[58] Werner H. Kelber, 'Jesus and Tradition: Words in Time, Words in Space', *Semeia* 65 (1995), 139–67 (159).

[59] John Miles Foley, 'Words in Tradition, Words in Text: A Response', *Semeia* 65 (1995), 169–80 (171).

[60] Werner H. Kelber, 'Modalities of Communication, Cognition and Physiology of Perception: Orality, Rhetoric, Scribality', *Semeia* 65 (1995), 193–216 (199–200).

more complex than simply dictating a final text. He also calls attention to Plato's anxiety about the use of writing – an anxiety that could hardly have existed unless speech and writing were conceived as distinct. He also argues that writing may have aided visualization, and that ancient theories of rhetoric, as reflections on the use of language, would scarcely have been possible without writing.[61]

In a further development Kelber discusses the relationship of manuscript to memory in what, following Mary Carruthers, he terms a 'memorial' culture (the scribal culture of late antiquity and the Middle Ages). Here he suggests that cultural memory can be likened to tradition, and (in a move that should now be familiar) that the study of memory can be fruitfully combined with the classic media studies of Lord, Havelock, Ong, Goody and Foley, adding that writing has greater power to reshape group identity since it is less subject to audience control than oral performance. On the one hand account should therefore be taken of the Gospels' ability to reshape communities, while on the other we need to take memorial processes into account, and not just intertextuality, in considering the composition of the Gospels. Moreover, in this context memory is not simply recall, let alone Gerhardsson's model of 'cold memory', or memorization of fixed material. For ancient authors such as Augustine, memory was a processing facility, not just a storage one, and involved the active imagination in the arrangement of remembered material.

Kelber goes on to say that while the Gospels do exhibit an overall narrative coherence, they are not fully plotted narratives like modern detective stories; their authors were not fully in control of their material, in part because they were deeply engaged with traditions that were live issues in their communities. While the process of Gospel composition may have involved some verbatim copying from sources, the Synoptic Problem should not be conceived purely in terms of literary relations between texts (here Kelber is evidently in full agreement with Dunn and Rodriguez). Kelber ends up by suggesting that a full account of the process of composing the Gospels may be beyond our ability to reconstruct.[62]

Conclusions

One of the common themes to have emerged from this chapter is the complex interplay of stability and flexibility in the Jesus tradition. Others

---

[61] Kelber, 'Modalities'.
[62] Werner H. Kelber, 'The Case of the Gospels: Memory's Desire and the Limits of Historical Criticism', *OT* 17 (2002), 55–86.

include the fruitfulness of combining social memory theory with Foley's work on metonymic referentiality, and the consequent emphasis on understanding the Jesus tradition as being performed in a 'biosphere' that consists, among other things, both of popular Israelite traditions (of salient themes such as the covenant and salient figures such as Moses, Elijah and David) and of the collective impact of earlier performances of the Jesus tradition.

Another theme is that of the close interplay of the written and oral forms of the tradition, so that the Gospels and Q (assuming such a document ever existed) should be seen as oral-derived texts thoroughly immersed in the oral tradition rather than as oral tradition's end products. The precise nature of the interface between the oral and the written in the Gospels remains uncertain, as, accordingly, does the extent to which any previous tradition of oral performances can be reconstructed from the written texts; where there is greater agreement is in the thesis that the dynamics of oral performance have a continuing role to play in the reception of these texts, so that they need to be interpreted in the light of metonymic referentiality to both Israelite tradition and a wider Jesus tradition.

There is also agreement that it is a mistake to understand the Synoptic Problem purely in terms of a literary relation between texts (particularly fixed texts unconsciously conceived in the likeness of those printed in a synopsis). While there probably is some kind of literary relation between at least the first three Gospels, theories of their composition also need to take into account the operations of memory and the dynamics of a continuing oral tradition. In other words, the Synoptic Problem may need to be rethought (but preferably without throwing the literary dependency baby out with the print-culture bathwater in the eagerness to embrace the insights of orality and memory studies).

These are all issues to which we shall return in the final chapter. In the meantime, there is one further issue to consider, namely the possible role of eyewitnesses not only in initiating the Jesus tradition but in maintaining it up to the point at which it began to be committed to writing. This will form the subject of the next chapter.

8

The role of eyewitnesses

In the last few chapters we have seen at least a partial convergence on the nature of the pre-Gospel oral tradition from social memory theory and developments in oral performance theory. Both perspectives focus on the functioning of memory and tradition in collectives. While it is recognized that the tradition must in fact have been performed by particular author-itative individuals, little attention has so far been given to who these individuals might actually have been, or to their possible relation to the original eyewitnesses. Conversely, while it is widely assumed that the Jesus tradition in some sense originated with eyewitnesses (however it may subsequently have been elaborated), so far little or no attention has been paid to whether any eyewitnesses to Jesus' earthly ministry may have played a continuing role in the transmission and maintenance of the Jesus tradi-tion, even up to the point when it first started to be written down. To be sure the majority view of New Testament scholarship is that the Gospels do not contain eyewitness accounts, but this may in part be due to a habit of thought arising from the long dominance of form-critical assumptions, which the previous chapters of this book have shown to be suspect. We thus need to consider afresh whether and to what extent a complete account of the pre-Gospel oral tradition needs to reckon with the ongoing role of eyewitnesses. To that end the present chapter will discuss the work of two scholars, Samuel Byrskog and Richard Bauckham who, albeit in rather different ways, have recently argued for the importance of eyewitness testimony to the Gospel accounts.

Samuel Byrskog – story and history

One of the main threads running through Samuel Byrskog's book *Story as History – History as Story* is the important of eyewitness testimony to ancient historiography.[1] A key concept here is that of autopsy, which Byrskog defines as '*a visual means to gather information about a certain*

---

[1] Samuel Byrskog, *Story as History – History as Story: The Gospel Tradition in the Context of Ancient Oral History* (Leiden and Boston: Brill, 2002).

object, a means of enquiry, and thus also a way of relating to that object'.[2] In accordance with Heraclitus' dictum that 'Eyes are surer witnesses than ears', the ideal of ancient historians was to write about what they had seen for themselves (direct autopsy) or what they could learn by questioning eyewitnesses (indirect autopsy). Even when a historian could not witness an event for himself, he could often carry out a measure of direct autopsy by examining significant sites, or inscriptions, or archaeological remains, but since no historian can be everywhere and see everything, eyewitness testimony was a vital resource. Byrskog proposes that this is analogous with (though not exactly identical with) the modern practice of oral history, in which the historian's raw material is the oral testimony of his subjects. The practice of autopsy was thus very much part of the New Testament environment.[3]

To be sure, ancient historians did also use written sources, just as they committed their own histories to writing, but ancient attitudes to writing were ambiguous. Writing was seen as a useful aid to memory and as a means of preserving a record for posterity when it might otherwise be forgotten, but it was not seen as a substitute for memory, which antiquity highly valued. Some historians were accused of simply reworking written sources to literary effect, without any living experience of their subject matter, but even historians who faithfully practised autopsy might employ written sources in a supplementary fashion, for example to acquire information that was not available to them from any other source. There was a tendency to prefer oral testimony, however; one could question an oral informant but not a written document. Where ancient historians compared and cross-checked sources they were far more likely to do so with their oral than their written sources.[4]

Modern oral historians are not concerned primarily or purely with getting at the objective facts behind the personal accounts of their informants, but are at least equally interested in their informants' perception of events, which is equally part of history. In a partially similar manner ancient historians' preference was not for the objective testimony of a detached eyewitness but for the involved testimony of active participants, on the basis that participants would be best placed to correctly understand and interpret the events they had witnessed. In the same way, the historian should write about the kinds of event of which he has some direct experience: on this way of thinking one cannot properly write about a battle,

---

[2] Byrskog, *Story*, 48 (italics original).
[3] Byrskog, *Story*, 26–30, 48–65, 93–9.
[4] Byrskog, *Story*, 107–27.

for example, unless one has experienced a battle for oneself. Although Byrskog does not quite put it this way, one might say that the kind of truth being sought was experiential truth, not the detached, objective truth of the post-Enlightenment ideal. It in any case follows that what is being sought is interpreted truth, and Byrskog recognizes two layers of interpretation at work.

First, as socially involved participants, the eyewitnesses inevitably interpreted events in the light of their own present interests and conceptual frameworks. Second, in constructing a coherent narrative out of the raw material of oral testimony, the historian would likewise be guided by his own ideological interests and conceptual frameworks, and would shape the material, for example, both by what he chose to include and omit, and by the (usually causal) explanations he gave to account for why things happened the way they did. Of course these remarks must apply to some extent to historians of any age, but Byrskog implies that ancient historians tended to give freer rein to their subjective preferences than modern ones would typically allow themselves. He notes, for example, that the practice of ancient historians was to include only what they considered worthy, but that what was considered worthy was purely a matter of subjective judgement.[5]

Byrskog considers but rejects the charge that ancient historians were not much concerned with truth. They were, he argues, well aware of the potential bias of eyewitnesses and generally tried to correct for it in their careful questioning. The fact that some historians were accused of being liars indicates the existence of a standard to which they could be held to account, and historians such as Thucydides and Polybius exhibited a great concern for historical truth, which Thucydides conceived of in terms of accuracy and clarity. To be sure, the truth they were after tended to be interpreted truth rather than raw fact, but this did not mean that ancient historians had no interest in factual truth. It is also true that by the first century historiography had increasingly come under the influence of rhetoric, and the prime function of rhetoric was not to instruct but to persuade. At first sight writers of this period appear to give self-contradictory advice on the extent to which fabrication is advisable in legal and historical rhetoric if it helps one carry one's point, but Byrskog resolves this apparent contradiction by suggesting that the rhetorically trained historian was expected to build a superstructure of narrative elaboration on a core of factual truth (although the line between the two

---

[5] Byrskog, *Story*, 26–30, 146–65, 254–62.

might admittedly be a bit fuzzy). In some historians claims to autopsy might be a rhetorical flourish to instil confidence in the target audience rather than an accurate description of what the historian actually did. But although Josephus is far from always reliable, his several claims to autopsy cannot all be dismissed as spurious; valid claims to autopsy thus continued into the first century (although not all claims to autopsy were valid).[6]

Byrskog's prime concern is to relate all this to the New Testament writings, particularly the Gospels. The point of his survey of ancient historiographical techniques is to demonstrate the environment in which the New Testament documents were written, an environment in which there was concern for historical truth and in which autopsy (direct or indirect) was the preferred means of arriving at it. To be sure, Byrskog argues that the historical truth that results is interpreted truth, but this enables him to make another important move: the fact that narrative texts such as the Gospels show heavy signs of theological interpretation does not automatically disqualify them from being based on autopsy.

Byrskog develops the application to the New Testament writings alongside his discussion of the Greek and Roman historians. Having established the ancient preference for autopsy as a means of enquiry, he discusses who the potential eyewitnesses to Jesus might have been, pointing out that many of them turned out not also to be informants of any consequence. Those that were included some local people in Galilean villages who spread rumours about Jesus, as reflected in Mark's narrative, some of the disciples, among whom only Peter, James and John are explicitly recorded as having played an active role after Jesus' death, Jesus' family (notably Mary his mother and James his brother), and Mary Magdalene (together with the other women who witnessed the crucifixion, burial and empty tomb). Of these, by far the most prominent appears to have been Peter. With the possible exception of Luke's infancy narrative, no specific family traditions are narrativized in the Gospels, and the women's testimony is legitimated by being subordinated to that of the male disciples (presumably because women's testimony was generally regarded as suspect).[7]

Byrskog's next key move in relation to the New Testament is to investigate the way in which claims to autopsy are incorporated into its narratives. He discusses the different ways in which such claims are used by Paul (for apostolic legitimation), Luke (as apostolic testimony), John (authorial legitimation) and 2 Peter 1.16–18 (pseudonymous legitimation). The fact

---

[6] Byrskog, *Story*, 179–90, 200–34.
[7] Byrskog, *Story*, 65–90, 190–8, 266–9.

that such claims are made does not automatically mean they are true (the last example is clearly not), since Byrskog has already acknowledged that spurious claims to autopsy could be used by first-century historians simply to boost their credibility. Byrskog also acknowledges that claims to autopsy become more explicit in later parts of the tradition (for example, Luke and John make much more of them than Mark), which could indeed suggest an apologetic motive. Byrskog nevertheless argues first that the need to establish eyewitness credentials would naturally become stronger with the passage of time as the events described receded further into the past, and second that compared with explicit claims to autopsy elsewhere, those in the New Testament are surprisingly modest, the implication being that anyone making false claims to autopsy for purely apologetic, polemical or rhetorical purposes would trumpet them far more stridently. He concludes, therefore, that although there may be an element of elaboration in the claims to autopsy found in Luke and John, say, they are based on a solid kernel of historical truth.[8]

Byrskog's final main move is to discuss the role played by Peter's eyewitness testimony, particularly in relation to Mark. Byrskog starts, naturally enough, from Papias's note that Mark was the interpreter of Peter, who after Peter's death wrote down all he could remember of Peter's teaching, although not in order (Eusebius, *Hist. eccl.* 3.39.15). Although Papias's note of this information he received from John the Elder is regularly dismissed by New Testament scholars as having little historical value, Byrskog maintains that the dismissal is unjustified. It may be that Papias's note has an apologetic intention, to counter Gnostic appeals to Peter, but in that case it is strange that there is little anti-Gnostic polemic elsewhere in Papias's surviving writings (a rather perilous argument from silence, one might feel). Furthermore, the reference to what John the Elder was in the habit of saying pushes this tradition back into the first century, and it claims nothing that is historically implausible (given what Byrskog has already established about ancient autopsy and oral history). In the absence of any clear evidence to the contrary, Papias thus deserves the benefit of the doubt.

Various other New Testament traditions link Mark and Peter, and Mark's narrative takes a special interest in Peter. Mark's shaky grasp of Galilean geography can be attributed to his being a native of Jerusalem without the benefit of maps to clarify the nature of what to him would be a comparatively distant region. Again, Byrskog claims, the outline of

---

[8] Byrskog, *Story*, 223–53.

Mark resembles the outline of Jesus' ministry given in Peter's speech at Acts 10.34–43 (although among a number of objections one might wish to raise against this point is the fact that it is in danger of proving too much if the narrativization of Jesus' ministry is to be attributed to Mark, as the logic of other parts of Byrskog's argument would seem to demand). Finally, Papias's notice could be read (says Byrskog) as implying that Peter taught in *chreiai* (pithy anecdotes illustrating the character of their subject in speech or action), and Vincent Taylor identified a number of Petrine *chreiai* in his commentary on Mark. At this point, however, Byrskog pulls back from arguing for much of a direct Petrine influence on Mark, for he finds, first, that the number of potentially Petrine *chreiai* in Mark is actually quite meagre, and second, that Mark gives the impression of having a tradition history that is too complex to be accounted for purely on the basis of Peter's eyewitness testimony. He therefore concludes that Mark combined direct knowledge of Peter's preaching with other Jesus traditions known in his community and some written sources such as a pre-Markan Passion narrative.[9]

Although Byrskog starts from a different theoretical base, much of what he says accords reasonably well with what has emerged in the previous two chapters, such as the complex interaction of orality and writing in antiquity, and the way in which present concerns and conceptual frameworks influence the interpretation of the past. While not primarily basing his argument on social memory theory, Byrskog does show awareness and qualified acceptance of it (particularly Halbwachs), acknowledging, for example, that all remembering takes place in a social context and that groups and societies supply many of the conceptual frameworks through which the past is interpreted. Where Byrskog is distinctive is in wanting to insist also on the role of the individual as against the anonymous collective; for all the importance of social context, especially in the less individualistic culture of antiquity, individual perspectives nevertheless play a significant role in the shaping of oral history, and (by implication) the role of individual eyewitnesses such as Peter is not to be neglected.[10]

There are places where Byrskog's reasoning feels forced and unconvincing. One example is where he takes the Epistle of James to be written by Jesus' brother and then argues that it shows James to be an important family eyewitness content to confine himself to echoing parts of the Jesus tradition that also emerge in the Sermon on the Mount; one ends up with

---

[9] Byrskog, *Story*, 265–92.
[10] Byrskog, *Story*, 153, 255.

the impression that Byrskog is trying to make a case for an eyewitness who may as well not have been an eyewitness.[11] Also unconvincing is where Byrskog, in the course of trying to argue for direct Petrine influence on Matthew, tries to account for the differences in the Markan and Matthean stances to the Torah by Peter's change of mind on the subject.[12] Quite apart from anything else, this seems to ignore Byrskog's own previous observations on the contribution of authorial ideology to the narrativization of tradition. Some parts of Byrskog's attempts to find traditions linking Mark with Peter are also questionable.[13] None of these parts of the argument are fundamental to the core of Byrskog's case, however, so we need not be detained by pursuing these objections any further.

A potentially more serious set of objections relates to Byrskog's use of ancient historians to illuminate the procedures of the Evangelists. Even on his own account, it is clear that not all ancient historians seriously aspired to live up to the ideals of Thucydides and Polybius, and as Byrskog admits, the early Christian writers did not set out to be historians.[14] The relation between the practice of autopsy by the most scrupulous historians and the practice of the Evangelists is thus unclear. One might suppose, for example, that their social situation might have made a significant difference. Ancient historians such as Thucydides and Polybius were presumably free to write on subjects of their own choosing in whatever manner they deemed appropriate. The Evangelists, on the other hand, were presumably constrained by their roles as ministers to the Christian community, not least to write what would be helpful and effective in their particular situations. Such constraints might well tip the balance more towards ideological appropriateness and rhetorical persuasiveness and away from strict factual accuracy than might be the case for many of the more scrupulous ancient historians.

Furthermore, there seem to be at least some gaps in Byrskog's argument that even rhetorically trained historians would be constrained to abide by a factual core, however much they went on to elaborate it. For one thing, Byrskog argues that an argument would be more rhetorically persuasive if it were based on facts rather than fabrication, but that presupposes that everyone is agreed on what the facts are. All Byrskog is really entitled to argue is that it is better not to be caught out in a lie. Any awareness of the political propaganda and media distortion recurrent over the past

---

[11] Byrskog, *Story*, 165–75.
[12] Byrskog, *Story*, 292–7.
[13] Byrskog, *Story*, 274–80.
[14] Byrskog, *Story*, 223–4.

century or so should soon dispel the notion that human beings generally equate rhetorical effectiveness with factual truth. Again the notion of 'factual core' and its distinction from 'narrative superstructure' is somewhat troublesome, since it appears to presuppose a notion of fact that is contradicted by Byrskog's own insistence that eyewitness testimony is always interpreted testimony, and that oral history delivers people's perception of events, what people imagined happened rather than what actually happened.[15] Moreover, the facts of the case may be precisely what are at issue in a legal debate or a historian's attempt to set the record straight.

These objections are not fatal to Byrskog's case, although they might require some qualification of emphases, for at least part of what Byrskog is trying to establish is what we have already encountered in the discussion of social memory theory, namely that the past is not wholly swallowed up in the concerns of the present, but continues to exert its influence on the present. Social memory theory discusses how the present may provide the kinds of narrative frameworks that are used to give an account of the past, but it may nevertheless be the past that is being narrated. That seems to be the key point that Byrskog is trying to make about the interplay of history (the past) and story (the narrative rendering of that past in the present). His appeal to the historian's need to preserve a factual core becomes less problematic if, on the one hand, 'factual core' is taken to mean not 'what actually happened' but rather 'what is commonly believed to have happened' and, on the other, to indicate a genuine intention to refer to past events. In the absence of the means to effectively dispute what is commonly believed to have happened, neither orator nor historian nor Evangelist could radically depart from it if they wished to be persuasive; Mark's Gospel would not have been received as authoritative, for example, if it contradicted too much of what its audience believed it knew about Jesus.

Interpreted this way, Byrskog's point becomes reasonably persuasive, and also becomes effectively equivalent to Rodriguez's appeal to Schwartz's notion of a stable core in social memory.[16] Since, however, such a stable core need not necessarily correspond to what modern people understand as historical fact, this may not quite be what Byrskog had in mind. Byrskog may nevertheless well be right both that the Gospels intend to refer to genuinely past events, and that to some extent they succeed in so doing, albeit in heavily interpreted form.

---

[15] Byrskog, *Story*, 26–30, 145–53.
[16] See p. 125 above.

Byrskog's proposal about Mark's relation to Peter's preaching ends up looking both modest and plausible. To be sure not every step in Byrskog's argument is equally persuasive, as we have already observed, but there are a few further points that could be urged in its favour. One is that not only is Peter known to have played a leading role in the primitive Church (as is apparent from Galatians 1.18; 2.6–14, even if one takes a radically sceptical view of the evidence in Acts) but that what we know of him suggests that he continued to be active into the early 60s CE, late enough, that is, for the author of a Gospel written around 70 CE to have encountered him in person. Another is that the preaching of such an authoritative figure who was known to have been an eyewitness to the earthly Jesus is likely to have been given considerable weight. Another is that the apparently ready acceptance of Mark's Gospel (on the assumption that both Matthew and Luke used it as the basis of their own accounts) might perhaps be accounted for if Mark was believed to have been personally familiar with Peter's testimony.

In conjunction with Byrskog's arguments about Papias's testimony, the idea that Petrine autopsy played a direct role in the composition of Mark's Gospel along with other, less direct, traditions is thus reasonably plausible (though far from proven). The main problem with it, apart from the absence of proof, is that we have virtually no way of knowing how reliable an eyewitness Peter may actually have been. Given what we now know about memory it would be naive in the extreme to suppose that Mark's acquaintance with Peter could be equated with his direct access to the historical Jesus. How far the possibility of such an acquaintance should be factored into our account of the pre-Gospel oral tradition is a subject to which we shall return in the final chapter. Our next task is to examine the work of a scholar who builds on Byrskog to present a rather more radical thesis about the place of eyewitnesses in the composition of the Gospels.

Richard Bauckham – *Jesus and the Eyewitnesses*

In a substantial if controversial book, Richard Bauckham has argued not only that eyewitnesses played a major role in transmitting and controlling the Jesus tradition, but that the canonical Gospels are based on direct eyewitness testimony.[17] There are several strands to Bauckham's argument, not all of which can be dealt with in equal depth here. In one strand,

---

[17] Richard Bauckham, *Jesus and the Eyewitnesses: The Gospels as Eyewitness Testimony* (Grand Rapids and Cambridge: Eerdmans, 2006).

Bauckham seeks to show that the Gospels of Mark, Luke and John all claim to embody eyewitness testimony. In another the evidence of Papias (the early second-century bishop of Hierapolis) is brought to bear, along with the slightly later writings of Polycrates and Irenaeus on John. A third strand, most directly relevant to the present book, examines models of oral transmission and the nature of eyewitness memory. A fourth strand examines the pattern of names used in the Gospels, arguing both that it reflects the pattern of names found in Jewish Palestine at the time (an indication of authenticity), and that it has a number of significant features in relation to the nature of the Twelve and the identity of potential eyewitnesses. At the beginning of the book Bauckham indicates that he is building on the work of Samuel Byrskog and addressing some of the perceived weakness in Byrskog's argument, such as its failure to develop criteria for identifying eyewitness testimony in the Gospels. At the end Bauckham concludes that the Gospels should be received (and trusted) as testimony, a particular kind of historiography that embodies the unique insider perspective on extraordinary events.

Most of the argumentation in the first strand is related to the Gospels of Mark and John, with a rather more cursory treatment of Luke. For all three of these Gospels Bauckham appeals to what he calls the *inclusio* of eyewitness testimony, the thesis that ancient authors sometimes signalled their eyewitness sources by naming them at the beginning and end of their accounts, a convention Bauckham also claims to have found in Lucian's *Alexander* and Porphyry's *Life of Plotinus*.[18] In Mark, Simon Peter is the first named disciple and the last to be mentioned by name (Mark 1.16; 16.7), indicating that Peter was Mark's eyewitness source (a thesis Bauckham goes on to support with other arguments). In John, it is the Beloved Disciple (identified with the anonymous disciple of John 1.35–40 and as the author of the Gospel at John 21.24) who plays this role. In Luke it is the women named at Luke 8.2–3 as following Jesus and at Luke 24.10 as visiting the tomb who provide the *inclusio* signalling the source of Luke's special tradition, although Luke also preserves a Petrine *inclusio* to signal use of the Petrine tradition he has taken over from Mark.

If this all seems somewhat oversubtle to the modern reader, Bauckham assures us that it would be much more apparent to an ancient audience who would expect there to be an eyewitness source named in the narrative. Nevertheless the argument seems particularly weak in relation to Luke, where the named women are introduced nowhere near the beginning of

---

[18] Bauckham, *Eyewitnesses*, 124–47.

the narrative, and not much better in John, where the alleged *inclusio* relies on John's audience having to decode a series of cryptic clues to the identity of a completely unremarkable unnamed disciple at John 1.35–40, surely a bizarre way to advertise one's eyewitness source.[19]

Bauckham bolsters his case in relation to Mark by appealing to a number of features of the Markan narrative, in particular its supposed Petrine perspective and the alleged plural-to-singular device. The latter refers to several places where the movement of an unspecified 'they' is followed by an account of the action of an unspecified 'he' (referring to Jesus), which Bauckham finds to be Mark's distinctive authorial way of drawing the reader into the perspective of the disciples following Jesus (and hence either Peter, James or John as one of the inner group of these disciples).[20] One might, however, question whether this is indicative of an eyewitness source or simply a natural way of narrating the activity of a notable figure being followed by a group of disciples.[21] Or even if it be granted that Mark is deliberately focalizing the narrative at certain points on the perspective of the disciples, this could surely just be an artistic device to draw the audience into the story, or to encourage them to identify with the disciples in a Gospel in which discipleship is one of the leading themes. Again, that Peter plays a major role in Mark's narrative is undeniable, and Bauckham makes a number of interesting observations about the role and charac-terization of Peter in Mark,[22] but whether this really amounts to the Gospel being narrated from a Petrine perspective as opposed to a Markan dramatic device is not so clear.

Part of Theodore Weeden's criticism of Bauckham's thesis is that Mark's Gospel gives us not the perspective *of* Peter but Mark's perspective *on* Peter, which Weeden takes to be thoroughly negative.[23] Bauckham responds that Weeden has not shifted his position on the role of the disciples from that expressed in his 1971 book *Mark – Traditions in Conflict* and has failed to respond to a number of telling criticisms of that position.[24] But even if one rejects Weeden's particular thesis on Mark as a polemic against a

---

[19] David Catchpole, 'On Proving Too Much: Critical Hesitations about Richard Bauckham's *Jesus and the Eyewitnesses*', *JSHJ* 6 (2008), 169–81 (175–8); Stephen J. Patterson, 'Can You Trust a Gospel? A Review of Richard Bauckham's *Jesus and the Eyewitnesses*', *JSHJ* 6 (2008), 194–210 (201–2).

[20] Bauckham, *Eyewitnesses*, 156–64.

[21] Patterson, 'Can You Trust a Gospel?', 202–3.

[22] Bauckham, *Eyewitnesses*, 165–70.

[23] Theodore J. Weeden, Sr, 'Polemics as Case for Dissent: A Response to Richard Bauckham's *Jesus and the Eyewitnesses*', *JSHJ* 6 (2008), 211–24 (218–21).

[24] Richard Bauckham, 'In Response to My Respondents: *Jesus and the Eyewitnesses* in Review', *JSHJ* 6 (2008), 225–53 (251–2).

divine-man Christology represented by the Markan disciples, Bauckham has still to explain why Mark appears to go out of his way to discredit his principal eyewitness source by repeatedly emphasizing the disciples' failure to understand.

A further objection is that the logic of Bauckham's argument about Peter would seem to apply just as strongly to Jesus. The *inclusio* of eyewitness testimony in the case of Jesus is formed by his being named at Mark 1.9 (almost right at the start of the narrative, well before Peter comes on the scene) and at Mark 16.6. Although Peter is referred to one verse later, verbs relating to what Jesus will do appear in Mark 16.7 after the final mention of Peter. Furthermore, Jesus is clearly the central character in the narrative. He is present for even more of its events than is Peter (occasionally to the seeming exclusion of any other witnesses, e.g. Mark 1.10–13, 35; 14.35–36); in addition the narrator is frequently privy to Jesus' thoughts and feelings (e.g. Mark 1.41; 2.5, 8; 3.5; 5.30; 6.6; 10.14, 21; 11.12; 12.34; 14.33) and on occasion narrates events explicitly from Jesus' point of view (Mark 6.45–48; 9.25; 12.41–42; 14.37, 40). Moreover, the ideological perspective of the Markan narrator is far more closely aligned with that of Jesus than that of Peter. The case could therefore be made that Mark's Gospel is written from a dominical perspective, and by Bauckham's reasoning we should deduce that Jesus was Mark's eyewitness source. Since this is clearly impossible no one has ever suggested it, but this must surely cast doubt on applying similar arguments to Peter.

A lesser difficulty with Bauckham's case in relation to Mark is that he also argues that where characters are named for no apparent reason (such as Jairus and Bartimaeus, against the tendency for beneficiaries of Jesus' miracles to be anonymous) they are to be understood as the eyewitnesses to the event in question.[25] Part of the problem here is conceiving how Mark is meant to have had access to the eyewitness testimony of such persons, something Bauckham never really explains. Did Mark receive their eyewitness testimony at first hand, using it to supplement what he obtained from the Petrine *chreiai*, or simply at the end of a chain of transmission of traditions in the name of these eyewitnesses? A more acute problem for Bauckham is that according to what he argues elsewhere, Peter should be the eyewitness for some of these events. For example, in the case of the raising of Jairus's daughter, Mark uses the precise plural-to-singular narrative device focusing in on the trio of Peter, James and John that Bauckham takes to be indicative of the Petrine perspective in

---

[25] Bauckham, *Eyewitnesses*, 52–4.

Mark's Gospel (Mark 5.37–39). So who is Mark trying to indicate as his eyewitness source here, Peter or Jairus? The logic of Bauckham's argument seems to demand both, but that surely tends to undermine its plausibility. While it is not impossible that Mark has combined information from more than one eyewitness source, this would then suggest that his use of sources went beyond the faithful reproduction of Petrine *chreiai* reported by Papias.

There are also difficulties with the way in which Bauckham envisages Mark accessing Peter's eyewitness testimony. Relying rather heavily on a close reading of the fragment of Papias preserved in Eusebius (*Hist. eccl.* 3.39.14–16), Bauckham argues that Mark translated the *chreiai* Peter used in his preaching for use in his Gospel over the course of several meetings specifically for that purpose, just as Peter remembered them.[26] Bauckham's argument here seems to squeeze a good deal of precise meaning out of a somewhat ambiguous report. It also presupposes that Eusebius has accurately recorded the precise wording of what Papias wrote, that in later life Papias accurately remembered and recorded precisely what he had gleaned from John the Elder in his youth, and that John the Elder's account of the relation of Peter's preaching to Mark's writing was precisely accurate. This set of assumptions would seem to be a trifle optimistic. It is also hard to square with Papias's view that Mark's account was not in order (according to Bauckham, in contrast to John's eyewitness account, which was), since if Papias thought that Mark had such direct access to Peter during the course of his Gospel, it is hard to see why he (Papias) would not also suppose Mark to have taken advantage of the fact to establish the order of events according to Peter. Bauckham thinks that Papias was in fact mistaken in supposing that Mark lacked order, so that this judgement may have been down to Papias rather than John the Elder,[27] but one is then left wondering what other parts of Papias's report may reflect Papias's own opinions.

A further problem Bauckham has to face is that nothing in Mark really has the character of eyewitness reminiscence, such as Peter would surely have been able to supply, to which Bauckham's response is that the Petrine testimony Mark uses is not Peter's reminiscences but Peter's preaching. This would seem to be in some tension with Bauckham's insistence elsewhere that the Jesus tradition was transmitted in isolation from its use (presumably for the purpose of preserving the tradition and handing it

---

[26] Bauckham, *Eyewitnesses*, 205–17.
[27] Bauckham, *Eyewitnesses*, 230–5.

on to authorized teachers),[28] for then one would have expected Peter to transmit this isolated tradition to Mark rather than *chreiai* honed for use in Peter's preaching. Overall, one may be left with the impression that Bauckham might have done better to argue a more modest case to the effect that Mark made use of his memory of Peter's preaching when he came to write his Gospel (although this would probably dilute what Bauckham wants to maintain too far).

Bauckham's arguments for the eyewitness authorship of John (by the Beloved Disciple, whom Bauckham identifies with the disciple John the Elder mentioned by Papias) follow a rather different course. In this case, the claim to eyewitness testimony is far more explicit (John 21.24), provided one accepts the final chapter of John as an integral and original part of the Gospel.

One difficulty with Bauckham's case is that, even on his own reckoning, the Beloved Disciple appears to be entirely absent from chapters 2 to 12, so that Bauckham is forced to hypothesize that the Beloved Disciple obtained much of this material from someone else in his circle.[29] In other words, he turns out not to have been a direct eyewitness to a great many of the events depicted in his Gospel after all (although Bauckham argues that he did have access to direct eyewitness testimony for these events).

A second difficulty is the almost cryptic way in which the Beloved Disciple appears to hide his identity within his narrative (if he is the author) while insisting on the truth of his own testimony. Bauckham tries to explain this as the result of the Beloved Disciple being such an obscure character that he needs to establish his credentials as the especially insightful disciple whom Jesus loved before revealing himself as author,[30] but this explanation feels contrived, in part because it is hard to envisage such an apparently noteworthy character being simultaneously so obscure, and in part because it seems at odds with Bauckham's insistence elsewhere on the transmission of testimony in the name of the relevant eyewitnesses, even when the eyewitnesses in question are such minor characters as Jairus, Bartimaeus or Simon of Cyrene.

Perhaps the greatest difficulty is that of reconciling the very different accounts of Jesus that appear in Mark and John if both are supposed to be based on reliable eyewitness testimony, not least the fact that the focus of the teaching of the Markan (and indeed synoptic) Jesus is the coming of the kingdom of God (to be understood, perhaps, in terms

---

[28] Bauckham, *Eyewitnesses*, 278–9.
[29] Bauckham, *Eyewitnesses*, 402–3.
[30] Bauckham, *Eyewitnesses*, 407–8.

of the restoration of Israel) while that of the Johannine Jesus focuses almost exclusively on his own role as the incarnate Son who alone reveals the Father.[31] Bauckham responds that in the case of John, the eyewitness in question has long reflected on the meaning of events, which he expressed through Christological discourses of his own composition, so that his narrative 'is not to be read as a straightforward chronicle', while 'the events themselves . . . are historical in a fairly straightforward sense'.[32]

Now Bauckham does make it clear that what he expects from eyewitness testimony is an insider (and *therefore* authentic) interpretation of events, seen in their true significance as only a participant could see them. He also makes it clear that ancient historians could exercise a degree of artistic licence with the details of their account for the purpose of narrative effectiveness so long as the gist of events remained intact, and that he is not expecting a higher standard of historical accuracy from the Gospel eyewitnesses than this (so that, for example, John may have reduced the number of female visitors to the tomb to just one for the sake of the narrative efficacy of focusing on Mary Magdalene).[33] At the same time, however, Bauckham wishes to maintain that subsequent interpretation does not take the tradition further away from the facts, but is simply a way of rendering the fact in intelligible and significant form.[34] The problem is that if Peter (through Mark) and the Beloved Disciple (in John) are both allowed to be sticking to the (albeit interpreted) historical facts, the notion of historical fact is in mortal danger from the death of a thousand qualifications. If, say, Jesus' exorcisms and preaching on the kingdom of God are to be regarded as peripheral details which John could dispense with while maintaining the essential historical core of what Jesus said and did, one wonders what is left to the essential historical core.

To be sure there is a good deal more to Bauckham's arguments than we have been able to cover here, but we must now move on to his treatment of issues more directly germane to the subject of this book, namely the transmission of the Jesus tradition and the related question of memory.

In this strand of his argument, Bauckham begins by borrowing Jan Vansina's distinction between oral tradition (collective tradition spanning a number of generations) and oral history (individual accounts given by still living eyewitnesses), while acknowledging that the distinction is a modern one and does not correspond to ancient usage. On this basis he

---

[31] Catchpole, 'On Proving Too Much', 178–80.

[32] Bauckham, 'In Response', 240.

[33] Bauckham, 'In Response', 236–7.

[34] Bauckham, *Eyewitnesses*, 305–10.

argues that Papias's preference for the 'living and abiding voice' related not to oral tradition (in Vansina's sense) but to oral history, implying that eyewitness testimony was still available at the time of Papias's youth (towards the end of the first century) and hence also when the Gospels were written.[35]

Bauckham subsequently goes on to discuss three models of oral tradition current in New Testament scholarship: form criticism, Gerhardsson's model of formal transmission on the rabbinic analogy, and the model of informal controlled tradition developed by Bailey and taken up by (among others) Dunn. Bauckham thinks that the form critics were correct in their observations that the form of pericopae in the Synoptic Gospels may be close to the oral forms they possessed previously and that the linking of pericopae in the Gospels may be due to the Evangelists rather than the tradition, but wrong about just about everything else.

Among Bauckham's criticisms of form criticism (many of which are akin to points made earlier in this book) are (1) that the assumption that traditions originated in pure form is highly questionable; (2) that there is no strict correlation between form and *Sitz im Leben*; (3) that the form critics greatly exaggerated what Jack Goody terms homeostasis (the notion that there is a perfect correspondence between traditions and their use in the society that transmits them); (4) that E. P. Sanders' work shows that there are no laws of tradition operating consistently throughout the Gospel tradition; (5) that the analogy with folklore is flawed, since the processes and timescale are quite different; (6) that folklorists have in any case abandoned the romantic notion of the folk as collective creator of folk tradition in favour of recognizing the roles of authoritative individuals; (7) that form criticism worked with a predetermined picture of the history of early Christianity which included a sharp division between the Palestinian and Hellenistic communities; (8) that the form critics assumed without proof that the Jesus traditions were circulated in purely oral form for several decades; and (9) that the form critics, especially Bultmann, employed an excessively literary model for understanding the processes of oral transmission.[36] One may quibble with details of this critique, such as whether Bultmann or any other form critic ever in fact employed such a thoroughgoing Goody-like model of homeostasis,[37] but overall Bauckham's points seem well made.

---

[35] Bauckham, *Eyewitnesses*, 5–8, 12–38.
[36] Bauckham, *Eyewitnesses*, 241–9.
[37] Patterson, 'Can You Trust a Gospel?', 205, 207.

Bauckham next discusses the theories advanced by Gerhardsson and Bailey (see Chapters 3 and 5 above), and questions Bailey's threefold typology of informal uncontrolled tradition (Bultmann), formal controlled tradition (Gerhardsson) and informal controlled tradition (Bailey). Part of the problem, he thinks, is that Bailey and, even more in following him, Dunn have confused the issues of formality and control, so that Dunn has adopted Bailey's model as a middle way because it allows more flexibility than Gerhardsson's model seems to while still guaranteeing a reasonable degree of stability. But, Bauckham argues, instead of simply assuming that greater formality correlates with greater stability, one has to ask a number of further questions. These include, not just whether a tradition was controlled, but, if so, why control was thought necessary, what the mechanisms of control were, whether different aspects of the tradition were treated differently and if so what was the relative balance of stability and flexibility in the treatment of these different kinds or aspects of tradition. One also needs to consider the extent to which eyewitnesses may have played an important role in controlling the tradition (as opposed to the more anonymous community model envisaged by Bailey). A further problem with the Bailey–Dunn model in Bauckham's view is that it regards informal controlled oral tradition as operating in Galilean villages, which may have been a plausible setting for such minor eyewitnesses as Bartimaeus and Jairus, but neglects what Bauckham takes to be the authoritative role of the Twelve in Jerusalem.[38]

Bauckham thus prefers something closer to the Gerhardsson model, in which recognized teachers passed on formal instruction to others. Memorization of the material would inevitably have played a part, since it formed such a universal part of ancient education. This did not necessarily mean verbatim memorization, since for some kinds of material (such as parables) it would be sufficient to memorize the gist, but it did imply a conscious effort to commit material to memory rather than simply relying on it happening to stick there. The fact that much of Jesus' teaching is cast in memorable form, together with the relative stability of the sayings material in the synoptic tradition, is partial evidence for this. Paul also furnishes evidence for the formal transmission of tradition in the terminology of tradition he employs (*paradosis* and cognates), the notice at Galatians 1.18 that he spent two weeks with Peter (presumably learning Petrine traditions) and the existence of teachers in the Pauline churches whose job it would have been to maintain the traditions within their various communities.

---

[38] Bauckham, *Eyewitnesses*, 249–63.

To be sure, variations would have occurred for all sorts of reasons, including performance variations, lapses of memory, and deliberate inter-pretative additions and alterations, but this does not justify an assumption of perfect homeostasis, the notion that the traditions were so thoroughly adapted to present use that the past of Jesus was lost sight of. Contrary to what is sometimes stated, oral societies can maintain a genuine interest in the past, and the primitive churches had religious reasons for doing so, not only in terms of their notion of self-identity as followers of Jesus (the sociological reason offered by Dunn) but on account of their theological interest in Jesus as the agent of salvation in fulfilment of God's promises to Israel. In any case, the transmission of Jesus traditions may not have been purely oral, since writing, at least in the form of private notebooks, may have played a role in stabilizing the tradition from the start.[39]

Bauckham's next step is to argue that traditions about Jesus were origin-ated and formulated by named eyewitnesses in whose name they were transmitted, and who remained the guardians and guarantors of the tradi-tion. Bauckham thus distinguishes himself from both the form-critical view and Dunn's view, both of which envisage a process of anonymous community transmission. He does not deny the existence of community tradition and 'collective memory', but wishes to assert the primacy of individual eyewitnesses in the handing on of tradition. In support of this, Bauckham argues that early Christian literature represents communities as the recipients of tradition, but never as its source, and that Papias expresses interest in tradition handed down by named individuals, not anonymous community tradition (although, as Dunn counters, Papias never contrasts named individuals with community tradition, since the latter is never in view in what he writes; Papias instead expresses the common ancient preference for oral testimony over written documents).[40]

In contrast to the Bailey–Dunn model with its focus on the traditioning process in Galilean villages, Bauckham suggests we should think of the Twelve as the principal (though not sole) authorizers of a body of Jesus tradition with Peter as their leading spokesman (Bauckham has by this point previously argued that since at least half the Twelve play no further role in the Gospels that name them, the point of listing their names can only have been that they played such a role). In Bauckham's view the relative mobility of the early Church leaders would have allowed the

---

[39] Bauckham, *Eyewitnesses*, 264–89.
[40] James D. G. Dunn, 'Eyewitnesses and the Oral Jesus Tradition', *JSHJ* 6 (2008), 85–105 (103).

eyewitnesses to control the transmission of the tradition, at least at one remove through their direct disciples, if not in person.

As an example, Bauckham points to the tradition of eyewitness testimony that Paul cites at 1 Corinthians 15.3–8. Once the eyewitnesses started to die out, the written Gospels took their place by preserving their testimony.[41] Dunn objects that once the Church expanded beyond a hundred small communities or so, there would not have been enough eyewitnesses to go round to exercise the kind of control Bauckham envisages.[42] The point is a reasonable one, but not fatal to Bauckham's main case, which does not depend on eyewitness-controlled tradition being available to every single member of every first-century community, but simply to the people who wrote the Gospels, who were likely to have been prominent teachers in prominent churches (or so Bauckham could argue) and thus more likely to have had access to the best available eyewitness traditions (which, Bauckham could also argue, might help to explain why their Gospels won acceptance). A more telling objection from Dunn is the lack of evidence for Bauckham's key assertion that traditions were generally handed on in the name of individual eyewitnesses, particularly when it comes to the sayings material.[43]

The final part of Bauckham's argument that need concern us here relates to his treatment of memory, both collective memory and individual eyewitness memory. Bauckham does not deny the existence or importance of collective memory, but regards Halbwachs's notion of it as too prone to social determinism, preferring Barbara Misztal's intersubjective approach. In this, Bauckham is effectively in agreement with much that has been said in the previous two chapters, so we need not labour the point here. Bauckham, however, goes on to distinguish between recollective memory (of what one has personally experienced) and memory for information (elsewhere termed 'semantic' memory), adding that much of what is called 'social', 'cultural' or 'collective' memory concerns the latter of these categories. Bauckham also wishes to distinguish between (1) the social dimension of individual recollection, (2) the shared recollections of a group, and (3) collective memory proper. In his view Misztal is quite right to stress that individual memory takes place in a social context. He also acknowledges the existence of the type of memory Dunn envisages in relation to the disciples, in which a group of people share recollections of common experiences. 'Collective memory' would then refer to the traditions circulating among people who had not themselves been eyewitnesses. One must,

---

[41] Bauckham, *Eyewitnesses*, 93–108, 290–310.
[42] Dunn, 'Eyewitnesses', 98–9.
[43] Dunn, 'Eyewitnesses', 100–2.

however, says Bauckham, be cautious about making unreflective use of what sociologists say about collective memory when considering the Jesus tradition, since the sociological use generally ignores the role of individual eyewitnesses.

The relevance for this to Bauckham seems to be in countering a 'presentist' understanding of collective memory in which the past of Jesus is totally absorbed and transformed by the present needs of the community, but here Bauckham is arguably attacking a straw man.[44] Perhaps of more concern is whether Bauckham is justified in separating individual and collective memory to the extent that he apparently wishes to, especially since he has acknowledged the social dimension to individual recollection and effectively appeals to at least one aspect of it in his treatment of individual eyewitness memory.

As has been discussed in previous chapters, in order to make sense of memories to ourselves and communicate them to others, we need to make use of the conceptual frameworks available in our culture. When it comes to recalling events, this involves shaping our memories according to schemata, or narrative scripts. Bauckham insists that schemata are not Procrustean beds into which our memories are forced; narrative scripts can be quite flexible and it is also possible to disrupt them. He also insists that the use of narrative scripts does not automatically lead to distortion of our memories, although distortions and omissions can occur, adding that when the employment of such scripts goes beyond the empirically verifiable in the quest for meaning it does not necessarily result in the distortion of the empirical. Nevertheless, he acknowledges, the social shaping of our memories occurs at all stages. All this should be broadly familiar from the previous two chapters. But Bauckham goes on to make a further point. The form critics, followed by Nineham, appealed to the forms of Gospel pericopae to argue that they were the product of long community use but, Bauckham points out, since psychological studies of recollective memory show that eyewitness accounts are rapidly honed into standard 'forms' (the narrative schemata available in that particular culture), the appearance of such forms in the Gospels cannot be used to argue for a long process of oral tradition.[45]

This argument appears fair enough as far as it goes, and is further supported by the fact that each rendering of a story in oral tradition is a fresh performance rather than a revised version of the rendering that

---

[44] Bauckham, *Eyewitnesses*, 310–18.
[45] Bauckham, *Eyewitnesses*, 335–8, 346–51.

immediately preceded it, which again implies that the form of an account says little about the length of the transmission process that led to it. Whether Bauckham is justified in separating out the non-empirical quest for meaning from the empirical facts narrated when it comes to narrativizing memories is another matter. One takes the point that narrativization is not necessarily distortion, since it is necessary to cast a memory in some narrative form in order to communicate at all, but in the case of stories such as the Gospel pericopae where events are frequently narrated without ostensible comment, it is hard to see how the quest for meaning could have influenced the narrative form without also reshaping the empirical facts to some extent, although in the light of what Bauckham says elsewhere his claim may be that such distortions as occur are not significant, since they do not affect the core meaning of the event.

Bauckham is concerned to argue that eyewitness memory is generally reliable, while allowing that it can also be fallible. He maintains that most of the incidents narrated in the Gospels would come under the category of recollective (or episodic) memory, and cites William Brewer in support of the view that recent recollective memories tend to be veridical, that recollective memories give rise to high confidence in the accuracy of their content, and that such confidence can frequently predict objective accuracy. Bauckham goes on to suggest (again following Brewer) that constructive theories of memory (such as were alluded to in Chapter 6 above) probably have to be combined with copy theories (while neglecting to add that the essay by Martin Conway that follows Brewer's essay in the same volume argues for a strongly constructivist view).[46] Bauckham then lists a number of factors that (he says) tend to make recollective memory more reliable and argues that they apply to the Jesus tradition.[47]

Not all of the factors listed by Bauckham are equally relevant, since in several cases he mentions factors such as the presence of irrelevant detail or the point of view only to admit the absence of evidence for their effect on the accuracy of recall. Some other factors, such as emotional involvement in an incident, seem ambivalent, since strong emotion can distort memories as well as preserve them, and the effects of emotion on memory can be quite complex.[48] He points out that salient, consequential and unusual

---

[46] Bauckham, *Eyewitnesses*, 319–35; cf. William F. Brewer, 'What Is Recollective Memory?' in David C. Rubin (ed.), *Remembering Our Past: Studies in Autobiographical Memory* (Cambridge: Cambridge University Press, 1995), 19–66 and Martin A. Conway, 'Autobiographical Knowledge and Autobiographical Memories' in Rubin (ed.), *Remembering Our Past*, 67–93.

[47] Bauckham, *Eyewitnesses*, 341–6.

[48] Sven-Åke Christiansen and Martin A. Safer, 'Emotional Events and Emotions in Autobiographical Memories' in Rubin (ed.), *Remembering Our Past*, 218–43.

events tend to be more memorable, and that the events narrated in the Gospels tend to be of this sort, but in this context, 'memorable' is an ambiguous term, since it is not clear from what Bauckham says whether 'memorable' here equates to 'accurately memorable'. Bauckham also fails to discuss the possibility that fictitious or highly distorted accounts may equally well describe events that *appear* salient, significant, unusual and emotional. In other words the fact that a story contains these features does not in itself constitute an argument for its having been based on reliable eyewitness memory.

Another problematic criterion Bauckham employs is that of frequent rehearsal of the material. He is almost certainly right to suggest that the kind of material that ended up in the Gospels would have been frequently narrated by the eyewitnesses, but frequent narration can be a mixed blessing. It can serve to fix one's memory of an event in the standard form in which one has narrated it, rather than the way one experienced it at the time, and one's recollection of the event can be influenced by the way one has narrated it in the past. Thus, for example, Jan Vansina, on whom Bauckham frequently relies elsewhere, cautions that 'frequent repetition does not of itself guarantee fidelity of reproduction'.[49] Again Bauckham appeals to the fact that episodic memories tend to be more reliable if one sticks to the gist of events rather than trying to recall peripheral details, and then makes the point that the Gospels rarely record the peripheral details of a scene. But, as we have seen, in Bauckham's view what Mark recorded was Peter's *chreiai* honed for the purposes of Peter's preaching, which might itself account for the lack of peripheral detail. If Bauckham is simply trying to argue that the kind of material that appears in the Gospels is the kind that the eyewitnesses *could* have remembered with reasonable accuracy, then in general terms his case is fair enough; but he has not shown that the eyewitnesses *did* or *must have* remembered everything with reasonable accuracy, let alone that everything that appears in the Gospels is the result of accurate eyewitness memory.

Bauckham nowhere supposes that eyewitness testimony or eyewitness memory gives access to a kind of photographic, objective record of brute historical facts, and he is thus concerned to give some account of the interplay of fact and interpretation in eyewitness memory. He notes that the ancients valued the participant perspective over the observer perspective, and that modern psychologists such as John Robinson insist that the

---

[49] Jan Vansina, *Oral Tradition as History* (London: James Currey, 1985), 40–1; cf. Geoffrey Cubitt, *History and Memory* (Historical Approaches; ed. G. Cubitt; Manchester and New York: Manchester University Press, 2007), 96–9.

subjective first-person perspective needs to be studied along with the objective third-person one.

Bauckham also notes that Robinson enquires why meaning in personal memories changes or remains stable over time, and proposes four factors: *the multiplicity of potential meanings, deferred meaning, changing meaning* and *negotiating meaning* (within a social context). According to Bauckham, Robinson holds that the rememberer's search for meaning does not part company with the objective past and that varying interpretations may be equally valid (although Robinson's actual point seems to be rather that the variations in an individual's explanations of the past may be due to factors other than egocentric revisionism).[50] Past and present come together in remembering, since those who recollect intend to recall the past rather than create it, while memories are recalled to serve present need.

Applying this to the Jesus tradition, Bauckham argues that the common model in Gospel scholarship that assumes that subsequent interpretation took the tradition further from the facts is therefore unjustified. He finds particular relevance in the concept of *deferred meaning* (where the significance of something only becomes apparent some time after the event), particularly in relation to John's Gospel (where it is a motif that explicitly occurs several times). Bauckham also points to the fact, previously noted by Gerd Theissen, that the healing and exorcism stories show little sign of eschatological meaning, which is provided only by the context in which they occur.[51] This, Bauckham claims, exemplifies the comparatively modest extent to which subsequent use and reflection has affected these pre-Easter stories. Here Bauckham arguably understates the extent to which healing and exorcism stories were made to serve the Evangelist's agenda (and so may not be such straightforward unvarnished accounts or pre-Easter events as Bauckham suggests), a particularly blatant example being the two-stage restoration of sight to the Blind Man of Bethsaida (Mark 8.22–26) which seems designed to comment both on the continuing blindness of the disciples and on its only partial correction in Peter's Confession (Mark 8.27–30).[52] He also seems to take a minimalist view of the extent to which the search for meaning might affect one's recollection of what actually took place, although he perhaps only gives the impression

---

[50] John A. Robinson, 'Perspective, Meaning and Remembering' in Rubin (ed.), *Remembering Our Past*, 199–217 (214).

[51] Gerd Theissen and Annette Merz, *The Historical Jesus: A Comprehensive Guide* (tr. John Bowden; London: SCM Press, 1998), 301–2; cf. Eric Eve, *The Healer from Nazareth: Jesus' Miracles in Historical Context* (London: SPCK, 2009), 123–5.

[52] Eric Eve, 'Spit in Your Eye: The Blind Man of Bethsaida and the Blind Man of Alexandria', *NTS* 54 (2008), 1–17; Eve, *Healer*, 105–6.

of leaning too far in this direction in his anxiety to combat excessive scepticism.

Perhaps the biggest problem with Bauckham's treatment of eyewitness memory remains, as suggested above, his apparent desire to insulate it too much from the wider social memory which would surely have influenced it in one way or another. Bauckham himself suggests that at least some of the eyewitness testimony, that of the Twelve, might have been shaped collectively in what he terms 'group memory'. He also notes that eyewitnesses such as Peter would have been responsive to audience feedback as they repeatedly narrated their recollected material. Although it would be implausible to suppose that eyewitnesses such as Peter were so suggestible that their memories of Jesus would be completely moulded by the communities to which they ministered, it is also unlikely that they would have been completely immune to social pressure.

The biggest problem with Bauckham's thesis overall is that he has tried to push it too far. He has not convincingly demonstrated as close a connection between the canonical Gospels and eyewitness testimony as he claims to have done, for the reasons outlined above (although there is rather more to his argument than there has been space to do justice to here). However, he has raised a number of important questions about the nature of the transmission of Jesus tradition in the primitive Church. It is completely fair to point out that the tradition was more likely to have been transmitted and controlled by certain individuals such as authorized teachers rather than simply passed round an anonymous collective, and it is entirely reasonable to suggest that recognized eyewitnesses were likely to have had a continuing role in this process for as long as they were around.[53] Any model of the oral tradition behind the Gospels therefore needs to take this possibility into account. What difference it makes in practice is another question, and a first step towards answering that question would be to probe the evidence to see what kind of theory provides the best fit. This task will be attempted in a small way in the next chapter.

---

[53] So also Patterson, 'Can You Trust a Gospel?', 197–9.

9

Probing the tradition

We have now examined a number of models of the oral transmission of the material that found its way into the Gospels. Each of them is speculative insofar as we lack any direct access to the way in which this material was in fact transmitted. Any theory thus has to rely on scattered clues in the extant sources together with analogies from the way memory and oral transmission have been observed to work elsewhere. As illuminating as such comparative studies of oral tradition are, there are no universal laws governing how oral tradition functions in all times and places; different societies handle different kinds of oral material in different ways. Theories of oral tradition drawn from other fields of study (general folklore, Balkan bards, African oral traditions, etc.) may thus be suggestive, but they fall short of being probative for the oral tradition behind the Gospels.

There is, however, one final step we can take before trying to come to any conclusions, and that is to probe the Gospel tradition to get some sense of its nature. Arguably we could have done this at the very start, but leaving it to the end means we may be able to get some sense of how the various accounts of oral tradition we have encountered measure up against what we find. Potentially this could be a substantial study in itself, requiring us to analyse most of the material in the New Testament and a number of other broadly contemporary sources. To keep things manageable this chapter will confine itself to just two probes, both in areas where we can compare aspects of the tradition as it surfaces in different and almost certainly independent sources. That way we can begin to gauge both the extent of the tradition and the kinds of transformation and constraint it was subject to. Again to keep things manageable we shall (broadly) restrict ourselves to one principal witness to the Gospel tradition (Mark) and compare that witness in turn to two rather different ones: Paul and Josephus.

Mark and Paul

On the assumption that there is no direct literary relationship between the New Testament Gospels and the Pauline Epistles, material that is common to both (not least teaching attributed to Jesus) should offer some indication of how such material was handled in the oral tradition.[1] At least two features of this material have been frequently observed. One is that the Epistles in general and Paul in particular seemingly show very little interest in the life and ministry of the earthly Jesus. There are, of course, a few exceptions: for example, Hebrews 5.7–8 looks like a reference to the prayer of Jesus at Gethsemane found in Mark 14.32–36 and parallels, while 2 Peter 1.16–18 clearly refers to the transfiguration story of Mark 9.2–8 and parallels. The other is that the New Testament letters, not least those of Paul and James, contain occasional echoes of and allusions to the teaching of Jesus found in the synoptic tradition, but that with a couple of exceptions in Paul, the material is not explicitly attributed to Jesus and often comes in the form of general paraenesis (moral exhortation and instruction) rather than the more distinctive and often poetic pronouncements the Gospels place on the lips of Jesus.

Whether or not Mark is directly or indirectly dependent on Paul, no one will suppose that Paul was dependent on Mark, and so Paul may be taken as a witness to traditions that were in existence prior to Mark. There are a number of indications that Paul knows of traditions that were not entirely dissimilar to those on which Mark drew. Paul knows of a tradition that Jesus was descended from David (Romans 1.3) even if he does not make much of it, while Mark perhaps knows of a similar tradition (Mark 10.47–48) without expressing much enthusiasm for it (Mark 12.35–37). It may be that Mark was simply reckoning with the Davidic associations of the title 'Messiah', but it is in any case undeniable that both Mark and Paul know that this title was used of Jesus, just as both refer to him as the 'Son of God' (e.g. Romans 1.4; Mark 1.1, 11; 9.7; 15.39). Again, even if for Paul 'Christ' sometimes seems to operate as a proper name, he is obviously aware of its titular significance (e.g. Romans 9.5) as Mark clearly is (Mark 1.1; 8.29; 12.35; 14.61; 15.32), and both agree in applying it to Jesus. Paul seems largely to take it for granted as a name or title for Jesus; Mark presents it as something more contentious, but his account nevertheless presupposes that it is how Jesus was designated. Both these titles for Jesus would thus appear to be common to the traditions known to both Paul

---

[1] For some fuller discussions of this material see, e.g., David Wenham, *The Jesus Tradition outside the Gospels* (Sheffield: JSOT Press, 1985); David Wenham, *Paul, Follower of Jesus or Founder of Christianity?* (Grand Rapids: Eerdmans, 1995); David Wenham, *Paul and the Historical Jesus* (Cambridge: Grove Books, 1998); Traugott Holtz, 'Paul and the Oral Gospel Tradition' in Henry Wansbrough (ed.), *Jesus and the Oral Gospel Tradition* (JSNTSup, 64; Sheffield: Sheffield Academic Press, 1991), 380–93; and notes 3 and 6 below.

and Mark (although arguably they would hardly be Christian traditions if this were not so).

When it comes to the content of Jesus' teaching, there are again points of contact between Mark and Paul which suggest at least some common or parallel traditions. Paul certainly knows of the term 'kingdom of God' as a Christian desideratum even if he does not make much of the term (Romans 14.17; 1 Corinthians 4.20; 6.9–10; 15.24, 50; Galatians 5.21; 1 Thessalonians 2.12; 2 Thessalonians 1.5), while Mark represents it as central to Jesus' preaching (Mark 1.15; 4.11, 26, 30; 9.1, 47; 10.14–15, 23–25; 12.34; 14.25). Paul tends to speak of 'inheriting' the kingdom of God while Mark more often speaks of 'entering' it, but in both cases the issue is what qualifies or disqualifies a person for the kingdom. The importance of the kingdom of God and whether or not one is fit for it are thus themes common to traditions known to both Paul and Mark.

Paul cites prohibition of divorce as a teaching of the Lord (1 Corinthians 7.10–11) which is a tradition also known to Mark (Mark 10.2–9). Paul's insistence on the centrality of the love commandment (Romans 13.8–10; Galatians 5.14) could well be a witness to the same tradition that lies behind the dominical summary of the law at Mark 12.28–31, though this is less certain, both because Paul says nothing about deriving this teaching from Jesus and because it would scarcely be stretching coincidence too far to suppose that an appeal to Leviticus 19.18 could crop up independently several times in a first-century Jewish-Christian milieu. Nonetheless, the use of this motif in other first-century Christian texts (notably Matthew) does make it somewhat unlikely that it was an idea that both Paul and Mark happened independently to hit on, but suggests that the appeal to Leviticus 19.18 was at least an established part of the Christian tradition, whether or not it was originally attributed to Jesus.

One could go on, especially if one extended the comparison to include Matthew and Luke, but the point has been made that Mark knew at least some traditions that were also known to Paul and that, at least at first sight, the tradition seems to have been reasonably stable, at least insofar as the gist of Jesus' teaching was concerned in particular instances.

According to Jens Schröter, however, the data could point to a very different conclusion. In his view, while material was sometimes attributed to Jesus, the purpose was not to record historical reminiscence but to give authority to a body of Church teaching that combined words of Jesus, the Hebrew Scriptures, Jewish-Hellenistic ethics and early Christian teaching supposedly authorized by Jesus, as is shown for example by Paul's attribution to the Lord of a saying at 1 Thessalonians 4.15 that manifestly was not a saying of the earthly Jesus. Schröter accordingly suggests that parallel material found in the Gospels and Epistles is indicative, not of the faithful preservation of the sayings of Jesus in Christian memory, but of the subsequent historicizing and attribution to Jesus of this common body of material. In his view there was originally no attempt to distinguish between genuine words of Jesus and other Church teaching; instead the primitive Jesus tradition was a free and living one.[2]

James Dunn sees the matter rather differently, however.[3] According to Dunn, the fact that much of the paraenetic material in Paul, James and 1 Peter that resembles Jesus' teaching is not explicitly attributed to Jesus is indicative of 'one of the ways in which the Jesus tradition was remembered and used'.[4] Such material did not need to be explicitly attributed since the target audience was already well familiar with it, and such unattributed use of familiar material is typical of in-group language which helps to foster the identity of the group. According to Dunn this also shows that Paul's letters were not the medium of initial instruction to his churches, which could be assumed to have acquired a fair amount of Jesus tradition by other means.

Dunn and Schröter thus have very different ideas of the nature of the Jesus tradition and of the role of memory within that tradition. They are not completely opposed: Schröter apparently allows that some genuine words of Jesus would have entered the mix, and Dunn presumably accepts the possibility that some extraneous material may have been attributed to Jesus in the course of remembering the impact he made. Dunn and Schröter also concur in envisaging a widely spread body of common tradition. A fundamental difference between them nevertheless remains: for Dunn, what is remembered in the tradition is principally Jesus' original impact on his contemporaries, while for Schröter what is remembered is primarily the construct of the second generation of Christians responsible for creating a historicized portrait of Jesus in the Gospels that met current need; Schröter thus tacitly espouses a largely presentist approach to early Christian collective memory.

---

[2] Jens Schröter, 'Jesus and the Canon: The Early Jesus Traditions in the Context of the Origins of the New Testament Canon' in R. A. Horsley, J. A. Draper and J. M. Foley (eds), *Performing the Gospel: Orality, Memory and Mark* (Minneapolis: Augsburg Fortress, 2006), 104–46; cf. Werner H. Kelber, 'The Work of Birger Gerhardsson in Perspective' in W. H. Kelber and S. Byrskog (eds), *Jesus in Memory: Traditions in Oral and Scribal Perspectives* (Waco: Baylor University Press, 2009), 173–206 (185–91).

[3] James D. G. Dunn, *Jesus Remembered* (Christianity in the Making, 1; Grand Rapids and Cambridge: Eerdmans, 2003), 181–4; James D. G. Dunn, *The Theology of Paul the Apostle* (London and New York: T. & T. Clark, 1998).

[4] Dunn, *Jesus Remembered*, 183.

The fact that the same evidence can be read in such different ways should caution us against overconfidence in constructing theories on the basis of such relatively meagre data. Dunn's position may seem initially the more plausible, if only because it seems easier to envisage the paraenetic material in the Epistles being derived from the kind of strikingly phrased sayings found in the Gospels than the other way around, but it is not impossible that the early Church contained gifted wordsmiths who could cast paraenetic material into more memorable form when putting it on the lips of Jesus.[5] We have no hard evidence that the historical Jesus was the sole or most gifted oral poet contributing to the Jesus tradition; it is simply an assumption scholars seem quick to adopt. It is also possible that there is truth in both positions. If one abandons the assumption that all or most of what Jesus said was highly distinctive, then there is no particular reason why the thrust of much of what Jesus taught should not have resembled the ethical material found in other contemporary sources, such as those suggested by Schröter, in which case the distinction between authentic Jesus material and paraenesis drawn from other sources could in many cases turn out to be one without much discernible difference.

While it is principally Jesus' teaching that has attracted the attention of scholars looking for Jesus tradition outside the Gospels, a case could be made for finding some echoes of Gospel narratives as well. For example, Dale Allison argues that at least an outline of the Passion narrative could be reconstructed from Paul alone.[6] There are places in this argument where one may suspect that Allison's reconstruction is aided by his knowledge of the Gospel Passion narratives, but he is nevertheless able to make the case that Paul was aware of some kind of Passion narrative.

L. Michael White takes a far more cautious, almost minimalist, approach to the same material, although he appears rather quick to assume that the tradition that Paul cites in his letters is the sum total of the tradition Paul knows, and his related assumption that oral tradition would have been transmitted purely in the form of the kind of summary found at 1 Corinthians 15.3–7 without any attempt at narrative expansion seems a curious one.[7]

Support for the early existence of some kind of Passion narrative is provided by Chris Keith's and Tom Thatcher's argument (against Kelber) that the primitive Jesus movement would have experienced an urgent need

---

[5] See, e.g., H. Benedict Green, *Matthew, Poet of the Beatitudes* (JSNTSup, 203; Sheffield: Sheffield Academic Press, 2001).

[6] Dale C. Allison, *Constructing Jesus: Memory, Imagination and History* (London: SPCK, 2010), 392–423.

[7] L. Michael White, *Scripting Jesus: The Gospels in Rewrite* (New York: HarperOne, 2010), 106–29.

to come to terms with Jesus' untimely and violent death by constructing a narrative that made sense of it.[8] Keith and Thatcher suppose that this would largely be a matter of keying Jesus' death to existing narrative patterns, but while Allison by no means wants to argue that the Gospel Passion narratives are straightforwardly factual accounts, he does accept some arguments in support of the case that at least some elements in them are historical.[9]

The upshot is that it seems likely that the Pauline Epistles reflect the existence of early traditions of Jesus' death, already in the form of some sort of connected narrative, that resemble the stories later found in the Gospels. It does not, however, show that such primitive Passion narratives were fixed in form or wording, or that they were written down before Mark (although the possibility is not excluded), or that they were historically accurate (beyond the fact of Jesus' execution).

To look briefly at the evidence, a first, if rather obvious, point of comparison is that both Paul and Mark agree that Jesus died on the cross (e.g. Romans 6.6; 1 Corinthians 1.23; 2.2; Galatians 2.19–20; 3.1; 6.14; Philippians 2.8; Mark 15.15–38), and, moreover, although crucifixion was a Roman punishment (explicitly so in Mark), both writers agree in blaming Jews for Jesus' death (1 Thessalonians 2.14–15; Mark 14.1–2; 14.53—15.15). Again, both writers concur in putting considerable emphasis on Jesus' death (although the emphasis on its significance is rather more developed in Paul than in Mark).

Both writers also agree that Jesus was raised from the dead. No resurrection appearances are narrated in Mark, but that Jesus is raised is clearly implied in several places (Mark 8.31; 9.9, 31; 10.34; 14.28; 16.6–7) just as it is quite frequently asserted by Paul (Romans 1.4; 4.24; 6.9; 8.11; 1 Corinthians 15.3–23; 1 Thessalonians 4.14). To be sure, correspondences in detail are notoriously hard to come by. Paul and Mark concur in stating that prior to his resurrection Jesus was buried (1 Corinthians 15.4; Mark 15.46), although whether Paul (or the tradition he is citing) envisages the type of burial in a tomb described by Mark is impossible to say. They also agree in placing the resurrection on the third day (1 Corinthians 15.4; Mark 16.1–2) although Mark confusingly

---

[8] Chris Keith and Tom Thatcher, 'The Scar of the Cross: The Violence Ratio and the Earliest Christian Memories of Jesus' in T. Thatcher (ed.), *Jesus, the Voice and the Text: Beyond the Oral and the Written Gospel* (Waco: Baylor University Press, 2008), 197–234. For Kelber's response see Werner H. Kelber, 'The Oral-Scribal-Memorial Arts of Communication in Early Christianity' in Thatcher (ed.), *Jesus, the Voice and the Text*, 235–62 (256–8).
[9] Allison, *Constructing Jesus*, 423–7.

has Jesus predict that it will occur 'after three days' (Mark 8.31; 9.31; 10.34).

Paul knows of a tradition that Jesus appeared first to Cephas (Peter), and then to the Twelve (1 Corinthians 15.5), and this may be echoed by Mark's young man, who directs the woman to 'tell his disciples *and Peter*' that they are to see the risen Jesus in Galilee (Mark 16.7, my italics), although it is more clearly (though not exactly) reflected in the resurrection accounts of Luke and John (Luke 24.33–49; John 20.3–7, 19–23). Mark's account neither contradicts nor confirms Paul's tradition of a further series of appearances to 500 believers all at once, James, all the Apostles and finally Paul himself. It is also significant that Paul knows of a group called 'the twelve' (1 Corinthians 15.5), a tradition also known to Mark (Mark 3.13–14; 4.10; 10.32; 14.10, 17, 43). That Paul has Jesus appear to the *Twelve*, not the Eleven, does not necessarily contradict Mark (although it would clearly contradict Matthew 28.16 and Luke 24.33), since by the end of Mark all the disciples have failed, so that in Mark's Gospel Judas's rehabilitation is not necessarily any more certainly ruled out than that of the others.

The person of Judas raises the issue of Jesus' betrayal and Paul's account of the Last Supper. That Mark narrates Judas betraying Jesus is clear (Mark 14.10–11, 17–21, 43–46). The question is then whether Paul knows of some such tradition when he dates the institution of the Eucharist to 'the night when [Jesus] was betrayed' (*en tē(i) nukti hē paredideto* – 1 Corinthians 11.23). Arguably, *paredideto* could mean no more than 'handed over' or 'arrested', an interpretation perhaps strengthened by the mention of an appearance to 'the twelve' at 1 Corinthians 15.5.

Nonetheless, whatever Paul meant by *paredideto*, he does appear to be presupposing a larger narrative than he is explicitly relating here. At 1 Corinthians 11.23 Paul states that this is a tradition he has already imparted to his recipients, so he is presumably reminding them of something they already know. 'In the night he was betrayed/arrested' thus implies (or metonymically references) a fuller narrative known to both Paul and the Corinthians that Paul has no need to spell out again. Furthermore, there are several indicators that this narrative (however brief) was closely related to Jesus' death. The sayings over the bread and cup suggest this (1 Corinthians 11.23–24), the fact that repeating these actions is seen as 'proclaim[ing] the Lord's death' (1 Corinthians 11.26) surely implies it, and the association of Jesus' actions with the night he was betrayed or arrested also indicate it, since the most likely significance of Jesus' betrayal/arrest was that it was this that led to his execution. The possibility that this refers to some other occasion on which Jesus was betrayed/arrested (but then escaped) is surely remote. The only reasonable alternative is that Paul knew of some account of events, however sketchy, in which the Last Supper was rapidly followed by Jesus' arrest and execution (as in Mark).[10]

Indeed, although the Pauline form of the words of institution is closer to Luke 22.19–20 than to Mark 14.22–24, overall there are several significant points of contact. Mark places the events in the evening (Mark 14.17) while Paul has them at night (1 Corinthians 11.23). Whatever Paul meant by *paredideto*, he mentions it just before the words of institution, just as Mark immediately precedes his account of the institution with the prediction that the Son of Man is about to be betrayed or handed over (*paradidotai* – Mark 14.21). Immediately following the words of institution in Mark, Jesus states, 'Truly, I say to you, I shall not drink again of the fruit of the vine until that day when I drink it new in the kingdom of God' (Mark 14.25), whereas Paul immediately goes on to state, 'For as often as you eat this bread and drink the cup, you proclaim the Lord's death until he comes' (1 Corinthians 11.26). To be sure, there are significant differences between these two sayings, but they both relate drinking to the theme of eschatological fulfilment. Thus, although Mark and Paul diverge in the detailed wording of what was said over the bread and cup, there is some agreement in the framing of the institution; sufficient agreement, at any rate, to suggest that the traditions available to Paul were reasonably similar to those available to Mark.

This is a convenient point at which to emphasize again what is already well known, namely that both here and in connection with the resurrection in 1 Corinthians 15 Paul is quite explicitly handing on traditions he has received, and appears to be using the technical language for imparting such traditions.[11] Paul is not simply giving his own opinion: he is quite explicitly talking about traditions that were available to him, and which he apparently regards as authoritative, expecting his audience to hold the same view. At both 1 Corinthians 11.23 and 15.3 he appeals to this tradition to make his point. It must therefore have had something of the status of an 'official version of events' within at least that branch of primitive Christianity to which Paul belonged.

---

[10] See also Marion L. Soards, 'Oral Tradition before, in, and outside the Canonical Passion Narratives' in Henry Wansbrough (ed.), *Jesus and the Oral Gospel Tradition* (JSNTSup, 64; Sheffield: Sheffield Academic Press, 1991), 334–50 (334–5).

[11] See, e.g., Birger Gerhardsson, *The Origins of the Gospel Traditions* (London: SCM Press, 1977), 27–41.

This brief survey suggests several things. First, it indicates that where Paul can be used as a check on Mark, Paul tends to support the existence of a tradition similar (but by no means identical) to that reflected in Mark. This in turn suggests that, where we have been able to check it, the tradition seems to have been reasonably stable between Paul's time and Mark's, and also that Mark has been reasonably conservative in his employment of it (since unless both conditions obtained, we should not see the degree of agreement that we do). This does not, of course, prove that Mark treated all his material in the same way, or that he did not invent anything, or that all the traditions available to Mark enjoyed a similar degree of stability from the time of Paul, but it does indicate that any model of the tradition and of Mark's use of the tradition has to take at least this degree of stability into account.

Second, Paul's own use of the tradition suggests that it was far from uncontrolled. It is something he cites as authoritative on more than one occasion, suggesting that he is to some extent constrained by it and expects his audience to be so also. The tradition matters to Paul because it conveys what he takes to be true (at least in the sense of authoritative); it would be surprising if Paul were alone in this attitude.

Third, although Paul never explicitly states where precisely he obtained his tradition from, his letters, particularly that to the Galatians, do provide some possible clues. To be sure, Paul does start by insisting that he obtained his gospel not from any human source, but 'through a revelation of Jesus Christ' (Galatians 1.12), but in that case what he means by his 'gospel' in this context can hardly include the full content of the tradition he refers to elsewhere. For one thing, he at once goes on to say that (prior to this revelation) he 'persecuted the church of God violently and tried to destroy it' (Galatians 1.13), something he would hardly have felt motivated to do if he had no idea what the Church stood for. For another, he tells us that 'after three years [he] went up to Jerusalem to visit Cephas, and remained with him fifteen days' (Galatians 1.18) and that although he saw none of the other Apostles, he did see 'James the Lord's brother' (Galatians 1.19). Since this was presumably not just a social call, it is highly probable that Paul would have obtained some of the traditions he later drew on during that visit, which probably took place in about 37 CE.[12] He may also have received some instruction from the church in Damascus following his conversion three years earlier (Galatians 1.15–17), though this is not made

---

[12] Robert Jewett, *Dating Paul's Life* (London: SCM Press, 1979), 99; John Knox, *Chapters in a Life of Paul* (rev. edn; London: SCM Press, 1989), 68.

explicit. It would, however, be strange if Paul conferred with no other Christians at all between his conversion in 34 CE and his first Jerusalem visit in 37 CE; indeed it would be utterly extraordinary if he made no attempt to seek a better understanding of the faith he had been so vigorously persecuting on becoming an adherent of it.

The rhetoric of Galatians 1 is designed to establish Paul's authority as an apostle, based on a divine call, not a human commissioning. Paul claims he is dependent on no mere human being for his saving knowledge of Christ, which came through a revelation; he does not say that his knowledge of the traditions of the Christian community came by the same route. In any case, whatever form the revelation of Christ took to him, it could have made no sense to him, could not even have been identified as a revelation of Christ, unless he already knew something of Christian beliefs about Christ prior to the experience. This puts Paul in touch with some form of Christian tradition at least as early as 34 CE (within four years of the most likely date of the crucifixion) and with a form of the tradition provided by Peter and James, two men who had known Jesus in the flesh, three years later.

In Galatians 2.1–10 Paul indicates that he returned to Jerusalem 14 years after his previous visit (i.e. in around 51 CE), to lay before 'those who were of repute' (presumably James, Cephas and John) the version of the gospel he had been preaching, 'lest somehow [he] should be running . . . in vain', and that the three 'pillar Apostles' were apparently happy with what they heard. This suggests that Paul's understanding of the tradition was still reasonably in step with theirs, although it does not indicate precisely what was discussed. The issues at stake seem to be more the terms on which the gospel was to be offered to the Gentiles than the details of the Jesus tradition, so it might be hazardous to make too much of this. Nonetheless, Paul's second Jerusalem visit surely afforded an opportunity to discuss the various parties' understanding of the tradition (and it is hard to see how a meaningful discussion of the issues could have lacked this element), so the indication is that over the course of his 14-year absence from Jerusalem, Paul's understanding of the tradition had not diverged too sharply from that of the three pillar Apostles based in Jerusalem (although this is, of course, more directly a statement about what Paul wanted his Galatian audience to believe than what actually happened).

We must guard against rushing to too hasty a conclusion from all this. It might be tempting to conclude that since Paul bears witness to traditions similar to some of those employed by Mark, and since the source of Paul's traditions can be traced back, at least in part, to Peter in 37 CE, if not earlier, Mark therefore has access to reliable traditions stemming from people who knew Jesus in the flesh. This has not in fact been shown, since there is no way of ascertaining whether the traditions Paul received from Peter are the same as those that later appear in his letters and that are in some agreement with Mark, or that what Peter told Paul was historically accurate.

We should also consider the degree of flexibility the tradition exhibits in the examples discussed above. For example, for all the points of contact, the words of institution at the Last Supper do differ quite a bit in detail between Paul and Mark; even if Jesus did in fact utter something of the sort on the night of his arrest the tradition was either unable or unconcerned to preserve his precise words. This is also apparent when Paul explicitly cites Jesus' sayings elsewhere; the wording never corresponds all that closely to anything we find in the Gospels, and the attribution of this or that tradition 'to the Lord' is potentially problematic since, as we have seen, Paul shows himself capable of claiming direct revelations from the risen Christ (Galatians 1.12; 2.2). Moreover, although Paul, Mark and the other Evangelists agree in the fact of the resurrection, they are quite at odds over the details. To call the Jesus tradition *stable* on the basis of a comparison of Paul and Mark is thus by no means to claim that it was *fixed*, but rather to suggest that its variability was constrained.

What we can say is that Paul is a possible witness to a tradition that stems from Apostles based in Jerusalem, and that this tradition has elements in common with that employed by Mark. But since Mark and Paul both belonged to the early Jesus movement, it is perhaps not surprising that they should show signs of familiarity with similar traditions which could well have been subject to similar constraints stemming from similar needs. A stronger test might be to compare Mark with someone quite independent of the Jesus movement, so that is what we shall attempt next.

Mark and Josephus

The most promising candidate for someone independent of the Jesus tradition to compare with Mark is probably Mark's contemporary, the Jewish historian (and propagandist) Josephus.

At a general level, Mark and Josephus have several points of contact. They both write about Israel, including places such as Galilee and Jerusalem and persons such as Pilate and Herod Antipas. This might seem trivial but for the fact that it confirms that Mark's narrative world does frequently reflect historical reality as one of his contemporaries perceived it. What this proves about Mark's traditions is less clear; the fact that some real persons and places are referred to does not necessarily mean that what is said about them either is or is intended to be factually accurate, let alone that what he says about anyone else is. All we can say on this basis is that Mark appears to have aimed at a reasonable level of verisimilitude, perhaps under the constraints of his tradition.

One might suppose that the most fruitful comparison between Mark and Josephus would be between Mark's overall portrayal of Jesus and Josephus's account of him in the *Testimonium Flavianum* (*Ant.* 18.63–64). But there are two reasons why this will not serve our purpose. The first is the difficulty of comparing like with like; to compare Mark's Jesus with Josephus's Jesus we should have to compare an extended narrative with a brief summary. This problem is not insurmountable, for to the extent that Mark and Josephus turned out to agree, we could argue that both must have been constrained by similar traditions, although the constraints acting on Mark, as a member of a Christian community, would surely have been very different from those acting on Josephus, who had no need to paint Jesus in a flattering light. But the more intractable problem is that the *Testimonium* has certainly been tampered with by a Christian hand (Josephus simply could not have written 'he was the Messiah' – *Ant.* 18.64 – or what he goes on to say about Jesus' appearing to his followers on the third day after his execution). In fact, the passage could well be a Christian forgery throughout.[13] Even if we were to suppose that Josephus wrote something about Jesus at this point in the *Antiquities*, we could not reconstruct it with any confidence, and we could not be certain that Josephus's information was free of any influence from Mark, even if that influence turned out to be as indirect as Josephus's acquaintance with Christian traditions that had been influenced by Mark.

If it is unprofitable to compare what Josephus and Mark have to say about Jesus, it may nevertheless be fruitful to compare what they have to say about John the Baptist. Not only is the material more comparable in nature and length, but there is no indication that Josephus's material on John the Baptist (*Ant.* 18.116–19) is in any way dependent on a Christian source, since there is nothing that links the Josephan John with Jesus or primitive Christianity.[14]

We may start by noting the points of agreement. First, both agree in identifying a John who is singled out from other Johns by being 'the baptizer'

---

[13] See K. A. Olson, 'Eusebius and the Testimonium Flavianum', *CBQ* 61 (1999), 305–22.

[14] See, e.g., John P. Meier, *A Marginal Jew: Rethinking the Historical Jesus*, vol. 2: *Mentor, Message, and Miracles* (New York: Doubleday, 1994), 19–21.

(*Ant.* 18.117; Mark 6.14 and possibly 1.4), presumably on account of his characteristic activity of baptizing people (Mark 1.4–5, 8), or, at the very least, urging them to be baptized (*Ant.* 18.117), an act both writers connect in some way with turning away from sins. According to Mark 1.4–5 the baptism was for 'repentance for the forgiveness of sins' and the people came 'confessing their sins', while according to *Ant.* 18.117 John's baptism was not to be used 'to gain pardon for whatever sins they committed' but as an outward sign that their souls had already been cleansed through reformation of conduct. They also concur in saying that John attracted substantial crowds (Mark 1.5; *Ant.* 18.118), and in evaluating him as a godly man (implied in Mark by the way John is introduced at Mark 1.4 directly after what is stated at Mark 1.1–3, and equally implied by Josephus calling John a 'good' man who encouraged justice and piety towards God and whose death God was popularly thought to have avenged, *Ant.* 18.117). Finally, both Mark and Josephus state that John was executed on the orders of Herod Antipas (Mark 6.27–28; *Ant.* 18.118–19).

The precise circumstances surrounding that execution form the most obvious differences between the Markan and Josephan accounts. The reason Mark gives for John's arrest is that John had told Herod (Antipas) that his marriage to Herodias was unlawful (Mark 6.17–18). Herod is subsequently tricked into having John beheaded against his better judgement by his wife and stepdaughter (Mark 6.19–28). This account with its somewhat gruesome conclusion reads more like a folk tale than sober recollection (with such stock folk tale elements as the king promising up to half his kingdom; compare Esther 5.3, 6; 7.2), although this does not in itself prevent its having been a popular account of the matter on which Mark drew. One could also see it as a means by which Mark or his tradition keys the persecution of John by Herod and Herodias to Elijah's clashes with Ahab and Jezebel (1 Kings 18; 19; 21).

According to Josephus, on the other hand, the decision to have John executed was based on sober political calculation: John was attracting too much of a popular following, and there was always the danger that this might turn into an uprising, so it seemed better to make a pre-emptive strike before trouble erupted (*Ant.* 18.119).

At first blush, Josephus's account looks the more sober and historical. In the Markan version Herodias is made to play Jezebel to John's Elijah, Herod's banquet is pointedly contrasted with Jesus' (Mark 6.30–44), and the whole episode is made to foreshadow Jesus' passion (Jesus is also executed against the better judgement of the official who orders his execution). Again, Mark's account of John's arrest looks suspiciously confused, with two appended explanations employing *gar* (for) in characteristically Markan style (Mark 6.17–18). The statement in Mark 6.17 is perhaps meant to imply that Herod Antipas had John arrested at Herodias's instigation. Mark 6.18 implies that John's offence was to tell Herod that his marriage was unlawful. Presumably this was not something John is meant to have said to Herod's face (if he had, Herod would not have needed to *send* anyone to arrest him). The fact that Herod thought John worth arresting suggests that the issue was what John was putting about among the general populace, but in that case what lies behind Mark's account may be a little closer to Josephus's version. Again, one has to wonder whether Herod really intended to detain John indefinitely in prison, or whether he had in fact arrested him with a view to execution from the start; given the somewhat contrived nature of the means by which the Markan Herod is forced to order John's execution, one may once again judge Josephus's version to be the more plausible.

On the other hand, one also needs to probe Josephus's version. For example, one wonders how Josephus knew what Herod's motives were. Does Josephus have access to inside information at this point, or is he merely continuing to report popular opinion on the subject, as he quite explicitly starts off by doing? Or is Josephus simply offering his own speculation and attributing to Herod the kind of motive that would make sense to his intended Graeco-Roman audience? Perhaps Josephus is pursuing his own characteristic agenda here, and his account of John is intended as a piece of apologetic. According to Josephus, John was a popular figure among Jews, executed (by Josephus's own account) for potential sedition, but Josephus does not want to give the impression that Jews in general favoured sedition, so he offers an explanation of how Herod came to execute a figure who was in fact politically innocuous (a move that parallels the way the Gospels tend to treat the execution of Jesus).

Again, although Josephus does not make the link absolutely explicit, even in Josephus's account there *is* a link between Herod's marital misadventures and the popular perception of John's death. According to Josephus, the popular view was that the defeat of Herod's army was a punishment for his execution of John the Baptist. The defeat in question was at the hands of Aretas, king of Petra, whose quarrel with Herod was that Herod had married Herodias, the wife of his half-brother, while being already married to Aretas's daughter. Josephus does not state the length of time that elapsed between John's execution and Herod's defeat; if one followed closely on the other this might explain the popular view that Herod's defeat at the hands of Aretas was a divine punishment for the unjust killing of John. But if the Gospels are right in putting John's death before Jesus' (i.e. probably before 30 CE), then some years will have elapsed between the two events (Herod's military defeat occurred in 36 CE).[15] It would at least be more obvious why the connection between these two events had been made if John was known (or believed) to have been an outspoken critic of Herod's marital arrangements. This remains the case even if the Gospels are simply wrong about the date of John's execution. It seems highly probable, then, that the popular perception of John on which both Mark and Josephus drew knew (or believed) John to have been an outspoken critic of Herod Antipas's marriage to his sister-in-law.

There remains to consider the discrepancies between what Josephus and Mark present John as having preached. As we have seen, Mark has John preach a 'baptism of repentance for the forgiveness of sins', but is not very specific about what this involved, beyond stating that people confessed their sins when they came to be baptized (Mark 1.4–5). Josephus is rather careful to explain that John did not employ baptism to effect forgiveness for past sins, 'but as a consecration of the body implying that the soul was already thoroughly cleansed by right behaviour' (*Ant.* 18.117). This almost reads as if Josephus is deliberately trying to distance John from a Christian understanding of baptism, although there is no apparent reason *why* he should be bothering to do this. Perhaps the point is rather, as John Meier puts it, that 'For Josephus' largely pagan audience, the Baptist is transformed into a popular moral philosopher of Stoic hue, with a somewhat neo-Pythagorean rite of lustration.'[16] On the other hand the way Mark handles John makes him principally the herald of the coming one (presumably Jesus, unless we are to understand the Baptist's prophecy in Mark 1.7 as referring to the coming of Yahweh). For this purpose John is made into an Elijah figure (Mark 1.6; 9.11–13), whose main prophetic utterance beyond predicting the coming stronger one is a protest against Herod's marriage to his sister-in-law. In Matthew, John becomes more obviously a prophet of coming judgement (Matthew 3.7–10); the same material is employed by Luke (Luke 3.7–9) who also, however, adds material that makes John look like a purveyor of ethical instruction (Luke 3.10–14), thus bringing him closer to the Josephan John.[17]

---

[15] According to the date given by Meier, *Marginal Jew*, 2.22.

[16] Meier, *Marginal Jew*, 2.20–1.

[17] For the argument that Luke had some knowledge of Josephus's works, see Steve Mason, *Josephus and the New Testament* (Peabody, MA: Hendricksen, 1992), 185–229. For a summary of other views on Luke 3.10–14, see Meier, *Marginal Jew*, 2.40–2, 61–2 (the latter passage dealing specifically with the similarities between Luke and Josephus at this point).

If one were to hazard a guess at what lay behind these conflicting accounts, it would probably be a tradition of a John who was popularly perceived as a prophet and who was executed by Antipas for being too outspoken or too popular. There is some similarity between the way Josephus described John and the way he describes other prophetic figures (the 'sign prophets') in that John attracts a popular following and is duly executed by the authorities for doing so. Since Josephus appears to approve of John, however, he does not use language that would associate him too closely with the false prophets he castigates elsewhere. Again, given that Josephus generally plays down Jewish eschatological expectations, we should expect him to play down any eschatological elements he found in the traditions of John's preaching.[18] Conversely, it may well have suited the Evangelists to play up such elements, drawing on John's popular status as a prophet to underline the imminent eschatological expectations fulfilled by Jesus. That the common traditions represented John as a prophetic spokesman for God, urging people to repentance, seems highly likely. To penetrate much further into the distinctive teaching either of the historical John, or John the Baptist as presented by the traditions about him, is probably impossible.

Since we have both Mark and Josephus, we have two seemingly independent sightings on the John the Baptist tradition. This does enable us to discern its general outline. It also suggests that, at least by the time of Mark and Josephus, there was a reasonably stable tradition about John that constrained both Mark and Josephus to present him in certain recognizable ways. But together with this fairly positive conclusion comes an alarmingly negative one. Despite the constraints of this tradition, Mark and Josephus are well able to present a John the Baptist who serves their very different purposes. The tradition proves equally malleable to both authors. Within certain fairly loose constraints, neither Mark nor Josephus finds it that difficult to make John the Baptist say what they want him to say. The constraints of the tradition thus prove to be not so much a limitation as a useful tool – they enable both Josephus and Mark (and, of course, the other three Evangelists) to draw on the authority of a prestigious figure and employ it to their own ends; one might even say that both Josephus and Mark prove well able to *exploit* the constraints of the tradition.

In terms of the models of oral tradition and social memory examined in previous chapters, this comparison of Mark and Josephus well illustrates

---

[18] So also Meier, *Marginal Jew*, 2.60–1.

the interplay of stability and variability that several scholars have drawn attention to. It also illustrates how a tradition can be made to serve different ends, even when many of its core elements are respected; what has sometimes been referred to as the variable 'periphery' (in contrast to the stable core) may be far from peripheral when it comes to determining the *significance* of tradition. The varying accounts of how John met his death are also unhelpful for Bauckham's theory of eyewitness testimony, since it is unclear who Mark's eyewitnesses are likely to have been for this event; Josephus is rather more likely to have been moving in the kind of circles where eyewitness memories of events at Herod Antipas's court could have been circulating, and his more sober account hardly supports Mark's more fanciful version.

Conversely, the Markan version quite neatly dovetails with a theory of oral tradition that involves keying and metonymic reference. Herod (called 'king' by Mark even though he was in fact only a tetrarch) and his wife Herodias are cast in the role of King Ahab and Queen Jezebel, who was reputed to have been responsible for the persecution of Elijah, while Mark makes it quite clear elsewhere that John the Baptist is to be in some sense identified with Elijah (Mark 1.6; 9.11–13). Of course, we cannot be sure how much of this is due to Mark rather than any oral traditions he employed, but the comparison with Josephus demonstrates that Mark had some access to traditions about John the Baptist, and the way he employs them suggests that he, and possibly others before him, developed them in ways consonant with the kind of model of oral tradition and social memory adumbrated in Chapter 7.

Conclusions

The sample of evidence surveyed here is clearly far too small to sustain any firm conclusion, but one further (perhaps rather obvious) point may be made. Compared with the variations in the way that Mark and Josephus treat John the Baptist, the variations in the Jesus tradition between Paul and Mark seem relatively restrained. There are some historical constraints on the ways Mark and Josephus treat John the Baptist, as there have to be if he is to be at all recognizable as the same figure, but the freedom available within those constraints is considerable. The portraits of John the Baptist presented by these two authors owes at least as much to their different ideological and narrative concerns as it does to the constraints of the tradition. That Mark and Paul seem closer in their presentation of common tradition than do Mark and Josephus, therefore, may be due largely to their operating under similar ideological or social constraints (they both needed to serve the needs of their respective Christian communities). Although this is hardly unexpected, it does provide some evidence that it was the needs and concerns of the primitive Christian communities that shaped the Jesus tradition into the relatively stable form we find quite as much as any putative historical conservatism in the tradition (*pace* Bailey). Conversely, the common elements in the John the Baptist tradition found in Mark and Josephus suggest that there were some limits; such traditions were not infinitely flexible – they did not need to be in order to be shaped to meet present need – and do not (in these instances, at least) seem to have undergone totally free invention.

The traditions we have sampled in this chapter thus exhibit the kind of mix of stability and variability described in previous chapters' discussion of social memory and oral traditions rather better than the kind of fixity suggested by Gerhardsson or the reliable eyewitness testimony urged by Bauckham. At the same time, the evidence tends to suggest that Mark and the other Evangelists had access to, and were to some extent constrained by, earlier traditions and did not simply invent all their own material. It does not, however, show that these traditions were necessarily being controlled for historical accuracy; as in the case of Bailey's data, Kelber's notion of preventative censorship, which accords well with social memory theory, would seem to be a better fit (provided it is not pushed to a radically sceptical extreme). Although it would be perilous to conclude too much from a mere pair of such probes, they do appear to lend general support to the convergence of the more workable ideas we reviewed in Chapters 4 to 7. In the final chapter we shall attempt to draw the threads together.

10

Conclusion

It may be that none of the models of oral tradition we have reviewed gives a totally comprehensive account of the tradition behind the Gospels. It is, in any case, quite likely that no one model applies to the whole process from the ministry of the Jesus to the writing of the Gospels.[1] It would be surprising if the tradition were handed on in precisely the same way as the social location changed from rural Galilee to Jerusalem to the cities of the empire. Moreover, we simply do not have direct access to any oral performances of the Jesus tradition in the primitive Church or to the social and memorial structures in which they were embedded. All that remains are the clues found in the relatively small number of texts that survive, clues which are perhaps patient of more than one interpretation. In particular we do not know who handed on the tradition to whom under what circumstances and in what social settings, or how long the chain of tradition was (in terms of the number of tradents involved) between Jesus and those who wrote about him. We do not even know the extent to which the Evangelists used oral or written sources or relied on their memory of both together. That some traces of Jesus tradition can be found in Paul, for example, suggests that Mark was probably not the first to set pen to papyrus, but how much Jesus tradition had been committed to writing before Mark, and how much influence it had on the tradition that reached Mark and the other Evangelists we have no way of knowing. We may form theories and make informed guesses about all these matters, but we can never know for sure; the evidence that would enable us to do so is simply no longer there.

Part of the problem lies with the potential circularity of any informed guesses we care to make. It seems equally possible to start with sceptical or with credulous presuppositions about the nature of the Jesus tradition and arrive at reasonably consistent results. If one approaches the tradition with radical scepticism, then it becomes possible to account for nearly

---

[1] On the need to recognize complexity in the process see also Terence C. Mournet, 'The Jesus Tradition as Oral Tradition' in W. H. Kelber and S. Byrskog (eds), *Jesus in Memory: Traditions in Oral and Scribal Perspectives* (Waco: Baylor University Press, 2009), 39–61 (41–2, 51–61).

everything in the tradition as late, secondary, unhistorical and shaped by the interests of the Church without obvious contradiction, since any evidence that might potentially challenge one's sceptical approach can be sceptically dismissed as suspect. Conversely, if one approaches the tradition with broadly credulous presuppositions, then one can consistently appeal to aspects of the tradition (the role of the apostolic witnesses and the speeches in Acts, say) that appear to support one's view.

That said, we saw in Chapters 6 and 7 that there is a measure of convergence between social memory theory and some of the more recent theories of oral tradition. Even though there may be grounds for reservations about some of Horsley's conclusions, a model combining the features of those advocated by Kelber, Dunn, Horsley and Rodriguez seems not only broadly plausible but also to be supported by the probing of tradition in Chapter 9. This in turn indicates that the proper approach to the Jesus tradition should lie somewhere between the extremes of credulity and scepticism. This follows from three theses about oral tradition and memory that flow from our study: (1) oral tradition typically exhibits both stability and change; (2) collective memory reflects both the impact of the past and the needs of the present; and (3) individual memory (insofar as it can be distinguished from social aspects of memory) is both generally reliable and capable of being seriously misleading.

Stability, change and the role of individuals

A further potential complication is that the relative stability of the Jesus tradition observable in the surviving sources may have been preceded by a period of rapid change as Jesus' first followers tried to make sense of what they or their informants had experienced (as may be illustrated, say, by the proposal that a Passion narrative was created early on in response to the need to make sense of Jesus' death). The need to make sense of other aspects of Jesus' life and ministry, such as the overall significance of his person, his most notable deeds and his teaching, may also have shaped (and probably did shape) the way Jesus was remembered from the start, for example by keying the stories about him to salient aspects of Israelite tradition that were already well known, such as tales about Moses, Elijah, Elisha and David. Such interpretative shaping of the memories of Jesus was probably well underway prior to the earliest appearance of Jesus traditions in any surviving writings, and thus cannot be traced. The move from the original Galilean setting of Jesus' first followers to the urban setting of Jerusalem and other cities of the empire will have given further impetus to reshaping the primitive Jesus traditions to meet the needs of a new context. Thus the relative stability of the tradition as it appears in its written remains cannot automatically be taken as an index of its historical reliability.

That said, Gerhardsson, Byrskog and Bauckham do raise a number of pertinent issues. It is, for example, perfectly reasonable to suggest that the formal process of handing on the tradition (to converts or potential teachers, say) might have been quite distinct from other aspects of its use (in Pauline paraenesis or preaching, say); the question is at least worth raising, not least because Paul does occasionally use the formal language of the handing on and receiving of tradition, and he does mention teachers, and the memorization of important material did constitute a significant part of ancient education. Moreover, if eyewitnesses did continue to be active in the primitive Christian community for some time after the crucifixion, it is plausible both that they would have been regarded as authoritative bearers of tradition and that they are likely to have helped stabilize the tradition. That there were too few eyewitnesses to go round to act as guarantors of the Jesus tradition in each and every Christian community may be beside the point; so far as the tradition available to Mark is concerned, for example, it would suffice for there to be one significant eyewitness (Peter, say) active in Mark's community.

The main problem with these suggestions is not their inherent implausibility, but the difficulty of squaring them with the material we in fact find in the New Testament. A subsidiary problem is that even eyewitnesses would have been subject to the kind of social pressures and constraints that shape collective memory, both in the way they originally perceived Jesus' deeds and words, and in the way they subsequently recalled them under new conditions. To put it crudely, if Peter found himself under pressure to conform his memories to group beliefs, he may have succumbed, at least in part, without any awareness that his memories were being in any way distorted.

We can amplify this point by means of a thought experiment. Suppose for the sake of argument that Mark met Peter in around 50 CE and was able to question him extensively about his memories of Jesus. What sort of version of events would he have received? Without knowing how suggestible, strong-willed or literal-minded Peter actually was we can never be sure, of course, but given what is known of the workings of human memory one thing we can be virtually certain of is that what Mark would *not* have received is an objective report of what actually happened, as if Peter (or any other eyewitness) would have acted as a high-fidelity recording device providing a transparent window onto the past. Peter's reminiscences would at the very least have been shaped by the way he had continually repeated them over the intervening 20 years, to the extent that the form in which he had come to narrate them would have fundamentally shaped the way he remembered them himself. Moreover, the fact that Peter occupied a prominent position in a social group whose entire raison d'être was bound up with what Jesus was believed to have said and done would mean that Peter's social and personal identity would have had a particularly strong investment in the way Jesus was remembered. It would be a miracle if this did not unconsciously distort the way Peter remembered Jesus so as to justify the present position of the Church and Peter's role within it.

This does not mean that Gerhardsson, Byrskog and Bauckham were wrong to challenge the dominant model of (more or less creative) anonymous community tradition derived from form criticism. It does seem likely that certain individuals would have been seen as the authoritative bearers and transmitters of tradition. But this may make less difference than is commonly supposed, since there is unfortunately no sure way of determining what role such persons actually played, or to what extent their memories were shaped by the social memories and needs of the communities to which they belonged. To the extent that they passed on their memories in oral performance, it seems likely that they will have been constrained to at least some extent by such factors as audience response and expectation, the conventions of the situation in which the oral performance took place, the performance tradition established by previous renderings of similar material, and their own roles within the community.

These are all factors that could promote both stability and adaptation. Overall, though, it does seem probable that the presence of such authoritative individuals in the community would tend to stabilize the tradition; there must be limits to what people who actually knew Jesus would have been prepared to attribute to him. That tendency would not, however, be enough to eliminate the flexibility of the tradition, and only in a fairly general sense would it help control for historical accuracy; it would probably control better for perceived congruence (in other words, accepting or rejecting material on the basis of how well it fitted with received portrayals of Jesus). It gives us a supporting reason for supposing that what we find in the Gospels does in some sense contain genuine memories of Jesus, but not that everything in the Gospels is a genuine memory in the sense of approaching what we would regard as objective historical fact.

Implications for historical Jesus research

The previous chapters' discussion of oral tradition and memory may also shed some light on the *sense* in which the Gospels may be said to contain genuine memories of Jesus. It should be apparent by now that a memory is not a photographic record of what actually took place, but a construction based on the original encoding of experience, the relating of that experience to oneself and others according to narrative frameworks and conventions supplied by one's cultural context, and the need to make sense of the past in the light of the present, and of the present in the light of the past. This does not mean that memory is radically unreliable; clearly for most everyday purposes it is anything but that; but it does mean that what is remembered cannot straightforwardly be equated with what actually happened. While it is most unlikely that the general course of Jesus' ministry would be seriously misremembered by those who witnessed it, and while it is highly likely that at least some details of striking events and sayings would also be retained with reasonable accuracy, distortions, reinterpretations, blending and confusion of separate incidents and even of the source of material apparently remembered would inevitably have occurred. To this must be added the tendency of oral narration to simplify, exaggerate and dramatize, to prefer stark contrasts and conflict, the need of oral poetics to cast its material in memorable form, and the tendency of both oral tradition and social memory to render the recent past usable in the present by relating it to other parts of the tradition by such means as keying, framing and metonymic reference.

This does not mean that the historical Jesus is forever lost to us, but it does mean that even under the most favourable conditions in which we suppose eyewitnesses to have played a key role in stabilizing the tradition, the Jesus who lived and walked and breathed in Galilee may be glimpsed only through a distorting lens. Moreover, while what we know of the typical workings of oral tradition and social memory may enable us to make a fair guess at the kinds of distortion that are likely to have taken place, they do not provide us with some kind of reverse lens through which the distortions may be undone. Here the way in which stories about John Hogg developed may offer an instructive parallel.

Thus, as scholars such as Rafael Rodriguez and Dale Allison have recently observed, the project of trying to separate authentic from inauthentic material in the Jesus tradition is fundamentally misconceived. The workings of memory and oral tradition simply do not allow such a neat separation. Of course there will be certain items in the Gospels which on other

181

grounds, such as those of general historical plausibility, we can judge to be historically either highly improbable or virtually certain (such as the appearance of resurrected saints walking around Jerusalem as described in Matthew 27.52–53 in the one case, or the fact that Jesus died by crucifixion in the other), but a great deal of the material that now appears in the Gospels will not be straightforwardly or demonstrably one or the other, but rather a blend of recollection, reinterpretation, reflection, conflation, confusion and distortion that simply cannot be reverse-engineered. The very concepts of authentic and inauthentic material need rethinking. If 'authentic' means a literal transcription of historical fact as it might have been recorded by a video camera, then little or nothing in the Gospels will count as authentic, but such an understanding of authenticity would be quite inappropriate to the material. If, on the other hand, 'authentic' is taken to mean reflective of the sort of things Jesus typically said and did, appropriately interpreted in the light of primitive Christian experience, belief and practice, then a great deal of the material that appears in the Gospels may be broadly authentic in this sense.

It may be thought that the oral tradition should have done a better job of preserving Jesus' words than other sorts of material, since these would have been in verbal form from the beginning (as opposed to the recollection of events), and Jesus could and probably did make a point of casting his teaching in memorable form. This is plausible up to a point, but only up to a point. While it is certainly the case that oral tradition is capable of transmitting such material with reasonable fidelity if it is judged sufficiently important, the evidence that the primitive Church employed any particular mechanisms to do so is in short supply. Moreover, the meaning of sayings material usually depends very much on its context, and so a method that would rip nuggets of sayings material from the supposedly secondary contexts in which the Evangelists or their tradition placed it risks leaving us with no context for interpreting it, or at least, no context other than one invented by the imagination of the investigator. Furthermore, it is highly probable that Jesus employed similar material in different contexts on different occasions, so that there is no original form of the saying, and no (uniquely) original context to be recovered.

Again, we should ask ourselves whether a saying or speech attributed to Jesus in the Gospels that faithfully represents the gist of what he said, but not the actual words he used, is to be judged more or less authentic than a collection of sayings that happens to preserve the very words that Jesus uttered on one or more occasions but so recontextualizes them as to completely distort their meaning. In terms of actually understanding the historical Jesus, the former is likely to be of more value than the latter. A further consequence is that it may not be so very important to distinguish what Jesus actually said from words subsequently attributed to him by persons sympathetic to his message; in any case, it is hard to see how we could ever be certain we had made the distinction accurately in any individual case.

None of this is intended to undermine the legitimacy or possibility of the quest of the historical Jesus; it is, however, to suggest that criteria of authenticity and the construction of (almost certainly highly speculative) tradition histories are the wrong tools for the job, since, quite apart from anything else, they take inadequate account of how oral tradition and memory are most likely to have functioned. A sounder method might be to look for recurring features of the tradition, to start with the (perhaps rather hopeful) working assumption that the Gospel narratives have not totally distorted the memory of Jesus (and so can be used with caution to interpret the material they contain), to gain as clear and detailed an understanding as possible of the particular social, political, historical, economic and religious conditions under which Jesus' ministry took place, and then to use one's critically informed historical imagination to construct a picture of the historical Jesus that fits these various constraints, and which can also explain the growth of the traditions about him. In the light of the picture that emerges one may go on to judge some materials in the Gospels to be more authentic than others, but this can hardly form the starting point of the enquiry (except to the extent that one judges certain items to be self-evidently unhistorical, but even then one needs to enquire why such items were felt to be appropriate at the time, and what they might have to say about the way in which Jesus was remembered and perceived).

Implications for source criticism and Gospel interpretation

Another obvious area of Gospel studies that may be impacted by our understanding of oral tradition is source criticism, and in particular the Synoptic Problem. In the past some scholars may have been too ready to employ somewhat vague invocations of oral tradition to help support their favoured theory of synoptic relationships. There is nothing wrong with the suggestion that oral tradition may have influenced the Evangelists' use of material also available to them in a written source; indeed, given the nature of the oral–scribal interface in antiquity this seems highly likely. The problem is rather with employing oral tradition as an epicycle on a source hypothesis fundamentally grounded in the assumptions of print culture, when what may be needed may be more in the nature of a Copernican revolution. It is far beyond the scope of this conclusion to attempt even a sketch of such a revolution here, except to say that the Synoptic Problem needs rethinking in terms not only of ancient compositional practices (as some scholars have started to do),[2] but also in the light of a fuller understanding of the interplay of scribality, orality and memory, and, indeed, of recent developments in text criticism. Whether such an exercise would end up supporting an existing source hypothesis or requiring the construction of a new one I am unable to predict.

A third area to consider is the interpretation of the Gospels. The oral tradition was not a stream flowing into the Gospel texts only to be frozen there; rather it was part of the biosphere in which the Gospels took shape and in which they were first used and performed. To the extent that the Gospels are oral-derived texts, in Foley's terminology 'Voices from the Past', they may originally have been intended to resonate with the ongoing oral tradition and social memory of the communities that employed them. We cannot now reconstruct more than fragments of either, but we should be alive to the possibility that hearing the Gospels in the light of their ambient tradition may be a more culturally sensitive way of appropriating them than reading them with the textual assumptions of print culture.

Conclusion

This book has examined a number of approaches to understanding the oral tradition behind the Gospels (or perhaps better, in which the Gospels were embedded), but while it has tended to favour some over others, and some attempt has been made to integrate studies of memory with studies of orality, no attempt has been made to come up with one definitive model as *the* way of understanding the oral Jesus tradition. There is probably no way in which such a definitive model could be arrived at, given both the great variety of ways in which oral tradition has been observed to operate under other circumstances and the absence of much specific evidence for how it actually operated in primitive Christianity. Valuable as cross-cultural studies from anthropology, folklore and the like may be, we must always bear in mind that their application to the first-century situation of the first followers of Jesus is bound to be speculative, and that we lack

---

[2] See especially R. A. Derrenbacker, *Ancient Compositional Practices and the Synoptic Problem* (BETL, 186; Leuven: Peeters-Leuven, 2005).

the detailed data to determine the specifics of how individual and social memory functioned in the pre-Gospel period, as opposed to an appreciation of what seems generally probable.

That said, it should by now be clear that thinking about the oral tradition behind the Gospels has moved on a long way since the days of classical form criticism. It also seems clear that any account of the pre-Gospel tradition has to reckon with the interplay between stability and flexibility, recollection and interpretation, novelty and conformity to cultural expectations, and the needs to understand the past in the light of the present and the present in the light of the past, and that this interplay is extremely unlikely to have resulted in either photographic recall or total invention. Finally, oral tradition has increasingly come to be understood within the context of social memory, and it may well be that in future research memory will turn out to be a more useful category than oral tradition.

Bibliography

Achtemeier, Paul J., 'Omne verbum sonat: The New Testament and the Oral Environment of Late Western Antiquity', *JBL* 109 (1990), 3–37.

Alexander, Loveday, 'Memory and Tradition in the Hellenistic Schools' in W. H. Kelber and S. Byrskog (eds), *Jesus in Memory: Traditions in Oral and Scribal Perspectives* (Waco: Baylor University Press, 2009), 113–53.

Alexander, Philip S., 'Orality in Pharisaic-Rabbinic Judaism at the Turn of the Eras' in H. Wansbrough (ed.), *Jesus and the Oral Gospel Tradition* (JSNTSup, 64; Sheffield: Sheffield Academic Press, 1991), 159–84.

Allison, Dale C., *Constructing Jesus: Memory, Imagination and History* (London: SPCK, 2010).

Assmann, Jan, *Cultural Memory and Early Civilization: Writing, Remembrance, and Political Imagination* (tr. David Henry Wilson; Cambridge: Cambridge University Press, 2011).

Aune, David E., 'Oral Tradition and the Aphorisms of Jesus' in H. Wansbrough (ed.), *Jesus and the Oral Gospel Tradition* (JSNTSup, 64; Sheffield: Sheffield Academic Press, 1991), 211–65.

Babcock, Barbara A., 'The Story in the Story: Metanarration in Folk Narrative' in R. Bauman (ed.), *Verbal Art as Performance* (Long Grove, IL: Waveland Press, 1984), 61–79.

Baddeley, Alan, Eysenck, Michael W. and Anderson, Michael C., *Memory* (Hove and New York: Psychology Press, 2009).

Bailey, Kenneth E., 'Informal Controlled Oral Tradition and the Synoptic Gospels', *Themelios* 20.2 (1995), 4–11.

Bailey, Kenneth E., 'Middle Eastern Oral Tradition and the Synoptic Gospels', *ExpTim* 106 (1994), 363–7.

Barclay, Craig R., 'Autobiographical Remembering: Narrative Constraints on Objectified Selves' in D. C. Rubin (ed.), *Remembering Our Past: Studies in Autobiographical Memory* (Cambridge: Cambridge University Press, 1995), 94–125.

Bartlett, F. C., *Remembering: A Study in Experimental and Social Psychology* (Cambridge: Cambridge University Press, 1995).

Bauckham, Richard, 'In Response to My Respondents: *Jesus and the Eyewitnesses* in Review', *JSHJ* 6 (2008), 211–24.

Bauckham, Richard, *Jesus and the Eyewitnesses: The Gospels as Eyewitness Testimony* (Grand Rapids and Cambridge: Eerdmans, 2006).

Bauman, Richard, *Verbal Art as Performance* (reissued 1984 edn; Long Grove, IL: Waveland Press, 1977).

Bauman, Richard and Braid, Donald, 'The Ethnography of Performance in the Study of Oral Traditions' in J. M. Foley (ed.), *Teaching Oral Traditions* (New York: The Modern Language Association, 1998), 106–22.

Black, C. Clifton, *The Disciples According to Mark: Markan Redaction in Current Debate* (JSNTSup, P27; Sheffield: JSOT Press, 1989).

Blackburn, Barry L., *Theios Anēr and the Markan Miracle Traditions: A Critique of the Theios Anēr Concept as an Interpretative Background of the Miracle Traditions Used by Mark* (WUNT, 2; Tübingen: Mohr [Siebeck], 1991).

Bradbury, Nancy Mason, 'Traditional Referentiality: The Aesthetic Power of Oral Traditional Structures' in J. M. Foley (ed.), *Teaching Oral Traditions* (New York: The Modern Language Association, 1998), 136–45.

Brewer, William F., 'What Is Recollective Memory?' in D. C. Rubin (ed.), *Remembering Our Past: Studies in Autobiographical Memory* (Cambridge: Cambridge University Press, 1995), 19–66.

Bultmann, Rudolf, *The History of the Synoptic Tradition* (tr. John Marsh; Oxford: Basil Blackwell, 1963).

Bultmann, Rudolf, 'The Study of the Synoptic Gospels' in F. C. Grant (ed.), *Form Criticism: A New Method of New Testament Research* (tr. Frederick C. Grant; Chicago and New York: Willet, Clark & Co., 1934), 11–75.

Byrskog, Samuel, *Story as History – History as Story: The Gospel Tradition in the Context of Ancient Oral History* (Leiden and Boston: Brill, 2002).

Carr, David M., *Writing on the Tablets of the Heart: Origins of Scripture and Literature* (Oxford: Oxford University Press, 2005).

Carruthers, Mary, *The Book of Memory: A Study of Memory in Medieval Culture* (2nd edn; Cambridge Studies in Medieval Literature; Cambridge: Cambridge University Press, 2008).

Catchpole, David, 'On Proving Too Much: Critical Hesitations about Richard Bauckham's *Jesus and the Eyewitnesses*', *JSHJ* 6 (2008), 169–81.

Christiansen, Sven-Åke and Safer, Martin A., 'Emotional Events and Emotions in Autobiographical Memories' in David C. Rubin (ed.), *Remembering Our Past: Studies in Autobiographical Memory* (Cambridge: Cambridge University Press, 1995), 218–43.

Collins, Raymond F., *Introduction to the New Testament* (2nd edn; London: SCM Press, 1992).

Connerton, Paul, *How Societies Remember* (Themes in the Social Sciences; ed. John Dunn, Jack Goody, Eugene A. Hammel and Geoffrey Hawthorn; Cambridge: Cambridge University Press, 1989).

Conway, Martin A., 'Autobiographical Knowledge and Autobiographical Memories' in D. C. Rubin (ed.), *Remembering Our Past: Studies in Autobiographical Memory* (Cambridge: Cambridge University Press, 1995), 67–93.

Crossan, John Dominic, *The Birth of Christianity: Discovering What Happened in the Years Immediately after the Execution of Jesus* (San Francisco: Harper, 1998).

Cubitt, Geoffrey, *History and Memory* (Historical Approaches; ed. Geoffrey Cubitt; Manchester and New York: Manchester University Press, 2007).

Davids, Peter H., 'The Gospels and Jewish Tradition: Twenty Years after Gerhardsson' in R. T. France and D. Wenham (eds), *Gospel Perspectives*, vol. 1: *Studies of History and Tradition in the Gospels* (Sheffield: JSOT Press, 1980), 75–99.

Derrenbacker, R. A., *Ancient Compositional Practices and the Synoptic Problem* (BETL, 186; Leuven: Peeters-Leuven, 2005).

Dibelius, Martin, *From Tradition to Gospel* (tr. Bertram Lee Woolf; London: Ivor Nicholson and Watson, 1934).

Donahue, John R. and Harrington, Daniel J., *The Gospel of Mark* (Sacra Pagina, 2; Collegeville, MN: Michael Glazier, 2002).

Dunn, James D. G., 'Altering the Default Setting: Re-envisaging the Early Transmission of the Jesus Tradition', *NTS* 49 (2003), 139–75.

Dunn, James D. G., 'Eyewitnesses and the Oral Jesus Tradition', *JSHJ* 6 (2008), 85–105.

Dunn, James D. G., *Jesus Remembered* (Christianity in the Making, 1; Grand Rapids and Cambridge: Eerdmans, 2003).

Dunn, James D. G., 'Kenneth Bailey's Theory of Oral Tradition: Critiquing Theodore Weeden's Critique', *JSHJ* 7 (2009), 44–62.

Dunn, James D. G., *The Theology of Paul the Apostle* (London and New York: T. & T. Clark, 1998).

Eve, Eric, *The Healer from Nazareth: Jesus' Miracles in Historical Context* (London: SPCK, 2009).

Eve, Eric, *The Jewish Context of Jesus' Miracles* (JSNTSup, 231; Sheffield: Sheffield Academic Press, 2002).

Eve, Eric, 'Meier, Miracle and Multiple Attestation', *JSHJ* 3.1 (2005), 23–45.

Eve, Eric, 'Spit in Your Eye: The Blind Man of Bethsaida and the Blind Man of Alexandria', *NTS* 54 (2008), 1–17.

Eve, Eric, 'The Synoptic Problem without Q?' in P. Foster, A. Gregory, J. S. Kloppenborg and J. Verheyden (eds), *New Studies in the Synoptic Problem* (BETL, 139; Leuven: Leuven University Press, 2011), 551–70.

Farrell, Thomas J., 'Kelber's Breakthrough' in L. H. Silberman (ed.), *Orality, Aurality and Biblical Narrative* (Semeia, 39; Decatur, GA: Scholars Press, 1987), 27–45.

Fentress, James L. and Wickham, Chris, *Social Memory* (New Perspectives on the Past; Oxford and Cambridge, MA: Basil Blackwell, 1992).

Finnegan, Ruth, *Oral Poetry: Its Nature, Significance and Social Context* (Bloomington and Indianapolis: Indiana University Press, 1992).

Foley, John Miles, *How to Read an Oral Poem* (Urbana and Chicago: University of Illinois Press, 2002).

Foley, John Miles, 'Memory in Oral Tradition' in R. A. Horsley, J. A. Draper and J. M. Foley (eds), *Performing the Gospel: Orality, Memory and Mark* (Minneapolis: Fortress Press, 2006), 83–96.

Bibliography

Foley, John Miles, *The Singer of Tales in Performance* (Voices in Performance and Text; ed. John Miles Foley; Bloomington and Indianapolis: Indiana University Press, 1995).

Foley, John Miles, *The Theory of Oral Composition: History and Methodology* (Bloomington and Indianapolis: Indiana University Press, 1988).

Foley, John Miles, 'Words in Tradition, Words in Text: A Response', *Semeia* 65 (1995), 169–80.

Gerhardsson, Birger, 'Illuminating the Kingdom: Narrative Meshalim in the Synoptic Gospels' in H. Wansbrough (ed.), *Jesus and the Oral Gospel Tradition* (JSNTSup, 64; Sheffield: Sheffield Academic Press, 1991), 266–309.

Gerhardsson, Birger, *Memory and Manuscript: Oral Tradition and Written Transmission in Rabbinic Judaism and Early Christianity* (combined edn; Biblical Resource Series; tr. Eric J. Sharpe; Grand Rapids: Eerdmans, 1998).

Gerhardsson, Birger, *The Origins of the Gospel Traditions* (London: SCM Press, 1977).

Gerhardsson, Birger, *The Reliability of the Gospel Tradition* (Peabody, MA: Hendrickson, 2001).

Gerhardsson, Birger, *Tradition and Transmission in Early Christianity* (combined edn; Biblical Resource Series; tr. Eric J. Sharpe; Grand Rapids: Eerdmans, 1998).

Goodacre, Mark, *The Case against Q: Studies in Markan Priority and the Synoptic Problem* (Harrisburg, PA: Trinity Press International, 2002).

Goody, Jack, *The Domestication of the Savage Mind* (Themes in the Social Sciences; Cambridge: Cambridge University Press, 1977).

Goody, Jack, *The Interface between the Written and the Oral* (Cambridge: Cambridge University Press, 1987).

Green, H. Benedict, *Matthew, Poet of the Beatitudes* (JSNTSup, 203; Sheffield: Sheffield Academic Press, 2001).

Gregory, Andrew, 'What Is Literary Dependence?' in Paul Foster, Andrew Gregory, John S. Kloppenborg and J. Verheyden (eds), *New Studies in the Synoptic Problem* (BETL, 139; Leuven: Leuven University Press, 2011), 87–114.

Güttgemanns, Erhardt, *Candid Questions Concerning Gospel Form Criticism: A Methodological Sketch of the Fundamental Problematics of Form and Redaction Criticism* (Pittsburgh Theological Monograph Series, 26; ed. Dikran Y. Hadidian; tr. William G. Doty; Pittsburgh: Pickwick Press, 1979).

Halbwachs, Maurice, *On Collective Memory* (The Heritage of Sociology; ed. Donald N. Levine; tr. Lewis A. Coser; Chicago and London: University of Chicago Press, 1992).

Hanson, R. P. C., *Tradition in the Early Church* (London: SCM Press, 1962).

Havelock, Eric A., *The Muse Learns to Write: Reflections on Orality and Literacy from Antiquity to the Present* (New Haven and London: Yale University Press, 1986).

Havelock, Eric A., *Preface to Plato* (Cambridge, MA: Harvard University Press, 1963).

Hearon, Holly E., 'The Implications of Orality for Studies of the Biblical Text' in R. A. Horsley, J. A. Draper and J. M. Foley (eds), *Performing the Gospel: Orality, Memory and Mark* (Minneapolis, Augsburg Fortress, 2006), 3–20.

Bibliography

Hearon, Holly E., *The Mary Magdalene Tradition: Witness and Counter-Witness in Early Christian Communities* (Collegeville, MN: Liturgical Press, 2004).

Henaut, Barry W., *Oral Tradition and the Gospels: The Problem of Mark 4* (JSNTSup, 82; Sheffield: JSOT Press, 1993).

Hengel, Martin, *Judaism and Hellenism: Studies in their Encounter in Palestine during the Early Hellenistic Period*, vol. 1 (tr. John Bowden; London: SCM Press, 1974).

Hirst, William and Manier, David, 'Remembering as Communication: A Family Recounts Its Past' in D. C. Rubin (ed.), *Remembering Our Past: Studies in Autobiographical Memory* (Cambridge: Cambridge University Press, 1995), 271–90.

Hogg, Rena L., *A Master-Builder on the Nile: Being a Record of the Life and Aims of John Hogg, D.D., Christian Missionary* (New York: Fleming H. Revell, 1914).

Holtz, Traugott, 'Paul and the Oral Gospel Tradition' in H. Wansbrough (ed.), *Jesus and the Oral Gospel Tradition* (JSNTSup, 64; Sheffield: Sheffield Academic Press, 1991), 380–93.

Hooker, Morna D., *The Gospel According to St Mark* (BNTC; ed. Henry Chadwick; London: A. & C. Black, 1991).

Horsley, Richard A., *Hearing the Whole Story: The Politics of Plot in Mark's Gospel* (Louisville, KY: Westminster John Knox Press, 2001).

Horsley, Richard A., *Jesus and the Spiral of Violence* (San Francisco: Harper & Row, 1987).

Horsley, Richard A., *Jesus in Context: Power, People, and Performance* (Minneapolis: Fortress Press, 2008).

Horsley, Richard A., 'Prominent Patterns in the Social Memory of Jesus and Friends' in A. Kirk and T. Thatcher (eds), *Memory, Tradition, and Text: Uses of the Past in Early Christianity* (SBL Semeia Studies, 52; Atlanta: SBL, 2005), 57–78.

Horsley, Richard A. and Draper, Jonathan A., *Whoever Hears You Hears Me: Prophets, Performance and Tradition in Q* (Harrisburg, PA: Trinity Press International, 1999).

Jaffee, Martin S., *Torah in the Mouth: Writing and Oral Tradition in Palestinian Judaism, 200 BCE–400 CE* (Oxford: Oxford University Press, 2001).

Jewett, Robert, *Dating Paul's Life* (London: SCM Press, 1979).

Kahl, Werner, *New Testament Miracle Stories in Their Religious-Historical Setting; A Religionsgeschichtliche Comparison from a Structural Perspective* (FRLANT, 163; Göttingen: Vandenhoeck & Ruprecht, 1994).

Keith, Chris, *Jesus' Literacy: Scribal Culture and the Teacher from Galilee* (LNTS, 413; ed. Mark Goodacre; New York and London: T. & T. Clark, 2011).

Keith, Chris and Thatcher, Tom, 'The Scar of the Cross: The Violence Ratio and the Earliest Christian Memories of Jesus' in T. Thatcher (ed.), *Jesus, the Voice and the Text: Beyond the Oral and the Written Gospel* (Waco: Baylor University Press, 2008), 197–234.

Kelber, Werner H., 'Biblical Hermeneutics and the Ancient Art of Communication: A Response' in L. H. Silberman (ed.), *Orality, Aurality and Biblical Narrative* (Decatur, GA: Scholars Press, 1987), 97–105.

Kelber, Werner H., 'The Case of the Gospels: Memory's Desire and the Limits of Historical Criticism', *OT* 17 (2002), 55–86.

Kelber, Werner H., 'Jesus and Tradition: Words in Time, Words in Space', *Semeia* 65 (1995), 139–67.

Kelber, Werner H., 'Modalities of Communication, Cognition and Physiology of Perception: Orality, Rhetoric, Scribality', *Semeia* 65 (1995), 193–216.

Kelber, Werner H., 'Narrative as Interpretation and Interpretation as Narrative: Hermeneutical Reflections on the Gospels' in L. H. Silberman (ed.), *Orality, Aurality and Biblical Narrative* (Semeia, 39; Decatur, GA: Scholars Press, 1987), 107–33.

Kelber, Werner H., *The Oral and the Written Gospel: The Hermeneutics of Speaking and Writing in the Synoptic Tradition, Mark, Paul and Q* (Voices in Performance and Text; Bloomington and Indianapolis: Indiana University Press, 1997).

Kelber, Werner H., 'The Oral-Scribal-Memorial Arts of Communication in Early Christianity' in T. Thatcher (ed.), *Jesus, the Voice and the Text: Beyond the Oral and the Written Gospel* (Waco: Baylor University Press, 2008), 235–62.

Kelber, Werner H., 'The Work of Birger Gerhardsson in Perspective' in W. H. Kelber and S. Byrskog (eds), *Jesus in Memory: Traditions in Oral and Scribal Perspectives* (Waco: Baylor University Press, 2009), 173–206.

Kelber, Werner H., 'The Works of Memory: Christian Origins as MnemoHistory – A Response' in A. Kirk and T. Thatcher (eds), *Memory, Tradition, and Text: Uses of the Past in Early Christianity* (SBL Semeia Studies, 52; Atlanta: SBL, 2005), 221–48.

Kirk, Alan, 'Memory' in W. H. Kelber and S. Byrskog (eds), *Jesus in Memory: Traditions in Oral and Scribal Perspectives* (Waco: Baylor University Press, 2009), 155–72.

Kirk, Alan, 'Social and Cultural Memory' in A. Kirk and T. Thatcher (eds), *Memory, Tradition, and Text: Uses of the Past in Early Christianity* (SBL Semeia Studies, 52; Atlanta: SBL, 2005), 1–24.

Kirk, Alan and Thatcher, Tom, 'Jesus Tradition as Social Memory' in A. Kirk and T. Thatcher (eds), *Memory, Tradition, and Text: Uses of the Past in Early Christianity* (SBL Semeia Studies, 52; Atlanta: SBL, 2005), 25–42.

Kloppenborg, John S., 'Variation and Reproduction of the Double Tradition and an Oral Q?', *ETL* 83 (2007), 53–80.

Knox, John, *Chapters in a Life of Paul* (rev. edn; London: SCM Press, 1989).

Kundsen, Karl, 'Primitive Christianity in the Light of Gospel Research' in F. C. Grant (tr. and ed.), *Form Criticism: A New Method of New Testament Research* (Chicago and New York: Willett, Clark and Co., 1934), 96–139.

Lord, Albert B., *The Singer of Tales* (2nd edn; Harvard Studies in Comparative Literature, 24; Cambridge, MA and London: Harvard University Press, 1960).

McCasland, S. V., 'Portents in Josephus and in the Gospels', *JBL* 51 (1932), 323–35.

Machen, Arthur, *The Angels of Mons: The Bowmen and Other Legends of the War* (2nd edn; London: Simpkin, Marshall, Hamilton, Kent & Co., 1915).

Marxsen, Willi, *Mark the Evangelist* (tr. James Boyce, Donald H. Juel, William Poehlmann and Roy A. Harrisville; New York: Abingdon Press, 1969).

Mason, Bruce Lionel, 'E-Texts: The Orality and Literacy Issue Revisited', *OT* 13 (1998), 306–29.

Mason, Steve, *Josephus and the New Testament* (Peabody, MA: Hendricksen, 1992).

Meier, John P., *A Marginal Jew: Rethinking the Historical Jesus*, vol. 2: *Mentor, Message, and Miracles* (New York: Doubleday, 1994).

Merenlahti, Petri, *Poetics for the Gospels? Rethinking Narrative Criticism* (Studies of the New Testament and Its World; ed. John Barclay, Joel Marcus and John Riches; Edinburgh: T. & T. Clark, 2002).

Misztal, Barbara A., *Theories of Social Remembering* (Theorizing Society; ed. Larry Ray; Maidenhead and Philadelphia: Open University Press, 2003).

Morgan, Robert C. and Barton, John, *Biblical Interpretation* (Oxford: Oxford University Press, 1988).

Mournet, Terence C., 'The Jesus Tradition as Oral Tradition' in W. H. Kelber and S. Byrskog (eds), *Jesus in Memory: Traditions in Oral and Scribal Perspectives* (Waco: Baylor University Press, 2009), 39–61.

Mournet, Terence C., *Oral Tradition and Literary Dependency: Variability and Stability in the Synoptic Tradition and Q* (WUNT, 195; Tübingen: Mohr Siebeck, 2005).

Nineham, D. E., *Saint Mark* (rev. edn; Harmondsworth: Penguin Books, 1969).

Olson, K. A., 'Eusebius and the Testimonium Flavianum', *CBQ* 61 (1999), 305–22.

Ong, Walter J., *Orality and Literacy: The Technologizing of the Word* (New Accents; London and New York: Routledge, 2002).

Patterson, Stephen J., 'Can You Trust a Gospel? A Review of Richard Bauckham's *Jesus and the Eyewitnesses*', *JSHJ* 6 (2008), 194–210.

Räisänen, Heikki, *The 'Messianic Secret' in Mark's Gospel* (Edinburgh: T. & T. Clark, 1990).

Riesenfeld, Harald, *The Gospel Tradition and Its Beginnings: A Study in the Limits of 'Formgeschichte'* (London: A. R. Mowbray, 1957).

Robbins, Vernon K., 'Oral, Rhetorical and Literary Cultures: A Response' in J. Dewey (ed.), *Orality and Textuality in Early Christian Literature* (Semeia, 65; Atlanta, GA: SBL, 1995), 75–91.

Robinson, John A., 'Perspective, Meaning and Remembering' in D. C. Rubin (ed.), *Remembering Our Past: Studies in Autobiographical Memory* (Cambridge: Cambridge University Press, 1995), 199–217.

Rodriguez, Rafael, 'Authenticating Criteria: The Use and Misuse of a Critical Method', *JSHJ* 7 (2009), 152–67.

Rodriguez, Rafael, *Structuring Early Christian Memory: Jesus in Tradition, Performance and Text* (LNTS, 407; ed. Mark Goodacre; London: T. & T. Clark, 2010).

Rubin, David C., *Memory in Oral Traditions: The Cognitive Psychology of Epic, Ballads, and Counting-out Rhymes* (Oxford and New York: Oxford University Press, 1995).

Sanders, E. P., *The Tendencies of the Synoptic Tradition* (SNTSMS, 9; Cambridge: Cambridge University Press, 1969).

Sanders, E. P. and Davies, Margaret, *Studying the Synoptic Gospels* (London and Philadelphia: SCM Press; Trinity Press International, 1989).

Schacter, Daniel L., *Searching for Memory: The Brain, the Mind, and the Past* (New York: Basic Books, 1996).

Schröter, Jens, 'Jesus and the Canon: The Early Jesus Traditions in the Context of the Origins of the New Testament Canon' in R. A. Horsley, J. A. Draper and J. M. Foley (eds), *Performing the Gospel: Orality, Memory and Mark* (Minneapolis: Augsburg Fortress, 2006), 104–46.

Schwartz, Barry, 'Christian Origins: Historical Truth and Social Memory' in A. Kirk and T. Thatcher (eds), *Memory, Tradition, and Text: Uses of the Past in Early Christianity* (SBL Semeia Studies, 52; Atlanta: SBL, 2005), 43–56.

Schwartz, Barry, 'Jesus in First Century Memory – A Response' in A. Kirk and T. Thatcher (eds), *Memory, Tradition, and Text: Uses of the Past in Early Christianity* (SBL Semeia Studies, 52; Atlanta: SBL, 2005), 249–61.

Shiner, Whitney, 'Memory Technology and the Composition of Mark' in R. A. Horsley, J. A. Draper and J. M. Foley (eds), *Performing the Gospel: Orality, Memory and Mark* (Minneapolis: Fortress Press, 2006), 147–65.

Small, Jocelyn Penny, *Wax Tablets of the Mind: Cognitive Studies of Memory and Literacy in Classical Antiquity* (Abingdon: Routledge, 1997).

Smith, Morton, 'A Comparison of Early Christian and Early Rabbinic Tradition', *JBL* 82 (1963), 169–76.

Soards, Marion L., 'Oral Tradition before, in, and outside the Canonical Passion Narratives' in H. Wansbrough (ed.), *Jesus and the Oral Gospel Tradition* (JSNTSup, 64; Sheffield: Sheffield Academic Press, 1991), 334–50.

Talmon, Shemaryahu, 'Oral Tradition and Written Transmission, or the Heard and the Seen Word in Judaism of the Second Temple Period' in H. Wansbrough (ed.), *Jesus and the Oral Gospel Tradition* (JSNTSup, 64; Sheffield: Sheffield Academic Press, 1991), 121–58.

Taylor, Vincent, *The Formation of the Gospel Tradition* (London: Macmillan, 1960; 1st edn, 1933).

Thatcher, Tom, 'Why John Wrote a Gospel: Memory and History in an Early Christian Community' in A. Kirk and T. Thatcher (eds), *Memory, Tradition, and Text: Uses of the Past in Early Christianity* (SBL Semeia Studies, 52; Atlanta: SBL, 2005), 79–97.

Theissen, Gerd, *The Gospels in Context: Social and Political History in the Synoptic Tradition* (Edinburgh: T. & T. Clark, 1992).

Theissen, Gerd and Merz, Annette, *The Historical Jesus: A Comprehensive Guide* (tr. John Bowden; London: SCM Press, 1998).

Bibliography

Theissen, Gerd and Winter, Dagmar, *The Quest for the Plausible Jesus: The Question of Criteria* (tr. M. Eugene Boring; Louisville, KY: Westminster John Knox Press, 2002).

Thompson, Michael B., 'The Holy Internet: Communications between Churches in the First Christian Generation' in Richard Bauckham (ed.), *The Gospels for All Christians* (Edinburgh: T. & T. Clark, 1998), 49–70.

Tonkin, Elizabeth, *Narrating Our Pasts: The Social Construction of Oral History* (Cambridge Studies in Oral and Literate Culture, 22; ed. Peter Burke and Ruth Finnegan; Cambridge: Cambridge University Press, 1995).

Tremlin, Todd, *Minds and Gods: The Cognitive Foundations of Religion* (Oxford and New York: Oxford University Press, 2006).

Tuckett, Christopher M., 'Form Criticism' in W. H. Kelber and S. Byrskog (eds), *Jesus in Memory: Traditions in Oral and Scribal Perspectives* (Waco: Baylor University Press, 2009), 21–38.

Vansina, Jan, *Oral Tradition as History* (London: James Currey, 1985).

Weeden, Theodore J., Sr, 'Kenneth Bailey's Theory of Oral Tradition: A Theory Contested by Its Evidence', *JSHJ* 7 (2009), 3–43.

Weeden, Theodore J., Sr, 'Polemics as Case for Dissent: A Response to Richard Bauckham's *Jesus and the Eyewitnesses*', *JSHJ* 6 (2008), 211–24.

Wenham, David, *The Jesus Tradition outside the Gospels* (Sheffield: JSOT Press, 1985).

Wenham, David, *Paul and the Historical Jesus* (Cambridge: Grove Books, 1998).

Wenham, David, *Paul, Follower of Jesus or Founder of Christianity?* (Grand Rapids: Eerdmans, 1995).

White, L. Michael, *Scripting Jesus: The Gospels in Rewrite* (New York: HarperOne, 2010).

Wright, N. T., *Jesus and the Victory of God* (Christian Origins and the Question of God, 2; London: SPCK, 1996).

Index of ancient and biblical texts

Index of modern authors

Index of subjects

Index of subjects

Sermon on the Mount 140
sermons 73, 74, 79
'sign prophets' 174
similitudes 23
Simon of Cyrene 148
sins 171, 173
Sitz im Leben 16, 17, 25, 28, 33–4, 49, 54, 150
social: entrepreneurship 125; identification 51, 52; identity 83; memory 2, 83, 86, 87, 91–101, 107, 109, 112, 116, 123, 124–5, 130, 139, 142, 158, 176, 178, 180, 181, 184
sociological reductionism 94
'source attribution' errors 91
source criticism 130–1
speech 2–8, 53; direct 56; memorable 51, 52
speeches 119, 121
stability and variability 54, 64, 83, 100, 111–12, 124, 126, 130, 132, 133, 151, 176, 178–80
stable core 125
stories *see the various types of story*
synoptic parallels 41–2, 45, 111–12
Synoptic Problem xiii, 126, 128, 129–30, 133, 134, 183–4; *see also* Two Document Hypothesis
Syrophoenicia 121

Tales 18–19
'Tam Lin' (Scottish ballad) 103–4
taxation 118
teachers 19, 35, 43, 87, 153, 179
Temple, destruction of 39
temptation narrative 38
Testimonium Flavianum 170
testimony 144, 149; apostolic 138, 178
Thucydides 137, 141
Tiberias 118, 121

tomb, empty *see* empty tomb
Torah 140; scroll 12
tradition: criticism 130; informal controlled oral xiv, 66–85, 110, 150, 151; isolation of 31–2; tendencies of 28
traditional referentiality 103–4, 107; *see also* metonymic referentiality
transitional texts 49
transcript: hidden 116; official 116
translation 38
triads 56
truth, historical 137, 139
Twelve, the 36–7, 45, 144, 151, 152, 158, 165
Two Document Hypothesis 60, 121–2, 130
typographic bias 51, 64

urinating incident 69, 74–6

verbatim: learning 40, 53; repetition 6
verse, measured 119
Vespasian 61
vile water incident 75–6
villains 7, 125
virgin birth 24
Voices from the Past 128

'War of the Ghosts' 90, 96, 98
wisdom sayings 22
women's testimony 138
'word-power' 106, 132
worship 92–3
writing 8–13, 39–40, 48–50, 51–2, 59–60, 115–16, 120, 124, 127–9, 132–3
written sources 25

Yugoslavia 5

Also by Eric Eve

The Healer from Nazareth: Jesus' miracles in historical context (SPCK, 2009)

'For many believers, Jesus' miracles testify straightforwardly to his divine nature. For many unbelievers they constitute a stumbling block to acceptance of Christian claims. In this clear, beautifully written book, Eric Eve gently shows both believers and unbelievers that things are more complicated but also more interesting than those positions imply.

Eve does a great service to pastors and scholars in clarifying the issues, and to the discipline of apologetics in highlighting what the Gospel stories of Jesus' mighty works do, and do not, suggest.'

Grove Biblical Studies Bulletin

'It is quite the best book I have read on the subject . . . At a time when Christian faith comes under fire from many quarters, and people dismiss it as irrational superstition, here is a book that offers a historically credible view of the miracles of Jesus . . . I warmly recommend this book.'

Methodist Recorder

'Eminently readable.'

Journal for the Study of the New Testament